TRUE TO LIFE

INTERMEDIATE

Ruth Gairns
Stuart Redman
with Joanne Collie

TEACHER'S BOOK

CAMBRIDGE
UNIVERSITY PRESS

PUBLISHED BY THE PRESS SYNDICATE OF THE UNIVERSITY OF CAMBRIDGE
The Pitt Building, Trumpington Street, Cambridge, United Kingdom

CAMBRIDGE UNIVERSITY PRESS
The Edinburgh Building, Cambridge CB2 2RU, UK   http://www.cup.cam.ac.uk
40 West 20th Street, New York, NY 10011–4211, USA   http://www.cup.org
10 Stamford Road, Oakleigh, Melbourne 3166, Australia
Ruiz de Alarcón 13, 28014 Madrid, Spain

© Cambridge University Press 1996
Fourth printing 2000

Printed in the United Kingdom at the University Press, Cambridge

ISBN 0 521 45632 0 Class Book
ISBN 0 521 45631 2 Personal Study Workbook
ISBN 0 521 45630 4 Teacher's Book
ISBN 0 521 45629 0 Class Cassette Set
ISBN 0 521 45628 2 Personal Study Workbook Cassette
ISBN 0 521 48576 2 Personal Study Workbook Audio CD

CONTENTS

INTRODUCTION

Who this course is for

True to Life is a three-level course designed to take learners from elementary to good intermediate level.

The course is specifically designed for adult learners. Topics have been chosen for their interest and relevance to adults around the world, and activities have been designed to provide adults with the opportunity to talk about their experiences, express opinions, use their knowledge and imagination to solve problems and exchange ideas so as to learn from one another.

True to Life Intermediate is for learners who have covered a basic course such as *True to Life Elementary* and *Pre-intermediate*. It provides between 60 and 80 hours upwards of classroom activity, depending on the time available and the options used.

Key features

True to Life incorporates the best of current classroom methodology by providing varied teaching materials to meet the needs of different learners and learning styles, but particular attention has been paid to the following:

1 Learner engagement and personalisation

We believe that learning is most effective when learners are actively engaged in tasks which they find motivating and challenging. Moreover, it is essential for learners to have opportunities to see the relevance of new language to their own personal circumstances. We have, therefore, provided a very large number of open-ended and interactive tasks which allow learners to draw on their knowledge of the world *and* to be creative. These tasks are used not just for fluency work but also in quite controlled tasks designed to activate specific language areas (vocabulary, grammar and functions).

2 Speaking and listening

It has been our experience that adult learners lay great emphasis on oral/aural practice in the classroom, often because it is their only opportunity to obtain such practice. We have, therefore, decided to limit the amount of reading material in the Class Book (but increase it in the Personal Study Workbook) so that we can devote more time and space to speaking and listening. Users should find that opportunities for speaking practice are present in most stages of the lessons.

3 Recycling

We have decided to employ the 'little and often' approach to revision. Instead of sporadic chunks, we have devoted one page in every unit to revision. This section is called *Review and development*; it gives learners a chance to review material while it is still relatively fresh in their minds, and ensures that material from every unit is formally recycled on two separate occasions, excluding the tests in the Teacher's Book. For example:

Unit 10

Lesson 1	Lesson 2	Lesson 3	Lesson 4
input	input	input	Review and development of Units 8 and 9

Unit 11

Lesson 1	Lesson 2	Lesson 3	Lesson 4
input	input	input	Review and development of Units 9 and 10

4 Flexibility

It is important that learners know what they are learning and can see a clear path through the material. It is also important, though, that teachers can adapt material to suit the needs of their particular class. We have provided for this with the inclusion of further activities in the Teacher's Book (called *Options*), and some of these contain worksheets which may be photocopied. This, then, gives teachers a clear framework in the Class Book, but with additional resources to draw upon in the Teacher's Book for extra flexibility.

5 Vocabulary

In *True to Life*, vocabulary is not treated as a separate section because it forms an intrinsic and fundamental part of every unit, and a wide range of vocabulary activities is included throughout the three levels. Moreover, great importance is attached in these activities to spoken practice of newly presented lexical items, so learners have the opportunity to use new words and phrases in utterances of their own creation.

In the Class Book and, even more so, in the Personal Study Workbook, vocabulary learning skills are introduced and developed, as are activities which make learners more aware of important aspects of word grammar. These include lexical storage and record keeping, contextual guesswork, word building, collocation, and so on.

6 The Personal Study Workbook

This aims to be as engaging on an individual basis as the Class Book is on a group basis. Personalisation is, therefore, carried through to the Personal Study Workbook, which provides a range of activities, both structured and open-ended, designed to motivate learners to continue their learning outside the classroom. Special features include:

Visual dictionary: pages of illustrations for learners to label. That is, a personal dictionary which is easy to compile, and genuinely self-access with the aid of a bilingual dictionary.

Speaking partners: The single thing most learners want to practise outside the classroom is speaking; unfortunately it is often the most difficult to organise. We have, therefore, continued the concept of 'speaking partners' throughout the Personal Study Workbook as in the previous level. Speaking partners invites learners to find a partner who they meet (or phone) on a regular basis outside the classroom, and practise speaking English with using ideas and activities suggested in the Workbook.

Components and course organisation

At each level, the course consists of the following:
Class Book and Class Cassette Set
Personal Study Workbook and Personal Study Cassette
   or CD
Teacher's Book

The Class Book and Class Cassette Set

The Class Book contains 22 units, each one providing three to four hours of classroom activity. Each unit is divided into four lessons and each lesson is designed to take 45 to 60 minutes. Teachers are, of course, free to explore the material in different ways (indeed we have indicated ways of doing this in the following teacher's notes), but each lesson has been designed as a self-contained, logical sequence of varied activities, which can be used as they stand.

The first three lessons contain the main language input. This consists of:
- a clear grammatical syllabus
- an emphasis on lexical development
- key functional exponents
- listening and reading practice
- speaking and writing activities

The final section of each unit provides review and development activities based on the two previous units; e.g. the final section of Unit 4 revises Units 2 and 3; the final section of Unit 5 revises Units 3 and 4.

At the back of the Class Book there is:
- a Grammar Reference section
- the tapescript of selected recordings for the Class Book
- a list of irregular verbs
- the phonetic alphabet

The listening material on the Class Cassette Set is very varied – scripted, semi-scripted and unscripted – and a particular feature is the regular inclusion of dual-level listening texts. These provide two versions of a listening passage, one longer and more challenging than the other. This feature allows teachers to select the listening material that best meets the needs of their particular learners, but it also gives more scope for exploitation. In some cases, the content of the listening in each version is different, so teachers may start with the easier listening and then move on to the more difficult one; in other cases where the content is the same but more challenging, the teacher could (if facilities permit) split the group and give a different listening to different learners. And there is nothing to stop a teacher doing

version 1 at one point in the course, and then returning to do version 2, days, weeks or even months later.

The Personal Study Workbook and Personal Study Cassette or CD

The Personal Study Workbook runs parallel to the Class Book, providing 22 units which contain further practice and consolidation of the material in the Class Book.

The exercises at the beginning of each unit concentrate on consolidating grammar and vocabulary; later exercises focus on skills development, with a space at the end of each unit for the learners to record their problems and progress in English.

The Personal Study Cassette or CD provides further material for listening practice, and there is a tapescript at the back of the Workbook along with an answer key for most of the exercises.

An additional feature is the visual dictionary, which provides pages of illustrations at the back of the book for learners to compile their own personal dictionary. The material is linked to the units in the Class Book, so learners complete it at regular intervals during the course.

The Teacher's Book

This offers teachers a way through the activities presented, but also provides a wide range of ideas that will enable them to approach and extend the activities in different ways. Some of these include worksheets which may be photocopied and distributed in class.

In addition, the Teacher's Book provides:
- guidance on potential language difficulties
- a complete answer key to the exercises in the Class Book.
- four photocopiable formal tests, each test covering a section of the Class Book
- tapescripts of the Class Book recordings which may be photocopied and given to learners

LOOKING BACK AND LOOKING FORWARD

I CAN VAGUELY REMEMBER ...

Introduction

The learners revise the past simple through a personalised activity talking about their memories, and then expand on the theme using the new vocabulary input of adjectives describing personal feelings. (It is important that a first lesson should not appear too daunting, but at the same time most learners want to go away from a first lesson feeling that they have learned something.) A listening activity concludes the lesson.

Suggested steps

How you begin this first lesson will depend very much on whether you already know the group, and whether they know each other. If the answer to either question is *no*, you may wish to start with an ice-breaker activity. Here is an example:

Option

If you are working with a *multilingual group* you will need copies of Worksheet 1A, which you will find on page 116. Give each member of the group a copy, put them in pairs of different nationalities, and get them to fill in their partner's name and country on their own questionnaire. Then tell them to fill in the rest of the questionnaire without asking their partners. Encourage them to guess anything they don't know and stress that there is no shame in not knowing the answers. When they have finished, they tell each other their answers and add to the information.

With a *monolingual group*, use Worksheet 1B, which you will find on page 116. Give each member of the group a copy, tell the learners to find a partner they don't know, then tell them to interview that partner to complete their questionnaire. When they have finished, tell them to find a new partner and talk about the person they have just interviewed.

1

Using the lesson from the book, you could begin by asking the learners if they have a good memory. If anyone says *yes*, test them with one or two questions from the list, e.g. their first English lesson or their first day at primary school. Then ask round the class, and after a few responses draw their attention to the phrases in the box, or write them on the board. In particular, explain the use of *not ... at all* and *vaguely*.

Go through the rest of the list to check that they understand, and then put them in pairs to complete the exercise. At this stage, emphasise that they should not go into detail, but simply use the target language from the box.

Option

If many of your learners are still at school/college, you may wish to change some items in the list which they will not have experienced. Here are some further suggestions for these learners:

– your first day at university
– your first bicycle
– your first important examination
– your first cigarette

- the first time you went to a disco
- the first time you had a shave/wore make-up
- the first time you went in a plane
- the first time you bought clothes with your own money

2

Give the pairs several minutes to look through the adjectives. Encourage them to explain words to each other and use dictionaries – they should have access to bilingual and monolingual dictionaries. At the end you will need to go over the words again and clarify certain items, but this is likely to be more effective if they have already familiarised themselves with the words. You will also have to check their pronunciation and make sure they know when the final -ed represents an additional syllable. You could even ask them to deduce a rule.

> ### Language Point
>
> -ed endings on past participles become an additional syllable if the verb ends in t or d (excluding a final e), e.g. *decided, reminded, persuaded, waited, started, disappointed*, etc.

Put the learners in small groups, so they can tell each other how they felt during some of the 'firsts' from Exercise 1. We want the learners to use the adjectives, but equally we would like to see groups extending the conversations in ways that interest them. The activity may take five minutes or fifteen minutes; stop it when you feel interest beginning to flag.

Give some feedback on the conversations, both positive feedback and error correction, and then introduce the listening.

3 ▭▭ ▭▭

There are two versions of the listening activity, one more difficult than the other. This feature is included throughout the course, and factors which differentiate the two versions may be length of text, organisation of information, difficulty of lexis and expression, speed of delivery, etc. Clearly you are the best person to help the learners decide which one to listen to, although you may decide to do both; the easier one to build confidence, and the more difficult one to provide additional exposure to natural language. In subsequent activities where there are two recordings, you may decide – if you have the facilities – to split the group and let the learners choose which they would prefer to do.

The tapescripts are on page 142.

Play the appropriate version of the recording, then put the learners in pairs to check their answers. If necessary, play the recording a second time, before going over the correct answers.

Answer key

Version 1:
1. Lyndham talks about his first driving lesson. He was very nervous and stalled the car after he had gone three feet.

2. Juliet talks about her first kiss. It was at a party. She was eight and the boy's name was Lee Portnoy. He kissed her very hard, and it was not a very nice experience for her.

Version 2:
1. Willie talks about his first flat. He had a large barrel of beer containing 40 pints (about 20 litres). It leaked and went through the ceiling into the flat below. When he opened the barrel, it was empty.

2. Julia talks about her first day at primary school. She was very excited, and on the way home she went upstairs on a double decker bus. Unfortunately, she fell down the stairs and refused to go to school the next day.

4

This final activity simply gives the learners an opportunity to talk about the experiences they listened to on the recording and recycle a few of the adjectives from Exercise 2.

Personal Study Workbook

1: Words with similar meanings: vocabulary
2: Something's missing here: irregular verbs
5: Famous people look back: reading

QUICK NOTES

This went well:

....

....

There was a problem with:

....

....

Things to think about:

....

....

HOW TIMES HAVE CHANGED

Introduction

The first lesson revised the past simple; this lesson has further discussion using the past simple but also revises ways of talking about the future and includes new vocabulary input. Practice takes the form of several personalised speaking activities, and in the final activity the learners have an opportunity to shape a short piece of writing involving past, present and future.

Suggested steps

1

You could start by recalling a few memories yourself (don't say much about the rest of the world otherwise the learners may not have any new information of their own to recall). Then put them in groups for the discussion.

Option

If your class are mostly around twenty years of age, you may feel that you will get more response if they talk about life fifteen years ago. With a middle-aged group, you could extend it to twenty-five years ago.

2

Give the learners two minutes to read through the list, look up new words and underline anything they still don't understand. Clarify any problems. You may also wish to highlight the use of comparative structures: comparative adjectives, *more/less* or *fewer* + noun group; *more* as an adverb.

3

The choice of time frame is still yours, although the potential for change is reduced if you discuss any period less than twenty years ago. At the end, get feedback from the groups to see if they agree, but avoid asking direct questions about the list, otherwise the learners will simply say *true* or *false* rather than using the language in the list.

4

Highlight the use of *will* and *won't* for predictions. You may also need to practise the pronunciation of *won't* and contrast it with *want*.

> **Language Point**
>
> Learners often say sentences like:
> *I think he won't come.*
> Most native speakers would prefer to make the first verb negative and say:
> *I don't think he'll come.*

Elicit some examples about the future, then ask the learners to work in groups. Monitor and conduct feedback.

5

Put the three time phrases on the board (*in the past*, *nowadays* and *in the future*) and ask the learners to predict which tenses would be used after each one. Then tell them to read the texts to see if they were correct. Clarify any vocabulary problems in the texts, then do the final activity. Allow the learners to work individually if they wish. Encourage them to read each other's work at the end; this is often extremely motivating.

Option

Instead of asking the learners to read the texts, read the first text aloud yourself (with their books shut) and stop at *in the future*. Ask them to predict the end of the text. You could do the same for the second text, or put the learners in pairs, asking one to read the first two sections of the handwriting text and the other to predict the ending.

Personal Study Workbook

4: Word stress in compounds: pronunciation
6: Looking back: recent history: listening

```
QUICK NOTES

This went well:
.............................................................
.............................................................

There was a problem with:
.............................................................
.............................................................

Things to think about:
.............................................................
.............................................................
```

NOW AND THEN

Introduction

The third lesson in this opening unit brings together different uses of the present continuous. The learners begin by matching pictures and dialogues, which are then used to analyse the different uses of the present continuous. A personalised speaking activity provides further practice, and in the final activity the learners' understanding of the concepts is further tested in their ability to make grammatical choices involving the present simple and/or present continuous; present continuous and/or *will*; and present continuous and/or *going to*.

Suggested steps

1

Follow the instructions in the Class Book.

Answer key

1. c   2. b   3. a

2

This is an opportunity for some creativity from the learners, but it also gives you the chance to highlight some useful words and expressions in the dialogues. When the pairs have extended the dialogues and compared with others, listen to some of their extensions and then highlight the following from the dialogues:

I haven't seen you for ages. (= I haven't seen you for a long time.)
How are things? (= How are you? / How's life?)
I haven't got long. (= I can't stop and talk a long time.)
We fixed it up. (= We arranged it.)

3

Ask the learners to complete the task individually and compare with a partner, then elicit answers.

Answer key

1. Dialogue 2: I'm working at the hospital right now.
2. Dialogue 3: I'm working at the hospital all week. (i.e. next week)
3. Dialogue 1: I'm working at the hospital in the casualty department at the moment.

4

Tell the learners to complete the table with real examples about themselves. When they have finished, put them in pairs for the practice/testing activity, and be prepared to help out if there is any disagreement over the answers.

Option 1

Instead of asking for truthful examples, you could ask the learners to include some real examples and some invented ones. Then, in the practice phase, listeners have to say a) which concept of the present continuous is being used, and b) whether they believe it is true or invented.

Option 2

At the end of the activity, you could ask the learners to repeat it, only this time the listeners respond to the statements and ask questions. For example:

A: *I'm wearing my father's watch.*
B: *Really. Do you often wear it?*
A: *I'm having lunch with my sister next week.*
B: *Oh. Where?*

5

This final activity tests the learners on their ability to distinguish between the present continuous and other structures (present simple, *will*, and the *going to* future). Elicit answers from the pairs and discuss any problems.

Answer key

1. b. is wrong   2. a. is wrong
3. a. and b. are both correct   4. a. is wrong
5. b. is wrong

Personal Study Workbook

7: Mixed tenses: writing

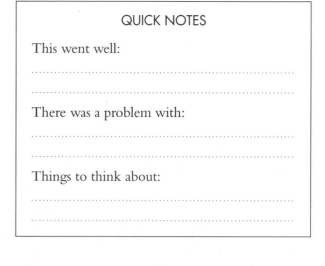

QUICK NOTES

This went well:

....

....

There was a problem with:

....

....

Things to think about:

....

....

REVIEW AND DEVELOPMENT

Introduction

In the rest of the book, the final lesson in each unit revises language from previous units; in this first unit, we consider revision techniques in general. The purpose is not to tell the learners how to revise, but to make them aware of different strategies, and to give them ideas which they could incorporate in their own learning.

Suggested steps

1

Ask the group if they think revision is important. If not, why not? (Make sure they know the meaning of *revision*.) Then let them read the text and get their responses.

2

Ask the learners to underline or highlight the words and phrases which mean the same as *revise*, then they can compare with a partner. Clarify any problems and highlight the use of *tend to* – it is a very common verb used to express a generalisation.

Put them in groups for the second part of the exercise.

Answer key

to go back and look at something
to review something
to have another look at something
to go over something
to look through something

Option

From your discussion of *when* the learners revise, you might like to try to agree on a timetable that seems reasonably effective without being too time-consuming; unrealistic goals are very demotivating. In *The Brain Book* (Routledge & Kegan Paul, 1979), Peter Russell suggests that new material should be revised briefly within 24 hours of initial learning, and then further revision should take place after a week, and then again after a month. The learners may feel that is a lot, but *little and often* is, in our opinion, the best strategy, and you can use the *Review and development* sections in the Class Book, the exercises in the Personal Study Workbook, and the tests in the Teacher's Book, to support this revision timetable.

3

This is an opportunity for the learners to explore and expand different ideas for revision. When individuals have written down a handful of ideas using the pictures and their own ideas, put them in pairs to compare and get more ideas, then encourage them to move around the class freely to see if they can gather any more. At the end, ask individuals to shout out any idea they got from someone else that they think would be useful. Put these ideas on the board or on a poster.

4 ▭

Play the recording and see if there are any new ideas not mentioned so far. Finally, create small groups so that the learners can sift through the ideas once more and decide on the best ones.

Answer key

See the tapescript on page 142.

5

This introduces the learners to the idea of going back over previous lessons with a specific learning purpose, rather than just aimlessly flicking through pages. Introduce the activity with a few ideas:
- Are there specific words and phrases which the learners would like to put in their notebooks? The list of things people did 20 years ago may be a good source here.
- Are there any passages the learners would like to read aloud, just to practise saying English sentences? The short texts on parking and writing are suitable for this.
- Are there any personal memories the learners would like to write down?
- Would the learners like to work in pairs so they can test each other?

When you feel the group have enough ideas, you can let them work on their own or with a partner for as long as you like.

Option

This would also be an ideal homework activity with the learners giving feedback at the beginning of the next lesson.

Personal Study Workbook

3: Grouping words by topic: vocabulary
8: Speaking partners
9: Visual dictionary

QUICK NOTES

This went well:

....

....

There was a problem with:

....

....

Things to think about:

....

....

2

HOW DOES THAT SOUND?

CONTENTS

Language focus:	comparative structures	
	countable and uncountable nouns	
	pronunciation	
Vocabulary:	adjectives	
	ways of talking	
	class words, e.g. *furniture*, *toys*	
Skills:	Speaking:	talking about pronunciation problems
		describing personal experiences
		identifying sounds and noises
	Listening:	how to improve your pronunciation
		people illustrating the meaning of words
		through sound, e.g. *shout*, *whisper*
	Writing:	sentence completion

HOW DO YOU SOUND IN ENGLISH?

Introduction

The learners are introduced to vocabulary items which are useful when talking about pronunciation, and then they listen to an expert giving some advice on practical ways to improve pronunciation. This is immediately followed by several exercises which enable the learners to work on both word stress and sentence rhythm, and in the process they will also acquire new vocabulary. We very much hope that this focus on pronunciation will encourage the learners to take their own pronunciation seriously, and that the advice they are given will prove useful to them throughout their learning. You may even wish to play the recording several times during your course.

Suggested steps

1

Most learners will be familiar with some of the terms in the box, so it's probably more interesting to put key words, e.g. *sound*, *syllable*, etc. on the board or OHP, then try to elicit definitions and examples from the group. And as you do this, keep the momentum going with choral and individual drilling of the examples to ensure that the group not only understand the terms but can also produce them.

Option

It is your decision whether you wish to teach phonetic symbols systematically, but we believe it does provide an invaluable guide for the learners, and the key symbols can be mastered very easily with just five or ten minutes'

practice over the first five or six lessons; then reinforced throughout the course as you provide phonemic transcriptions alongside much of the new vocabulary.

Now put the learners in groups and let them discuss questions 1–3. We have found that the length of the discussion here can vary enormously, so be prepared to move on quite quickly or just sit and listen for ten or fifteen minutes. At the end, enlist the help of the different groups to summarise the main points arising, and put them on the board (this may help with the listening in Exercise 2).

2 ▭▭ ▭▭

Introduce the listening and then play the appropriate version of the recording. As the learners are making notes, you may wish either to pause the recording at certain points or play the whole passage twice. At the end, let them compare with a partner, then elicit answers. The tapescript is on page 142.

Answer key

1. Listen carefully to examples of English for five minutes a day and focus on a special feature each time, e.g. a sound, or the rhythm and stress of English, or how high and low the voice goes.
2. The quickest way to improve is through work on stress. When you learn a new word, check the stress on the word and make sure you can say it correctly. Also, make regular stress on phrases and sentences when you are speaking.
3. Try 'shadowing'. Listen to a speaker of English and repeat phrases just after the speaker has said them.
4. Watch speakers of English and try to imitate the way they look: their mouths, position of head, body movement, etc.

3

Show the learners clearly how stress can be marked on individual words, and encourage them to do the same in their own notebooks. They can make a start with the lists of words in the book, which are all a common source of error for different nationalities and for different reasons. When they have finished, check their answers and practise the pronunciation if necessary.

Answer key

Jobs	*Countries*	*Concrete nouns*
policeman	Italy	vegetable
engineer	Japan	calculator
professor	Egypt	magazine
secretary	Brazil	certificate
photographer	Iran	machine

Abstract nouns	*Adjectives*
development	necessary
industry	interesting
advantages	reliable
career	Arabic
democracy	comfortable

4

This is an opportunity to check that the learners can get the stress right when a word is embedded in a sentence, but it is also a chance to work on sentence stress with some very common sentence patterns, e.g. *Do you know anyone who is …?* When individuals have finished, listen and drill some of their examples before putting them in pairs for further practice.

5

Move round and monitor the pairs carefully and correct where necessary.

If you feel this focus on pronunciation has been useful and engaging for the learners, you could extend it with Worksheet 2 on page 117, which focuses on individual sound problems.

Personal Study Workbook

  5: Weak forms: pronunciation
  6: Hearing dogs for the deaf: reading
10: Visual dictionary

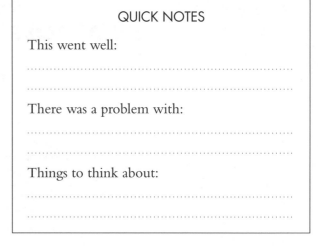

QUICK NOTES

This went well:

....

....

There was a problem with:

....

....

Things to think about:

....

....

WHAT A VOICE

Introduction

The lesson begins with the presentation and practice of words describing the different ways we talk, and progresses to a focus on different comparative structures. These two areas of language input then converge as the learners listen to people talking in a variety of ways and use comparative structures to talk about them. The lesson ends with the learners experimenting with different ways of talking.

Suggested steps

1

Play the recording of the first sound. Ask the group what the person is doing. When you have the answer and they know what is expected of them, play the rest of the recording. If they are not sure, they can write *I think the person is …* . Check the answers at the end and clarify any problems.

Answer key

1. Someone is shouting.
2. Someone is crying.
3. Someone is whispering.
4. Some people are cheering.
5. Someone is yelling.
6. Someone is mumbling.
7. Someone is whistling.
8. Someone is screaming.

> *Language Point:* **shout** *and* **yell**
> These words are obviously very close in meaning, but *yell* suggests that the shouting is very loud (hence the common expression *yelling at the top of his voice*) and the person is in an emotional state of excitement or anger.

Option

For further practice, put the class into groups of three, and ask one person to do each of the things in the box, i.e. shout, mumble, whisper, and so on. The other two in each group are in competition to see who can identify the sound first. This will produce a fairly noisy and chaotic classroom for a couple of minutes, but it's fun.

2

This consolidates the vocabulary in a more analytical and restrained way, but may also create the need for additional lexical items. For example, some learners may wish to say that people *usually whisper when they are being secretive*, but without actually knowing the word *secretive*. You may be called on to help in this way. At the end, listen to different examples round the class, then put them in pairs to personalise their sentences. If you hear anything very amusing or interesting, ask that person to tell the class at the end.

3

The learners should be familiar with comparative structures, so the first part of the exercise is simply to check that they do understand the basic rules governing the use of the different ways of forming comparatives in English.

Answer key

1. His voice is **louder than** mine.
2. correct
3. It's **worse than** mine.
4. correct
5. She's **better than** the other assistant.
6. correct
7. The children are **happier** now.
8. correct

There is probably nothing in the second part of the exercise that the learners have not seen before, but in our experience learners at this level often do not make use of these modifying structures.

4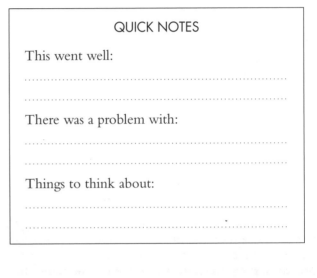

Play the example first, without referring to the book, and see if you can elicit the right answer. If the learners seem unsure, do the next pair of sentences as well. After that, play the rest of the recording, pausing after each one for the learners to write their answers. Then put them in pairs to compare. The tapescript is on page 143.

Answer key

The learners may have different but legitimate answers to some pairs of sentences. These are possible answers.
1. The second speaker is louder / more excited than the first.
2. The first speaker is younger than the second.
3. The second speaker's voice is deeper than that of the first speaker.
4. The first speaker is more polite than the second.
5. The second speaker is softer / more attractive/seductive than the first.
6. The second speaker is more anxious than the first.

5

Follow the instructions in the Class Book. As the learners say their sentences, monitor their general pronunciation and correct their word stress and sentence stress where necessary.

Personal Study Workbook

2: Much more interesting than I thought: comparatives and superlatives
3: Opposites: superlatives
4: In a soft voice: adjectives and adverbs

QUICK NOTES

This went well:

....
....

There was a problem with:

....
....

Things to think about:

....
....

DOES IT MAKE A NOISE?

Introduction

Much of the lesson is spent identifying things that make specific noises, or noises in specific locations. The theme is used to assist the learners in understanding new vocabulary, and it also provides the context in which the learners use various countable and uncountable nouns. This is the main language focus of the lesson, with specific attention being paid to nouns which are uncountable in English but countable in many other languages, e.g. *weather* and *training*.

Suggested steps

1

If you would like to make this first exercise more communicative, you could ask the learners to underline all the words in the list they know, and circle the words they don't know (or are not sure about). They can then move round the class enlisting the help of other learners with the items they don't know. With a monolingual class, this is one situation where the learners should be able to make use of the L1 if a simple clear translation equivalent is available. If you speak the learners' L1, you will also be in a position to know whether their translation is accurate. And if it is not accurate, you can use this situation to talk about the pros and cons of translation. Clarify any problems at the end.

2 ▭

The recording is a series of questions testing the vocabulary in Exercise 1. Play it through once and then let the learners compare answers. If necessary, play it a second time, then check with the whole group. The tapescript is on page 143.

Answer key

1. yes
2. yes
3. yes
4. industrial machinery
5. electric drill
6. putting butter on toast
7. wind, rain, hail stones, some snow
8. no (not usually)
9. air conditioning
10. It can do.
11. no (not usually)
12. a toy car, a train, a gun, a rattle (for babies)
13. no (unless it's the chimes of a clock)
14. someone brushing their teeth
15. no

3

Look at the dictionary entries with the group. If your class have access to monolingual dictionaries which are different from the ones represented in the book, you should ask them to tell you how their dictionaries show countable or uncountable nouns.

4

Go through the examples first. If you do not have enough dictionaries to share one between two, use groups instead of pairs. (It is important that the learners have access to dictionaries because dictionary training is a vital part of the activity, and without them the learners will simply be guessing a lot of the time with no context to help them.)

In feedback you will need to focus particularly on the items which your learners find most difficult, e.g. in monolingual groups, any problems of L1 interference; and on the items which are both countable and uncountable with different senses (e.g. *a paper* = a newspaper or an academic document; *a room* = part of a building, but *room* = space; *toast* = toasted bread, but there is also *to drink a toast* in tribute to someone, etc.).

Answer key

Countable	Uncountable	Countable/Uncountable
toy	furniture	room
bomb	weather★	experience
lorry	luggage	time
electric drill	research	hair
hammer	training	toast
	scenery	paper
	accommodation	work
	machinery	
	equipment	
	traffic	
	advice	
	air conditioning	

★ except in the phrase *in all weathers*; not, we feel a high frequency item relevant to learners at this level.

5

It would be sensible to put the example sentence on the board and ask the learners to make it plural. Continue until they have made both noun and pronoun plural, then they will understand what they have to do. Emphasise that some sentences cannot be changed, otherwise the learners may try to change things which they know cannot be changed.

Option

If the group have enjoyed Exercise 5, you could put them in pairs to write some sentences of their own, which another pair must then make plural where possible. They should obviously try to mix countable and uncountable nouns in their sentences as in Exercise 5.

Answer key

1. no change
2. We put our luggage next to the escalators.
3. Their advice was very helpful.
4. no change
5. The lorries were destroyed by the bombs.
6. no change
7. Have they had any training for this work?
8. Their research involved special equipment.

6

This draws together the grammar point of the lesson with the theme of the lesson and unit, i.e. noise, sound and speaking. Follow the instructions in the Class Book, first eliciting one or two examples from the group to give them the idea and get them started. Check answers at the end.

Answer key

Possible answers

	Countable noun	Uncountable noun
1.		
no noise at all	a photo	air
a slight noise if you drop it	a pen	sugar
a noise you don't like	a drill	chalk on a blackboard
2.		
reminds you of a season	an electric fan (summer)	ice (autumn)
a noise in the street	a lorry	traffic
a quiet continuous noise	a computer	air conditioning

Personal Study Workbook

1: *Hair or hairs?*: uncountable nouns
7: *Where would you hear it?*: listening
8: *Sound story*: writing
9: *Speaking partners*

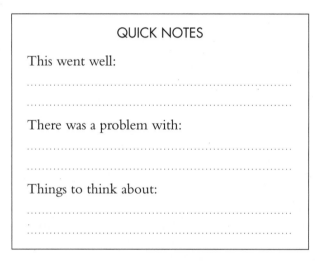

```
QUICK NOTES

This went well:
.........................................................
.........................................................

There was a problem with:
.........................................................
.........................................................

Things to think about:
.........................................................
.........................................................
```

REVIEW AND DEVELOPMENT

REVIEW OF UNIT 1

1

If your learners (or some of them) are familiar with bingo, ask them to explain the game to you or anyone who isn't familiar; this is very good language practice and often provides the context for useful language input. Then follow the instructions in the Class Book.
If the game is successful, you could repeat it with different verbs and by recording fifteen sentences yourself. (After a reasonable time lapse, you could probably repeat this same exercise from the book. Most learners will have forgotten the sentences and the order in which they occur.) The tapescript is on page 143.

2

Follow the instructions in the Class Book.

Answer key

1. We only eat vegetables **in** season.
2. I didn't like the film **at** all.
3. I'm not looking forward **to** Monday morning.
4. Could you look **after** the children while I go shopping?
5. **In** general people don't write many things **by** hand.
6. The couple get married **at** the end of the book.
7. I'm afraid the manager is away **on** holiday right now.
8. **In** the past many homes didn't have central heating. **In** fact, they didn't have much heating **at** all.

3

Some books make a clear distinction between the /t/ and /d/ ending in the past tense of different verbs. We do not feel this is a serious issue in *connected speech*, but if you wish, you could ask your learners to subdivide the first group into these different endings. For the rest of the exercise, follow the instructions in the Class Book.

Answer key

/t/ *or* /d/	/ɪd/
embarrassed	excited
scared	delighted
surprised	interested
relaxed	disappointed
shocked	
frightened	
confused	
astonished	

```
QUICK NOTES

This went well:
.........................................................
.........................................................

There was a problem with:
.........................................................
.........................................................

Things to think about:
.........................................................
.........................................................
```

3

GAMES PEOPLE PLAY

CONTENTS

Language focus: expressing likes and dislikes, preferences and opinions
verb + -ing form or infinitive; preposition + -ing form
defining and paraphrasing

Vocabulary: sport and leisure activities
verb and adjective + preposition
describing character

Skills: Speaking: giving opinions about sport
discussing game shows
qualities of game show contestants
playing a guessing game

Listening: people talking about leisure interests
people playing a guessing game

Reading: a text about game show contestants

Writing: describing your own sport and leisure interests

I'M NOT VERY KEEN ON IT

Introduction

The lexical focus of the lesson is sport, but as there are many people who do not like sport of any kind, we have created an additional focus on different ways of expressing likes and dislikes, and different ways of giving opinions. We hope this will give everyone an interest in the lesson whether they like sport or hate it. With the focus on likes, dislikes and opinions, most of the lesson revolves around a series of personalised speaking activities which provide opportunities to practise the target language.

Suggested steps

1

Setting a time limit for this warm-up activity will introduce a competitive element which your learners may enjoy. You may also need to remind them that they should try to answer the questions without using the same sport more than once.

Answer key

Possible answers
- horse racing, darts, swimming, gymnastics, skiing
- football, basketball, baseball, volleyball
- tennis, squash, badminton
- motor racing, athletics
- table tennis, snooker (billiards)
- boxing
- golf

2

The twelve sentences will contain new vocabulary for your group, but if you pre-teach any of it, the activity will be superfluous. We would therefore suggest that you put the learners in small groups, equip each group with dictionaries (if possible, bilingual and monolingual), and let them get on with it. During feedback, ask groups to justify their answers and be prepared to spend quite a bit of time highlighting and clarifying the target language, as there are a number of potential problems:
- new vocabulary, e.g. *barbaric*, *stimulating* and *competitive*;
- common errors, e.g. *good at* (not *good in*);
- word stress and pronunciation difficulties, e.g. *complicated*, *favourite* /feɪvərɪt/;
- false friends, e.g. *terrific* means *terrifying* in some languages;
- common word combinations, e.g. *I can't see the point of it* should be learned as fixed expressions. See also the following Language Point.

During feedback, you may also need to remind the learners that they will have a chance to express their own personal opinions.

Answer key

Positive: 3, 5, 7, 9
Negative: 1, 4, 6, 8, 11, 12
Neutral: 2, 10 (You could argue that sentence 5 is also neutral.)

Language Point: adding emphasis

1. We can use *at all* at the end of a negative sentence to add emphasis to the point we are making. The second sentence here is much stronger in tone than the first.
   I didn't like the film.
   I didn't like the film **at all**.
2. We can also use either *much* or *far* before a comparative structure to add emphasis:
   The book was better than the film.
   The book was **much/far** *better than the film.*

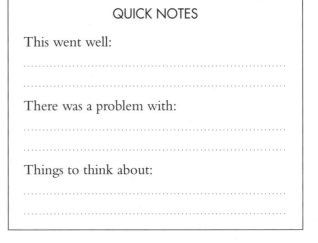

QUICK NOTES

This went well:

....

....

There was a problem with:

....

....

Things to think about:

....

....

3

Now the learners can express their own opinions. Put them into small groups (if you know them well, try to put them with people who will probably have different views), then let them exchange opinions. You could give one or two examples yourself, showing how the names of different sports will replace the pronoun *it* in the sentences, e.g. *Personally, I think boxing is barbaric; ice hockey requires a lot of skill*, etc. Monitor the groups and then conduct a short feedback on the ideas and language use.

4

Matching the words and pictures can be done with the whole group, before allowing pairs or groups to discuss the task.

Answer key

A dominoes   B Monopoly   C chess
D backgammon   E playing cards   F pinball
G majong   H crossword puzzles

5

You could include this task in Exercise 4 so that the group can engage in an extended speaking activity without interruption. Equally, you may wish to separate the tasks in order to give each one a clearer focus. Much will depend on your group and how they like to work.

6

This is a very free activity to end the lesson, and can be omitted if you are short of time or if your learners seem to be fully engaged in discussing Exercises 4 or 5. Do it another time in this case.

Personal Study Workbook

5: Women are catching up: reading
7: Speaking partners
8: Visual dictionary

I NEVER LIKED GAMES AT SCHOOL

Introduction

The learners complete a gapped text through an intensive listening activity, and this text is then used as the source to illustrate and focus on two uses of the *-ing* form: after certain verbs, and after prepositions. Verbs commonly followed by an infinitive are also included as a contrast with the verb + *-ing* form. Finally, the learners have an opportunity to use some of these verbs in a writing activity, using the listening texts as a model.

Suggested steps

1

You could begin by giving a personal example, then put the class into small groups for further discussion. Conduct a short feedback if there are any interesting reasons for people either taking up or giving up different games or sports. This is also a natural context for *used to* + infinitive, so you could make a note of whether it occurs in the conversations, and if so, if it is used correctly.

2

Play the recording, pausing after each speaker so that the learners have time to write down their answers. If necessary, play each one a second time. Let the learners compare answers, then check with the whole group.

Answer key

See the tapescript on page 144.

3

Check the meaning of any new verbs in the list – *avoid* and *persuade* may be new for most of the group – then allow the learners to complete the task. When they have finished they can check their answers by looking back at Exercise 2. Make sure they cover the text first before doing Exercise 3.

Answer key

decide to do	persuade somebody to do
avoid doing	imagine doing
enjoy doing	want to do
manage to do	can't stand doing
spend time doing	learn to do
refuse to do	

4

If the learners are having difficulty with this task, you could give them a clue and tell them that the key to the answer is in what comes before each *-ing* form. You could then follow up with further examples, e.g. *I'm tired of learning English*; *I can't go without speaking to her.*

5

If you insist on the use of three *-ing* form or infinitive constructions, you may restrict your learners in what they want to say. So, use the rubric as a guideline only and simply encourage them to try to incorporate the target verbs and structures.

If you wish to provide further practice of verb + *-ing* form or infinitive and/or extend the range of such verbs, you could do Worksheet 3 (on page 118) at this point.

Personal Study Workbook

1: What are you talking about?: *-ing* form or infinitive?
2: Are you good at sport?: word + preposition

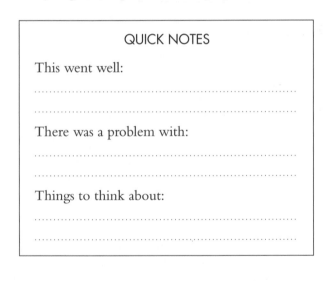

QUICK NOTES

This went well:

....

....

There was a problem with:

....

....

Things to think about:

....

....

GAME SHOWS

Introduction

The group has to consider the qualities required of good game show contestants before reading a text about this subject. This is followed by the introduction of some vocabulary and key expressions used in defining and paraphrasing. A listening activity reinforces these expressions and provides the model for a guessing game which the learners play to give them further practice of the new expressions and lexis.

Suggested steps

1

Put the learners in groups and provide a little prompting if they are having difficulty guessing what the games are; this may be the case if they do not have a comparable game show in their own country.

Option 1

With a multinational group, there may be quite a lot of interest in the different game shows in different countries. If Exercise 1 does stimulate a lot of discussion, you could ask the learners to think about other game shows on television in their country and then explain the game to other members of the group. Are there any games which appear in every country?

Option 2

With a monolingual group, ask them to make a list of all the game shows on television that they can recall, with their feelings about them, e.g. *I like it, I hate it, I never watch it, it's stupid*, etc. Then put the class into small groups to exchange opinions.

2

Instead of giving them the example from the book, you could introduce Exercise 2 yourself and try to elicit one or two examples from the group; this will help to draw them into the activity. They are unlikely to be able to think of a lot of characteristics, so make this quite brief and then tell them to go on to the text.

After they have completed the text you could check their understanding by asking for a list of qualities that make good game show contestants. Put these on the board so that the groups can then use it in their discussion of suitable class members for game shows. This may actually be more fun as a whole-group activity.

3

The learners can do the vocabulary activity individually, followed by a quick feedback. Check pronunciation at this stage.

Answer key

Very frightened means the same as *scared stiff.*
Awful is the opposite of *fantastic.*
Chess is a type of board game.
A *library* is the place where you borrow books.
An *architect* is someone who designs buildings.
A *key* is the thing you use for locking a door.
Suntan lotion is the stuff you use to protect your skin in
    summer.

4 📼

Play the first recording. This not only shows the learners how to play the game, but also highlights most of the expressions from Exercise 3, which are so important in defining and paraphrasing other lexical items. The tapescript is on page 144.

> *Language Point:* things *and* stuff
>
> We often use these very vague words when we cannot think of the name of something at the moment of speaking. We also use them when the listener knows what the speaker is talking about, so the speaker does not need to name it. We usually use *thing(s)* for countable words and *stuff* for uncountable words:
>
> *Put that thing (bowl) in the cupboard, will you?*
> *Where are my things (papers, books, files, etc.)?*
> *What's that stuff (aftershave) you're wearing?*
> *I have to take this horrible stuff (cough medicine in a bottle) three times a day.*

Answer key

See the tapescript on page 144.

5

Play the second recording. As a way of coaxing the learners into the spirit of the game, make sure you encourage them to shout out the answers as quickly and as loud as possible. The tapescript is on page 144.

Answer key

1. to wake up   2. perfume, aftershave, etc.
3. journalist (also reporter)   4. post office   5. giraffe
6. towel   7. often

6

Organise the class into teams of about five. The first team comes to the front, one member of the team is given a set of words to define and the others in his/her team shout out their guesses. Once they have guessed accurately, the team leader goes on to the next word. If they have any problems with a word, they leave it and go on to the next. Set a time limit of two minutes. Then the next team comes to the front and does the same, etc.

You may wish to make up your own list of words for each group to define (based on your previous teaching), but here are a few suggestions:

Set 1	Set 2	Set 3
optimistic	poker (the game)	a tennis court
golf	a stadium	a nurse
a TV studio	confident	a potato
a contestant	shampoo	pessimistic
soap	a chess champion	to revise
shy	to enjoy	face cream
a calculator	a suitcase	a camera

Option 1

If this works well, you can obviously repeat the game throughout the course. It is an excellent way of revising vocabulary and it provides continual reinforcement for this important language of defining and paraphrasing.

Option 2

You may decide to play the game in groups of three, giving each person in each group one of the lists above to define for the other two.

Personal Study Workbook

3: A wall of sound: pronunciation
4: Full of skill or skilful?: vocabulary and listening
6: What does that mean?: writing

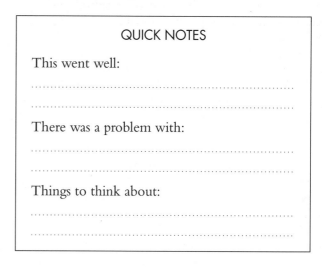

```
QUICK NOTES

This went well:
.............................................
.............................................

There was a problem with:
.............................................
.............................................

Things to think about:
.............................................
.............................................
```

REVIEW AND DEVELOPMENT

REVIEW OF UNIT 1

1A

Make sure the learners write down the sentences they hear, i.e. including the mistakes. The tapescript (with the mistakes) is on page 144.

1B

Now they can correct the sentences and compare them with a partner.

Answer key

1. She didn't know any students at all.
2. I want to meet a few people.
3. I'm not looking forward to next week.
4. We listen to music every day.
5. I might see him this evening.
6. He's worried about his exam results.
7. They're going to meet him at five o'clock.
8. I would like to find a new job.

2

When you go through the answers to this exercise, make sure the learners read out their sentences so that you can check their pronunciation. There are a number of recurrent problems:
pronouncing the final -ed as a separate syllable in *shocked* or *embarrassed*.
nervous /nɜːvəs/
vague /veɪg/
worried /wʌrid/

Answer key

1. upset   2. worried   3. great   4. scared stiff   5. vague
6. nervous   7. embarrassed   8. delighted

GAME SHOWS   19

REVIEW OF UNIT 2

1

This serves as a reading comprehension exercise, but the main point is to see if the learners remember the meanings of some of the uncountable nouns, e.g. *equipment* and *scenery*, and whether they remember to use a singular verb after them. Remind your learners to try to answer the questions without repeating words from the text – this will be a test of their understanding of the vocabulary and provide them with a useful paraphrasing task.

Answer key
1. He thought the public transport was good.
2. He thought the furniture was very basic and not very good.
3. The weather was perfect for skiing.
4. He thought the scenery was wonderful.
5. The children learned to ski very quickly.
6. He thought the traffic was awful.
7. The equipment they hired was very expensive.
8. He felt that some of the people in the skiing class were silly.
9. He thought the advice given to them at the travel agency was extremely useful.

2

Follow the instructions in the Class Book.

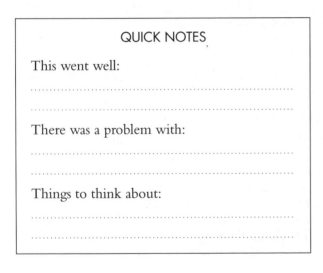

QUICK NOTES

This went well:

....

....

There was a problem with:

....

....

Things to think about:

....

....

4

NEWSPAPERS AND MAGAZINES

CONTENTS

Language focus: past simple and present perfect
for, since and *yet*

Vocabulary: social issues
newspapers
adjectives describing people

Skills: Speaking: conducting a magazine survey
choosing articles for a magazine
newspapers in your own country
Listening: facts about *¡Hola!* and *Hello!* magazines
Reading: a magazine survey
matching newspaper extracts with the
articles they come from
Writing: readership profiles
past actions and experiences

WHAT'S IN THE NEWS?

Introduction

Most adult learners are interested in newspapers and newspaper vocabulary, and with a multinational group it is potentially a very interesting topic for cross-cultural comparisons. The lesson begins with a focus on vocabulary and then develops through a series of activities combining reading and writing with personalised speaking.

Suggested steps

1

Ask the group if they have read a newspaper today, and if so, can they remember the headline (explain the word *headline* if they don't know it). Next, tell them they are going to look at some more vocabulary items associated with newspapers. Put them in pairs and let them do the first part of the task.

Answer key

1. True
2. False.(An editor makes decisions about the articles that will appear in the paper, and may also edit some of those articles.)
3. True and false (Most news journalists are looking for scoops, but journalists who have a daily or weekly column about specific subjects may not.)
4. True
5. False (They have short articles and lots of photos.)
6. False (A caption is the words accompanying a photograph.)

When you have checked their answers, the learners can choose two words from the remaining list and write true or false sentences. Monitor their sentences while they are working, then let them work with another pair.

2

This is of particular interest to multinational groups as newspapers can vary around the world and learners are usually very interested in the type of press enjoyed by other nationalities. In our experience the discussion may go beyond the questions set and soon range over many possible issues. Be prepared to let it flow and make a note of any interesting ideas or language points to bring out in feedback at the end.

With a monolingual group you may get more response with a slightly different approach. See the option below.

Option

With a monolingual group, ask half the class to bring in the two most downmarket daily papers, while the other half brings in the two most upmarket papers. Divide the class in half (or into groups of four if you have more than twelve), and ask the learners to compare the contents page in the book with their national papers (either the downmarket ones or upmarket ones). When they have answered the first three questions, the two halves can compare their results, and then together they can discuss question 4.

3

Ask the learners to explain why extract a is from the financial news section, then tell them to match the rest of the extracts and texts, and be prepared to explain their reasons. They can compare with a partner before you check with the group and clarify any problems of vocabulary.

Answer key

a	– Financial news	g	– International news
b	– TV and radio	h	– Obituary
c	– Reviews	i	– Home news
d	– Crossword	j	– Sport
e	– Letters	k	– Classified advertisements
f	– Weather	l	– Features

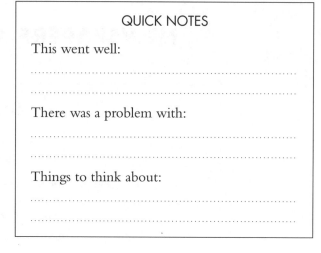

4

Follow the instructions in the Class Book. When you check the answers point out that most are very clear examples of collocation and often co-occur with other words in the extract, e.g. *cloudy and showers*; *reach an agreement*; *strength and courage*; *score a goal*; and so on.

Answer key

a. ... cause problems for shareholders who invested in the *company*

b. ... new seven-part serial starring the talented *actress*

c. ... who remains on stage throughout the play, gives a magnificent *performance*

d. 14. People wear them in *bed* (7)

e. ... in reply to your article last Thursday, which greatly distorted the *facts*

f. ... dull and cloudy with occasional *showers*

g. ... hope that foreign ministers will be able to reach an *agreement*

h. ... will always be remembered for her strength and *courage*

i. ... will be deciding who to vote for in the local *election*

j. ... defeat looked certain in the second half after the third *goal*

k. ... unwanted gift. Will accept £50 or nearest *offer*

l. ... the stresses of modern life are thought to be one of the main reasons for the rise in *divorce*

5

This could be given for homework. If so, ask the learners to write not just the sentence after the extract, but also the first part of the sentence leading into the extract. Ask them to do that for several of the extracts. You can compare answers in the next lesson.

If your group is particularly interested in newspapers, you could also follow up with Worksheet 4 on page 119.

Personal Study Workbook

2: The press in Britain: vocabulary
3: Grouping words by topic: vocabulary

READING HABITS

Introduction

The magazine survey provides an extended speaking activity for the first part of the lesson. But it also includes examples of the past simple and present perfect, which the learners analyse to establish differences in use. These differences are tested in a controlled activity, and then practised in a freer personalised speaking activity to finish the lesson.

Suggested steps

1

Ask one member of the group these questions about magazines, then get the learners to interview each other in a similar way.

Option

In the *Review and development* section for Unit 6 there is a group of magazine titles from England (some real, some invented), and the learners have to try to guess what each one is about. You could take a small selection of these and do the same activity as a warm-up.

2

Introduce the survey, and get the learners to complete it individually. Then put them in groups to compare and discuss their answers. Monitor and note down correct or incorrect uses of the past simple and present perfect simple.

3

Put the two example sentences on the board in separate columns, and ask the learners to tell you what the tenses are called. If they seem unsure, elicit further examples until the forms are clearly established. (This should, however, be revision.) Then ask them to shout out further examples from the survey. Put them on the board in the appropriate column and add one or two correct examples you noted down in the discussion, e.g. *I read* Time *magazine last month.*

Then put them in pairs again to complete the second task, making it clear that you simply want the learners to match these definitions with the examples you have written on the board. When they have finished, elicit answers.

Answer key

1. Have you ever read it? Have you heard of it? Have you ever written anything for a magazine?
2. Have you read any other magazines this week?
3. How long have you had your subscription?

4

Now put the learners back into pairs to analyse the examples of the past tense and decide why they are used. Encourage them to think about the present perfect examples and how they are different from the uses of the past simple. Check with the group when they have finished.

Answer key

1. The first speech bubble describes something that happened during a time period which is finished, i.e. *yesterday*.
2. The past simple in the second speech bubble also refers to actions which happened during a finished time period, i.e. *last week*.
3. The past simple in the third speech bubble refers to something that happened in a period of time which is finished, i.e. the period *before* the last ten years.

5

This is a straightforward testing exercise. You could set it for homework if you do not wish to use up class time for this exercise, but if you do, you will need to monitor the next exercise carefully to ensure the learners have a clear grasp of the different concepts.

Answer key

1. has worked; started; moved; wrote; enjoyed; left; has been; became
2. Have you written; finished; Has the editor seen
3. has he had; has been; bought

6

This final exercise keeps the focus on the same point of grammar, but the learners now have the opportunity for more personalisation. Encourage a range of answers, but tell the learners to be truthful. Monitor while they are writing and help if necessary. When they are ready, let them exchange information and ask further questions.

Personal Study Workbook

1: How long?: past simple and present perfect
6: What do you read?: listening

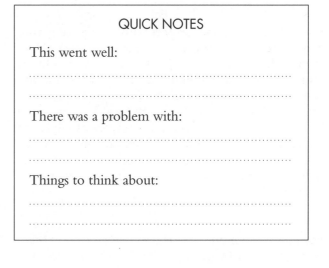

QUICK NOTES

This went well:

....

....

There was a problem with:

....

....

Things to think about:

....

....

¡HOLA! (AND HELLO!)

Introduction

The theme of magazines continues with a look at a phenomenon in magazine publishing: the Spanish magazine *¡Hola!* and the British version *Hello!* The lesson has quite a long listening activity in which the learners find out different facts about the two magazines, and then moves into an extended role play in which they must take the part of magazine editors and choose the best stories for their readers. There is also quite a lot of new vocabulary about social issues and practice of dates and numbers.

Suggested steps

1

Many European groups will be familiar with *¡Hola!*, but if you are working outside Europe, the first exercise may not provoke much response. If so, you could direct the group to the pictures in the book and ask them to tell you what kind of magazine it is, and whether or not it is likely to be very popular.

2 ▭▭ ▭▭

Play the appropriate recording, pausing it if you feel the learners need more time to write down their answers. Let them compare their answers with a partner before you go through the answers with the whole group. You may also wish to highlight the fact that certain answers will require the past tense, and others the present perfect. The tapescript is on page 144.

Answer key

1. 1944
2. has been the boss
3. 675,000; £10m
4. they are never attacked or criticised in the magazine, so they trust it
5. 1988
6. the end of 1990
7. sales have continued to rise
8. 25%

3

Look at the readership profiles with the whole group, explaining new vocabulary as necessary. You could ask them if they know any magazines which would fit these profiles in their own countries. Then put them in pairs to write a readership profile of *¡Hola!/Hello!* readers, using the same framework, i.e. the sex, age, and social background of the readers, and the types of subject they are interested in. Monitor the pairs carefully. Several pairs can read out their profiles (preferably ones which differ), and the group can discuss which is the most accurate.

Option

For groups from one country, you could extend this writing activity by getting them to write profiles of magazines that the whole group will be familiar with.

4

Introduce the role play. Let the learners individually choose one of the magazines, and then from their decisions, you can organise them into groups. Whichever magazine they choose, they must assume they are choosing stories for readers from their own countries (this should cause some disagreements in multicultural groups as certain topics will be popular in one country but not another). You will need to go through the list of stories first and explain new vocabulary, e.g. *cope with* and *cancer*, and you may also wish to say something about the grammar of newspaper headlines.

> **Language Point: newspaper headlines**
>
> Headlines have their own grammar rules, and this can make them difficult to understand:
> 1. Verbs are often omitted and the headline is just a string of nouns and adjectives, e.g. *New drug treatment for premature babies.* (Not *There is a new drug treatment …* or *A new drug treatment for premature babies has been found.*)
> 2. When verbs are used they are often in the present simple when referring to past events, e.g. *Leading politician reveals …* (This obviously means that a leading politician *has revealed …*). For future events, the full infinitive is normally used: *Clinton to meet Republican Senators* (Clinton is going to meet them).
> 3. When complex verb forms are used, the auxiliary verbs are often omitted, e.g. *Son of Hollywood film star arrested …* (not *has been arrested*).
> 4. Articles are usually omitted, e.g. *(The) son of (a) Hollywood film star …*

When the group understands the new language and they are clear about the purpose of the activity, let the role play continue for as long as possible if they are clearly enjoying the discussion. Monitor their language while they work. Conduct a feedback on both their decisions and their language use.

Option

If you would like further practice of the vocabulary in these headlines, you could do this writing activity.

The first sentence or two of an article usually expands on the information condensed into a brief headline. For example, the opening of the story with the headline *Son of Hollywood film star arrested for drug taking*, might be: *Bart Miller, the teenage son of famous film star Miles Miller, was arrested last night outside his home in Los Angeles. Police said the boy was in possession of cocaine.*

Now get the learners to take more headlines and write the openings of the stories.

Personal Study Workbook

4: When and where?: prepositions
5: *Women & Guns*: reading
7: Personal questionnaire: writing
8: Speaking partners

> ### QUICK NOTES
>
> This went well:
>
> ....
>
> ....
>
> There was a problem with:
>
> ....
>
> ....
>
> Things to think about:
>
> ....
>
> ....

REVIEW AND DEVELOPMENT

REVIEW OF UNIT 2

1

This revises vocabulary from the unit and has scope for pronunciation work, but it is clearly designed to be a fun activity, so do encourage the group to enjoy themselves and try to think up interesting stage directions for the actors.

In addition to acting out their own dialogues (it will be much more effective if you can get everyone to learn their lines), you could get the learners to swap dialogues, and then their task is to read the dialogue and simultaneously take account of the stage directions which have been written in by another pair.

2

Put the example exchange on the board without the answers, and then try to elicit possible answers (more than one if possible). When you are sure the learners have got the idea of the activity, let them complete it in pairs. If you have a large class, it may be more practical for pairs to read their dialogues to other pairs.

Answer key

Possible answers
1. oranges; bananas
2. post office; garage
3. Colombia; Ecuador
4. ruler; briefcase
5. economics; banking

REVIEW OF UNIT 3

1

Just follow the instructions in the Class Book, but go through the examples carefully so the learners understand what they have to do.

Answer key

Possible answers

	Synonym	*Opposite*
worried	anxious	relaxed
complicated	complex, difficult	simple, easy
to improve	get better	deteriorate, get worse
shy	timid (especially animals)	self-confident
fabulous	marvellous, wonderful	terrible, awful
to refuse	to reject	to accept
to win	to triumph	to lose
boring	dull	exciting, interesting
frightened	afraid, scared	calm
keen (on)	fond (of)	
unusual	strange, uncommon	common, typical
wet		dry

2

Give the learners a chance to complete their sentences and monitor that they are using the correct *-ing* or infinitive form after the verbs. Then put them in groups and follow the instructions in the Class Book. If they have produced many similar sentence endings, you could ask them why they think the endings were so predictable.

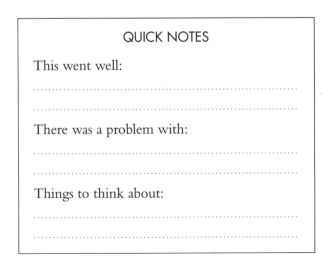

QUICK NOTES

This went well:

....

....

There was a problem with:

....

....

Things to think about:

....

....

5

RELATIONSHIPS

```
                              CONTENTS

    Language focus:   probability and possibility
                      prepositions in wh- questions
                      revision of question forms
                      's for possession

    Vocabulary:       family relationships
                      verb + preposition

    Skills:   Speaking:   describing a family tree
                          talking about family relationships
                          discussing effects of birth order
                          talking about close relationships
              Listening:  marking sentence stress on questions
                          a family tree
                          people talking about 'star' diagrams
              Reading:    a text about birth order and its influence
                          on children's characters
```

WHO WAS OONA MARRIED TO?

Introduction

In this lesson, the learners listen to a recording and complete a family tree. This revises and extends the vocabulary of relationships and leads into question practice as the learners exchange information about their own families. The lesson concludes with a focus on the rules governing the use of 's and further practice.

Suggested steps

1

You could begin by asking the learners to name any famous families, i.e. where there is more than one famous person in the family. Obvious examples are royal or political families, but there are many examples in Hollywood (Kirk and Michael Douglas; Michael Jackson and his brothers and sisters), and artists and writers: Picasso and his daughter, Paloma; Ernest Hemingway and his actress daughter, Mariel. In monolingual classes, the learners will draw on examples from their own country.

Then ask them to look at the family tree in their book and work out what relation the people listed were/are to Charlie Chaplin.

Answer key

Oona O'Neill: Chaplin's wife *[his fourth wife]*
Hannah Chaplin: his mother
Lita Grey: Chaplin's wife *[his second wife]*
Sydney Earle Chaplin: his son

2 ▢▢ ▣▣

Give the learners a few moments to look at the family tree in Exercise 1. If family trees are culturally new to them, explain how they work. Go over the task, then play the recording (Version 1 or 2), more than once if necessary. Do feedback on the answers after the learners have compared in groups. The tapescript is on page 145.

Answer key

See the completed family tree on the opposite page.

3

Do the first two examples together, then let the learners continue in pairs, using dictionaries if necessary to check any new words. Alternatively, you could ask them to look through the exercise and ask about unknown items before they begin. Provide feedback on answers at the end.

Answer key

1. Charles Chaplin
2. Shane
3. Shane
4. Aurelia and James
5. Charles Junior and Sydney Earle
6. Aurelia
7. James O'Neill

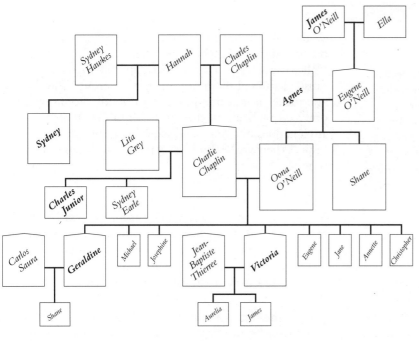

4

Allow 5–10 minutes for the learners to draw their own family trees. Impress on them that if they prefer, they can draw a tree of someone else they know well. This might be advisable in any case if your learners know each other very well socially and know each other's families; otherwise there will be little real communication happening. Monitor and make sure that they are leaving some question marks as in the Chaplin tree.

When they have completed their trees, demonstrate with one learner in front of the group what they have to do, i.e. you ask the learner questions about the missing information. Then let them continue in pairs. Monitor and collect examples of language points you wish to deal with in feedback afterwards.

5

Before you begin, look at the example together and highlight the possessive *'s*. Oral practice of this would be useful to reinforce the point – you could drill the sentences a and b.

Do the first one or two together, then ask the learners to write and speak their answers together. In feedback at the end, correct any errors with *'s*. These may be due to pronunciation rather than grammar – some nationalities find it difficult to add an *s* in this environment. Make sure they can hear the *s*, and help them to produce it in simple examples first.

Answer key

1. Your mother's brother or your father's brother
2. Your mother's mother or your father's mother
3. Your uncle's daughter or son, or your aunt's daughter or son
4. Your sister's husband or your husband's/wife's brother
5. Your brother's daughter or your sister's daughter
6. Your mother's son by another father or your father's son by another mother

6

This rounds up the use of the apostrophe, and includes examples of plurals. Give the learners a few moments to reflect on the answer in groups before feedback.

Answer key

We use *'s* when the noun before it is singular.
the child's mother (There is only one child.)
We use *s'* when the noun before it is plural.
the boys' father (There are two or more boys.)
With irregular plurals, we add *'s*.
the children's grandparents

Option

At the end of the lesson, ask the learners to list all the family vocabulary using the material on the page and the tapescript. Then ask them to see how many times the sound /ʌ/ occurs (e.g. m<u>o</u>ther, s<u>o</u>n).

Personal Study Workbook

1: Who's your father-in-law?: vocabulary
4: Consonants: pronunciation of /s/, /z/ and *th*
5: I was the youngest: listening

QUICK NOTES

This went well:

....

....

There was a problem with:

....

....

Things to think about:

....

....

Introduction

This lesson deals with a range of structures and lexical items around the theme of possibility and probability. The learners begin by ranking phrases in order of probability. They are then led into the topic of the reading text through personalised discussion. The text is then read intensively, and the learners practise the expressions of possibility and probability by discussing the content of the text. Finally, the learners make their own statements about relationships for discussion.

Suggested steps

1

You could begin by saying something about yourself which may or may not be true, e.g. *I've met the President of X*; *my father was a famous gymnast*; *I can speak Swahili*; and so on. Ask the learners to guess whether each statement is true, probably true, might be true, etc. This will lead into Exercise 1.

Ask the learners to put the expressions in the diagram, making sure that they understand they are ranking in terms of probability.

Answer key

It is definitely true.
It is probably true. / It is likely to be true.
It may be true. / It might be true.
It is unlikely to be true. / I doubt if it is true.
It definitely isn't true.

Language Point

Word order may be a problem for the learners here. *Probably* and *definitely* usually go after the verb *to be* in affirmative sentences, and in negative sentences if *not* is used in its full form.
It is probably (not) true.
It is definitely (not) true.
However, in negative contractions, these adverbs go before the verb.
It probably isn't true.
It definitely isn't true.

Elicit the answers and put them on the board; then highlight the problems with word order. There are a number of pronunciation problems in the expressions, so provide oral practice of the forms, correcting and highlighting the pronunciation of *(un)likely*, *doubt*, *might* and *definitely*, in particular.

2

Follow the instructions in the Class Book. If you want more controlled practice, do Worksheet 5 on page 120 instead.

3

With discussion activities of this kind, you may find that one group finishes while the others are still going strong. If that happens, you can redistribute the ones who have finished and tell them to join another group. You should also make clear at the outset that nobody should feel obliged to talk about their position in the family. If anyone does not want to disclose such information, respect their wishes and just ask them to listen to the others.

4

You could pre-teach a few items from the text before the learners read. Useful items might be: *strict*, *persuasion*, *power*, *bossy*, *pressure*. Check that everyone understands *first born* and *later children*, then ask the learners to read the text, but make it clear that some of the facts are not true.

Discuss the first point together, asking them to use the expressions from Exercise 1. When they have responded to the first point, tell them the answer (it is not true). Then ask them to continue in a similar way for the other points in small groups. Reinforce the fact that you want them to practise the probability expressions and monitor to ensure that they are doing so. They will of course need to use other language to back up their opinions.

Answer key

Parents talk to first-born babies **more** than to later children.
Parents are less strict with later children than with their first child.
First-born children use physical power to get what they want, whereas later children make more use of persuasion.
First-born children are more bossy than **later** children.
Later children also tell tales to their parents and teachers about other children.
First-born children identify more strongly with their parents and are more influenced by them.
First-born children have more communication with their parents than **later** children.
First-born children are under more pressure to do well at school.
Psychologists have a clearer idea of the personality of first-born children than of other children.

At the end, ask them to read the answers on page 171. Allow time for reactions to this – they may wish to disagree or comment on the statements.

5

The lesson ends with a personalised activity in which the learners can offer more opinions of their own. Give them a few minutes to read and complete the sentences in their own way (making clear that this task is open-ended and they can write what they like). Remind them once again of the expressions they have been using from the first exercise, then put them in groups for discussion. Monitor and provide feedback at the end.

Personal Study Workbook

3: Me and my future: future predictions
7: Reference words: writing
8: Speaking partners

QUICK NOTES

This went well:

....

....

There was a problem with:

....

....

Things to think about:

....

....

WHO ARE YOU CLOSEST TO?

Introduction

This lesson presents verbs with 'dangling' prepositions in question forms. After a contextualised gap filling activity, the learners practise the questions in a personalised way. They then draw a diagram to represent their own or someone else's relationships, and describe them to other learners. At the end, they listen to some people describing their star diagrams and return to practice of the prepositions.

Suggested steps

1

Pre-teach the meaning of the following items, without focusing too much on the prepositions they are followed by: *to confide (in someone) to rely (on someone) to lie (i.e. tell a lie)*. Then ask the learners to complete the questions, using the prepositions in the box.

Answer key

1. Who could you talk to?
2. Who could you confide in?
3. Who could you spend a week with?
4. Who would you call upon/on for help?
5. Who would you turn to for advice?
   Who could you borrow money from?
6. Who could you rely on to keep your secret?
7. Who would you be prepared to lie for/to?

Language Point: prepositions at the end of clauses: 'dangling prepositions'

It is normal in everyday English for prepositions to come at the end of clauses, and this is particularly common in question forms:
Who is she talking to? is more common than *To whom is she talking?* which sounds very formal in English.

Many learners find this strange and are uncomfortable with it, either because this word order is not the same in their own language, or in some cases because they may previously have learnt from a more 'bookish' grammar.

2 ▢▢

Play the recording and check the learners have marked the main stress on the verb and not the final preposition. Drill one or two of the sentences then let the learners repeat the sentences to themselves quietly. Move round and monitor at this point and listen to their pronunciation; correct where necessary.

3

When you are happy with the learners' pronunciation, move on to the personalised activity in pairs. Conduct a short feedback at the end.

4 ▢▢

Ask the learners to read the text and study the diagrams. Then play the recording, and ask them to write in their answers. The tapescript is on page 145.

Answer key

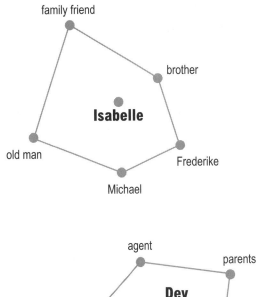

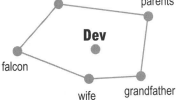

3

The explanation in the box is there for reference, but it may be more effective if you go through the analysis on the board and elicit the example sentences after explaining each rule. You might similarly wish to do the practice activity round the class, and if you do, make sure the learners are linking the words together, e.g. *turn it on*.

4

This extends the lexical set even further by adding more phrasal verbs and also verbs which use the prefix *un-* to reverse an action. Put the learners in pairs for this activity and then go through the answers with the whole group. Put them back into pairs for the practice, but first demonstrate the activity yourself using different learners. The activity is most effective if the pairs keep up the momentum with fairly swift exchanges, so tell the group to keep practising until they can ask and answer the questions without hesitation.

Answer key

turn off   undo   unwrap   unplug   untie   unload
get out (of)   unfasten   unpack   put out   unlock

5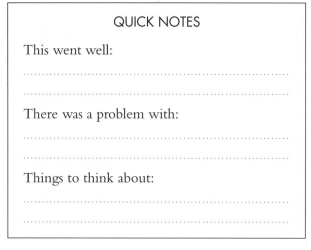

Choose the most appropriate version of the listening and play it to the group. Let them compare answers in pairs before you check with the whole group.

Answer key

Version 1:
1. How to tie your shoelaces
2. Wrapping up presents

Version 2:
1. Packing
2. Lighting a barbecue

6

It may help to show your learners the tapescript for Exercise 5 in order for them to see a clear model. The tapescript is on page 145. You will also have to move round and monitor weaker learners who may find it difficult to disguise the activity they are describing. If you are short of time, ask them to write a paragraph individually for homework.

Personal Study Workbook

2: Plug in the TV: verb + noun collocation
6: Guess what she's talking about: listening

I WAS JUST PLUGGING IT IN WHEN ...

Introduction

The initial activity presents new vocabulary, and much of it involves the use of reflexive pronouns and *get* + past participle, so this is highlighted for the learners in the second exercise. The rest of the lesson concentrates on the use of the past continuous, beginning with a focus on the concept and then followed up with a testing exercise to consolidate understanding. Finally, the learners have an opportunity to use the structure in a more personalised way in stories which also allow practice of the new vocabulary from the beginning of the lesson.

Suggested steps

1

You could begin by asking your learners what accidents may happen when you are making a hot drink. With luck this will elicit *spill it* or *scald yourself*, although you will probably have to teach one or both of these words in English (they are more likely to use gesture for *spill* and *burn* instead of *scald*). After this, they can continue with the exercise, individually or in pairs. When they have finished, check the answers with the group and clarify any new items.

Answer key

1. d   2. a   3. g   4. f   5. c   6. b   7. e

2

Write the two sentences on the board and elicit the difference. This should not present a problem, although you may have learners who will immediately ask the difference between *get* + past participle and the passive, i.e. verb forms of *to be* + past participle.

This structure is sometimes used with a passive meaning in informal English:

I got mugged on the way to the underground.
He got caught by the police for speeding.

You cannot always construct passive sentences with *get* + past participle. For example, you *cannot* say:

~~*The book got written by Martin Amis.*~~

Generally we use *get* + past participle for something that is done suddenly or unexpectedly (*mugged* or *caught by the police*).

There are also a few situations where we use *get* + past participle in preference to a reflexive pronoun for something we do to ourselves, e.g. *get dressed.*

The short activity at the end of the exercise will help to consolidate the two structures, but if you want more practice of *get* + past participle, try Worksheet 6 on page 121.

Answer key for Worksheet 6

He got lost, he got changed and *he got undressed* are reflexive. The rest are passive.

3

Your group should be quite familiar with the past simple and continuous, so this is just a quick check. But understanding a grammar point is one thing, being able to explain it quite another, so you may find it easier to move on to Exercise 4 without spending too long on abstract discussion.

Answer key

1. The past continuous
2. This is explained fully in the Grammar Reference at the back of the Class Book on page 161.

4

While your learners are doing the exercise individually, move round and monitor so you can see who is having difficulty. If it is just one or two learners, try to give as much personal help as you can. (You can tell the rest to compare their answers, and if necessary, to do a further practice exercise, e.g. *Consequences* in the *Review and development* section of Unit 7 on page 53.) If you suspect a number of learners are having difficulty, it would be better to tackle the problems with the whole group at the end of the activity.

Answer key

The mistakes are as follows:
We were having a lovely time should be *We had a lovely time* because the dinner with friends was finished.
When I walked home should be *When I was walking home* because the speaker is describing a longer activity which is then interrupted by a series of actions.
But I was telling him should be *but I told him* because it is simply one completed action in a series of completed actions.

5

If the group has handled all the language input without too much difficulty, you can give them as much freedom as you like for this final activity. If they still seem unsure about some of the structures, encourage them to try them out even if it means restricting their creativity at this point. You may also decide to give your learners the added support of developing a story in pairs. If so, make sure you split the pairs for the final activity in which they tell their stories in groups and guess which stories are true.

Option

The best way to introduce the final activity is probably to tell a story yourself and get the group to guess if it is true.

Personal Study Workbook

1: Diary extract: past simple and past continuous
3: Can you do it to yourself?: *get* + past participle and reflexive pronouns
8: Speaking partners

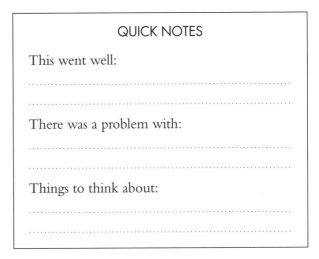

```
QUICK NOTES

This went well:
..............................................
..............................................

There was a problem with:
..............................................
..............................................

Things to think about:
..............................................
..............................................
```

DO YOU QUEUE?

Introduction

After two intensive lessons of language input, this lesson offers mostly a range of skills activities: cross-cultural speaking activities on the subject of queuing; a reading text and listening text; and further personalised speaking activities as the learners discuss how they would respond in a number of different situations.

Suggested steps

1

Start by asking the whole class the first part of question 1. Ask each learner to write down their answer, then conduct a quick feedback, and while you do so, ask for examples of what they queue for. As soon as you have established an interest in the subject, teach them the expression *to jump the queue*, then put them in pairs to

COURSES

CONTENTS

Language focus:	uncountable nouns ending in *s*	
	defining relative clauses (1)	
	adjective + infinitive	
	ask/tell + object + infinitive	
	obligation in the past	
Vocabulary:	education	
	household activities	
Skills:	Speaking:	educational backgrounds/experiences
		duties of a butler
		imagining you had your own butler
		qualities required for different jobs
		qualities required in your own job
	Listening:	how butlers remove a drunken guest
		actors describing drama school
	Reading:	a text about becoming a butler
	Writing:	sentence completion about education and
		doing the duties of a butler

TURNING POINTS

Introduction

The lesson presents a large group of vocabulary items connected with academic subjects and success and failure in education, and these are practised through several personalised speaking activities. In addition, there is a focus on two language points which can be common sources of error – uncountable nouns ending in *s*, and relative clauses. There is also a dual-level listening activity.

Suggested steps

1

The majority of learners will have few problems with the meaning of these words, but the pronunciation is another matter. In some cases the problems are specific to a word, e.g. *psychology* /saɪkɒlədʒi/, but this is a good opportunity to pass on certain general patterns of English pronunciation which will help with these and many other items:

– the /tʃə/ sound for words ending *-ture*, e.g. /ægrɪkʌltʃə/
– the /tri/ sound for words ending *-tory*, e.g. /hɪstri/ or *-tary*, e.g. /elɪmentri/
– the stress on most words ending *-ics* is on the syllable before, e.g. *econŏmics* and *statĭstics*
– the stress on words ending *-ology* or *-osophy* is on the third syllable from the end, e.g. *psychŏlogy* or *philŏsophy*

Make sure your learners have plenty of opportunity to say the words and achieve acceptable pronunciation before they go into groups to discuss the subjects with reference to school or university in their own country.

2

It is an easy mistake for learners to see the *s* ending and assume a plural verb is required. If you are working with a monolingual group who might make this mistake through L1 interference, highlight this point very clearly. And also highlight the fact that this group of nouns has an *s* ending; an equally common error is for the learners to talk about ~~math~~ or ~~physic~~ (although *math* without an *s* is correct in American English).

3

The learners could work individually or in pairs on this activity; but if they are on their own, they should really have access to dictionaries to help them. Go over the answers carefully, clarifying any important differences. See the following Language Point.

Language Point: degree, diploma, certificate

In Britain, a *degree* refers specifically to the title which is given by a university for the successful completion of the course. If a British person says they have a degree, they mean that they have a BA (Bachelor of Arts) or BSc (Bachelor of Science).

A *diploma* is awarded for other types of course and exam, e.g. a diploma in marketing or hotel management.

A *certificate* is an official piece of paper which verifies certain facts, e.g. *a birth certificate*. It is also very common to receive a certificate verifying that you have passed an exam or completed a course.

Put the class into groups to talk about their experiences. This is obviously an opportunity to use the vocabulary from the previous activity and Exercise 1, but don't worry too much if the learners are engaged in discussion but not using the target language very much. Make a note of any further vocabulary they obviously need to express their ideas, and highlight it for the group at the end of the activity if you think it is likely to be useful for most of them.

Answer key

1. take; fail
2. certificate
3. bad; brilliant
4. badly
5. enrol

4 ☐☐

Pre-teach *turning point*, i.e. when something happens that has a radical effect on you and changes the course of your life in some way, and draw the learners' attention to the questions they must think about while listening. Play the recording. If necessary, play the recording a second time, and make sure they have sufficient time to write down their answers. At the end, they can compare with a partner before you go through the answers with the group *or* let them check themselves using the tapescript on page 146.

Answer key

1. When she was 12 or 13.
2. She refused to learn Latin and learned German instead.
3. She couldn't go to university.★

★ In the past, you could not study certain subjects at university unless you had a base in Latin. This is no longer true.

5

You could put the learners in pairs or write the two sentences on the board and try to elicit the answer from the group as a whole.

Answer key

You must include *that* if it is the subject of the relative clause (as in 1); but you can omit it if it is the object of the relative clause (as in 2).

6

Give the learners the task individually so that you can check they understand, and monitor the group while they are working.

Answer key

1. You can omit *that*.
2. You cannot omit *that*.
3. You can omit *that*.
4. You can omit *that*.
5. You can omit *that*.
6. You can omit *that*.
7. You cannot omit *who*.

Finish with the personalised speaking activity. Give the learners time to complete the sentences and then put them in groups for the discussion.

Option

If your group are all adults who left school many years ago, it may be of more interest to them to talk about their work in Exercise 6; this just entails changing the sentences slightly. For example:
The thing that interests me most in my job is …

Personal Study Workbook

1: I studied maths and chemistry: *s* ending
2: The person I most admire: relative clauses
4: Text reading aloud: pronunciation
5: A turning point in my life: writing

QUICK NOTES

This went well:

....

....

There was a problem with:

....

....

Things to think about:

....

....

TURNING POINTS

Introduction

If you feel the subject of training to become a butler is not of interest to your particular group, you may wish to omit this particular lesson. We have found, however, that most learners are intrigued by this topic, which also lends itself to some interesting discussion on the subject of 'service'. The theme is developed through a listening and reading text, around which the learners have several personalised and creative speaking activities. There are also more structured tasks involving the manipulation of various verb structures, and adjectives commonly followed by an infinitive.

Suggested steps

1

You could mime being a butler, e.g. open a door to let someone in, take their coat, walk round the class with an imaginary tray of drinks, offering a glass to various learners in the process; and from this elicit the job you are miming and, if possible, the name of the job. After that, introduce the task, illustrate through the example, then give the learners several minutes to complete their sentences before they discuss them in groups.

2

Elicit or explain the key vocabulary items in the pictures (they also appear later in the reading text), then put them back into groups to discuss the easiest and most difficult to learn. Encourage the learners to give reasons for their answers, and check that they are using superlatives accurately.

Answer key

The pictures all show duties a trainee butler has to learn. The pictures show the following:
1. ironing a newspaper
2. learning to open and pour champagne
3. polishing the silver
4. serving food
5. bowing to guests
6. packing a suitcase

3

Tell the learners to read the text and think about their answers to the two pre-set questions. Put them in pairs to discuss their answers, then conduct a short group feedback.

Answer key

1. Trainees learn how to bow, iron the morning paper, present and pour wine, pack a suitcase and remove badly-behaved guests. Some butlers may also perform the traditional skills of polishing silver and supervising staff.
2. Nowadays a butler is more of a manager. He or she has to be more mobile, move around from house to house, handle accounts, make travel arrangements, etc.

Option

You could ask the group if there are any skills they think a butler would require in their country that are not mentioned in the text. This might be interesting with both monolingual and multinational groups.

4

Omit this exercise if you think it will offend any of your learners. With the vast majority of groups this can be an enjoyably light-hearted activity with considerable scope for humour.

5 ▭

Play the recording. You can pause at several points for the learners to write answers, but it is probably better to play the whole thing twice with time at the end to complete the sentences. Check answers with the group or let them look at the tapescript on page 146. You may wish to highlight the verb patterns (*ask/tell someone to do something, explain that … + clause*) more formally on the board.

Answer key

1. to deal with the situation
2. to return to the dining room in five minutes and announce a phone call
3. to take the phone call in another room
4. and say there is no call
5. that the host is worried that the guest is embarrassing himself
6. to leave
7. to give him his car keys
8. a taxi

6

Go through the examples first and highlight the use of *would* here for hypothetical statements. Monitor the groups and make a note of the most humorous and interesting comments to tell the whole class at the end.

Personal Study Workbook

3: Please don't tell me what to do!: *ask/tell somebody to do something*
7: Back on course: reading

```
QUICK NOTES

This went well:
.............................................
.............................................

There was a problem with:
.............................................
.............................................

Things to think about:
.............................................
.............................................
```

Introduction

This is another lesson that peeps into a world your learners may be very interested in, but know little about: the training of an actor. After a warm-up activity in which the group discuss their favourite actors, a reading text on the skills of acting forms the central part of the lesson. This is followed by a discussion on the necessary skills for other related professions, e.g. politicians and writers, in which the learners are also encouraged to use various modal verbs, e.g. *have to* and *don't have to*. A listening text on acting school recycles these modals, this time in the past tense, and the lesson ends with a personalised speaking activity on the skills your learners require in their work.

Suggested steps

1

Follow the instructions in the Class Book.

2

You could introduce the text by referring back to the discussion in Exercise 1. Ask the group if they like their favourite actors/actresses for their natural talents and abilities, or for the qualities that they have developed over years of training and experience. Then give them the text to read. The task at the end includes some vocabulary they may not know, e.g. *agile* and *sensitive*, but the purpose of the task is for them to extract the general meaning from a dictionary and then refine that understanding by finding illustrations of the concepts in the text.

After they have worked individually and compared their answers in pairs, you can then check with the whole group and clarify any problems.

Answer key

Actors may have to be good mimics. (scripts … now require a greater variety of voices and accents)

Actors have to be fit. (acting … makes great demands on the actor in terms of physical movement)

Actors have to be agile. (they may even find themselves working in performances which involve dancing, falling and acrobatics)

Actors have to be observant. (they have to look and learn; they have to represent not only many types of people but also objects and machines)

They may have to be sensitive. (… be responsive to the character's use of language; … recall and recreate emotion … learn to work with each other, the director and the audience)

3

Divide the class into small groups and establish with each group that they must first decide on two of the jobs. Go through the example and then let them do it themselves. Naturally, if any group finishes before the others, tell

them to choose and discuss another of the jobs. Encourage them, as always, to try to justify their answers.

4 ▢▢ ▢▢

Explain the task, then choose the appropriate version of the recording for your group. Let the learners compare their answers while you monitor. If they appear to have missed anything, play the recording a second time. Check the answers. The tapescript is on page 146.

Answer key

Version 1:
1. She had to learn to fall.
   She had to learn to laugh and cry.
   She didn't have to learn to dance.
2. He had to learn 'rib reserve breathing' (a special breathing technique).
   He didn't have to learn to sing.

Version 2:
1. She had to learn to fence (to do stage fights).
   She didn't have to be a professional level (fencer).
2. He had to learn to develop characters: to explore emotions and use personal experiences to understand characters he was playing.
   He didn't have to learn to speak verse or sing or dance.

5

This is the type of activity which may last five or twenty-five minutes. If you are short of time but the group seem genuinely interested in the topic, try to return to it in a future lesson.

If the subject of acting has been of interest to the group, and they all come from the same country, you may also wish to try Worksheet 7 on page 121.

Personal Study Workbook

6: Listen and answer: listening and vocabulary
8: Speaking partners
9: Visual dictionary

QUICK NOTES

This went well:

....

....

There was a problem with:

....

....

Things to think about:

....

....

REVIEW OF UNIT 5

1

Some groups may find it difficult to discuss these questions cold; others may not have many ideas of their own without a bit more prompting. If you have doubts about your class, you may wish to begin with the text in part B, complete the controlled activity which tests understanding and draws attention to the language used to express different degrees of probability, and then finish with their personal response to the text and the initial questions.

2

Give the groups a time limit or tell each group to shout out when they have reached 20. If the learners respond well to this type of activity, you could reproduce it for other lexical areas, e.g. make a list of all the things that butlers have to learn at their training school. Don't stop until you have at least eight, then turn to the text on page 49 to check.

REVIEW OF UNIT 6

1

Look at the example with the class and brainstorm as many possible explanations as you can. When you have got at least four or five, put the learners in groups for the activity. Monitor the groups while they are working and make a note of anything important for feedback, e.g. a useful word or phrase that one group used, an error you think is worth highlighting, etc. In feedback, you could also ask the group to vote on the most unusual, amusing or likely explanation.

Answer key

Possible answers
1. Perhaps she was having a shower.
2. Perhaps he was sitting in church.
3. Maybe he was trying to light a candle.
4. Perhaps she was swimming.
5. Maybe he was driving home after a party.
6. Perhaps they were talking about a football match in class.
7. Maybe she was riding a bicycle and she wasn't concentrating.
8. Perhaps he was carrying a cup of coffee upstairs.

2

Follow the instructions in the Class Book. Some learners might spend ages trying to recall when they did something, so it is a good idea to maintain momentum by telling each group that if one person cannot think of an answer fairly quickly, the next person can respond instead. Later, the question can revert back to the first person for their response.

QUICK NOTES

This went well:

....
....

There was a problem with:

....
....

Things to think about:

....
....

ALL IN A DAY'S WORK

CONTENTS

Language focus:	link words: concession and addition making and refusing requests asking for and refusing permission
Vocabulary:	work verb + noun collocation fixed phrases
Skills:	Speaking: practising everyday situations; asking for and refusing permission pros and cons of being self-employed and working in a large company problem solving and management decisions
	Listening: people role playing a difficult interview
	Reading: a text on management styles
	Writing: using link words to write a paragraph on the pros and cons of being self-employed

HOW DO YOU COPE?

Introduction

The opening activity asks the learners to think about a series of situations they may have experienced, and through this personalisation we hope they will be motivated to find out how to handle these situations in English. The rest of the lesson examines the language needed for these situations, including a listening activity, before finishing with an opportunity for the learners to practise using role play.

Suggested steps

1

The learners will need time to think about these situations and it will also help if you can begin with your own examples – this will show them that the situations may be quite significant, e.g. you tell someone that a friend has had an accident, or very mundane, e.g. you ask someone to open a window and they clearly are reluctant. Check that they understand the situations, then put them in groups after a few minutes of reflection, and monitor their discussion carefully. In feedback try to draw out the interesting points in the discussion you heard, and encourage them to reflect on the most difficult or sensitive of these situations and how they felt.

2

Without explaining any of the phrases, see if they can work out the answers to the task in pairs, and remind them that they can also use an expression in more than one situation.

Answer key

Asking someone to do something they didn't want to do:
I'm afraid that …
I'd be grateful if you could …
Would it be possible for you to …?
Do you think you could …?
I'm very sorry but …
Getting information over the phone:
Do you think you could …?
I'd be grateful if you could …
Would it be possible for you to …?
Giving bad news:
I'm afraid that …
I'm very sorry but …
Asking for permission:
Would it be all right if I …?
I wonder if I could …?
I'd very much like to …
Do you mind if I …?
Refusing permission:
I'm afraid that …
I'm very sorry but …
I'm afraid that's out of the question.

3 ▭

You might save yourself some time here by quickly explaining any items you anticipate will be new, e.g. *keen, cutback, training budget*. Then give the learners time to read through and digest the situations.

Play the recording and put the class into pairs to discuss their answers, before doing feedback with the whole class.

Answer key

1. Situation 2
2. Some of the expressions used on the recordings are slight variations on those in the book. They are as follows:
   Dialogue 1:
   I wondered if …
   I'd be grateful if you'd …
   out of the question
   Dialogue 2:
   I wonder if I could …
   I'd really like to …
   I'd be grateful if you could …
   Would it be all right if I …?
   I'm afraid that's out of the question.
   I'd very much like to.
3. This is a matter of opinion, but the person making the request in the first situation seems a little less pushy and the boss seems a little more understanding.

4

If the pairs can incorporate most of the phrases from Exercise 2 in their role play, so much the better. However, it is important that their involvement in the activity is not stifled by constant prompting to use the target language. So, just move round the pairs, prompting if you feel it will help, and giving advice or encouragement as required. You should also be in a position to know which pairs have the most interesting exchanges for the others to listen to. At the end, give them feedback on their language with positive comments and some error correction if it is significant.

Option

If most of your group do not have jobs, they may not be very interested in practising the remaining situations and may not have the background to know how to handle the situation. In this case, you may prefer to use Worksheet 8 on page 122, which is a parallel activity using non-work situations.

Personal Study Workbook

1: Do you think you could …?: functional language
4: Putting it nicely: permission and requests
7: Dear Sir/Mrs Lewis/Bunty: writing

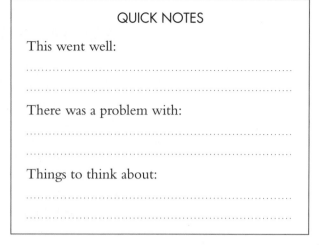

QUICK NOTES

This went well:
....
....

There was a problem with:
....
....

Things to think about:
....
....

PROS AND CONS

Introduction

The lesson begins by presenting common fixed phrases which refer to positive and negative features (e.g. *pros and cons*), and ends with a number of link words and phrases used to connect a piece of writing about advantages and disadvantages. The actual context for this contrast in the main part of the lesson is whether it is better to be self-employed or part of a company. This context allows a good deal of personalised discussion and also introduces a range of vocabulary items on the subject of work.

Suggested steps

1

Go straight into the exercise, and in feedback point out that these are form phrases in which the order is fixed, i.e. you can have *pros and cons* but not *cons and pros*.

Answer key

theory and practice
pros and cons
ups and downs
advantages and disadvantages
for and against

Option

If your group already knows the phrases from the first exercise, you could increase the input by asking them to name any other fixed phrases they know in which two words are joined by *and*. You can also look at Exercise 2 in the Personal Study Workbook, which is devoted to these fixed phrases.

2

If you have a mixed group in which some learners work and some don't, you can decide whether to mix the two or keep them separate. By monitoring the groups you will also see how much vocabulary they already know in relation to this subject. But as it is the focus of the next activity, you need not dwell too much on correction or input at this stage.

3

The learners can work on the task individually provided they have access to dictionaries; then they can discuss their answers in groups. Individual circumstances will obviously influence these factors a great deal (some people who are employed by others do not receive sickness pay; and some self-employed people cannot be very flexible about their holidays), so the answer key below is only there as a guideline. Give the learners feedback on their contribution at the end, add any further ideas to the list of sentences, and clarify any problems they have with the sentences.

Answer key

Possible answers
Pros:
You have more choice about the work you do.
Nobody above you gives you orders.
You can organise your working hours to suit yourself.
You can be flexible about holidays and days off.
There is no limit to what you can do.
Cons:
You don't receive sickness pay.
You don't have paid holidays.
You have nobody to share your problems with.
You have to manage your own financial affairs.
You lack job security.

4

Even though the learners have a model framework for the paragraph and the expressions to fill it, you will still find some learners who have difficulty grafting the content onto the various cohesive devices. Move round and help where necessary.

When the learners compare their answers, they can comment on both the construction and the content.

Option

You could do Exercise 4 using a different, i.e. non-work context if you think it would be more suitable. For example, one of the parents in a family (currently living in a big industrial city) has been offered a good job in a small town in the country. It is a very nice town, but the other parent might not be able to find a good job there, and there is a sixteen-year-old daughter to consider as well. Ask the class to think about the pros and cons of this situation in pairs and then write a paragraph about it.

5

You may want to start with one or two examples with the whole class before putting them in groups.

6

This is ideal for homework, either as a writing activity or as preparation for a short speech to start the next lesson. If you prefer to do it as a speaking activity,

encourage the learners to rehearse what they are going to say at home, and if you have access to an OHP, let them make their own OHTs for use during their speech. They could do this individually, or some learners could work in pairs. (This is often a wise tactic if you have any learners who would find it very intimidating to have to address the whole class without any help.)

Personal Study Workbook

2: It's in black and white: fixed phrases
3: Pros and cons, good and bad: work vocabulary

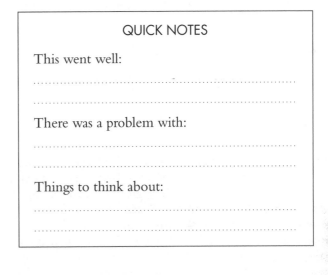

QUICK NOTES

This went well:
....
....

There was a problem with:
....
....

Things to think about:
....
....

DEMOCRATS AND AUTOCRATS

Introduction

As this lesson examines different styles of management, it is clearly most suitable for a group of learners who have had significant work experience and are in a position to comment on the possible pros and cons of different styles. Even so, the text on styles of management does provide the learners with a framework which should enable them to discuss the problem situations without the benefit of too much work experience. You must clearly use your own judgement here to decide if this lesson is suitable for your group.

Suggested steps

1

The learners will have an opportunity to see and use the target verbs later in the lesson, so this first exercise is to provide an initial guide to meaning. No pre-teaching should be necessary – the context, a dictionary and a process of elimination should be enough for most learners to arrive at the right answers and have a fair grasp of meaning. The exception might be the word *evaluate*, which you could explain as *examine and judge*. A useful synonym to teach at the same time is *assess*, and you may also decide to add the derived nouns *evaluation* and *assessment*. (*Continuous assessment* forms part of the education system in many countries and some learners may wish to know this expression.)

Answer key

1. solve   2. share   3. make   4. get   5. evaluate
6. consult   7. reach

2

You could introduce this activity by eliciting the meaning of *democrat* and *autocrat*. Then explain that the five styles of management cover the spectrum from one to the other, i.e. from a very democratic style to a very autocratic style. The learners' task is to read the five texts and put them in order. When they have finished you can check their answers and ask for responses based on their own work situations.

Answer key

DEMOCRATIC				AUTOCRATIC
4	1	5	3	2

3

It may be easier to tackle these situations one at a time. Put the class into small groups and give them a minute to read through the first situation. Clarify any problems and then let them work in their groups. Monitor and make notes. When they have clearly exhausted the subject, let the groups give each other feedback on their ideas and then give them some feedback on their use of language. Where possible, give them correction or input which may help them in the next situation.

Repeat the procedure for the second situation.

4

If the discussion has lasted quite a long time, you could give this activity for homework. If not, put the learners in pairs, and encourage them to organise the input into meaningful groups, and not just lists of words down a page. You can also encourage them to think of vocabulary not just as individual words, but more often combinations of words, phrases, expressions and sometimes whole sentences. For example:
One of the advantages of being self-employed
working for a company
reach an agreement
solve a problem
take time off work
theory and practice
training budget
make some/a lot of cutbacks
manage your own financial affairs
etc.

Personal Study Workbook

5: Listen and answer: listening and vocabulary
6: What's good about it?: reading
8: Speaking partners

REVIEW AND DEVELOPMENT

REVIEW OF UNIT 6

1

Look at the two examples for the first sentence and see if the group can add any other likely endings. Remind the learners that their sentences should give some indication of the meaning of the target vocabulary; if necessary, give an example of a sentence that does not do this, e.g. *I burnt myself yesterday morning.* When you are confident they have the right idea, let them complete the task individually before they get into groups to compare their answers. You could ask them to decide if there are any sentence endings which do not demonstrate in any way the meaning of the key words at the beginning of the sentence.

2

Follow the instructions in the Class Book.

REVIEW OF UNIT 7

1

Follow the instructions in the Class Book.

Answer key

1. When I was a child I did very **badly** at English.
2. At school we **didn't have to** wear a uniform.
3. The person who inspired me most was my art teacher. (No *he.*)
4. I apologised **for** my mistake.
5. The examiner asked me **to** read a text aloud in my oral interview.
6. Another student explained the rule (to me).
7. Someone told me not **to** use the front door.
8. At university we didn't **have** to go to lectures every day.

---

2 💿

Make sure your learners know how stress is indicated in
their dictionary. Sometimes the main stress is underlined;
sometimes there is a very small vertical dash ('); and
some dictionaries do not indicate stress at all.

Answer key

See the tapescript on page 147.

```
┌─────────────────────────────────────────────┐
│               QUICK NOTES                     │
│                                               │
│   This went well:                             │
│   .......................................     │
│   .......................................     │
│                                               │
│   There was a problem with:                   │
│   .......................................     │
│   .......................................     │
│                                               │
│   Things to think about:                      │
│   .......................................     │
│   .......................................     │
│                                               │
└─────────────────────────────────────────────┘
```

FROM THE CRADLE TO THE GRAVE

CONTENTS

Language focus: present simple passive
obligation, prohibition, permission

Vocabulary: ages and stages in life
birth, marriage and death
race, nationality, religion; wedding customs

Skills: Speaking: telling others about your family
discussing the best age to do certain things
what matters to people at different ages
talking about laws in your country
weddings in different countries

Listening: different people describing what is
important to them at their age

Reading: texts about weddings in different cultures

Writing: defining words and phrases

AGES AND STAGES

Introduction

The learners are taught the names of different ages and stages in life and many of the activities associated with them. This vocabulary is practised through personalised speaking activities and then further consolidated through a listening text in which native speakers of very different ages talk about the things that concern them at their stage of life. The lesson finishes with the learners doing the same activity with reference to their own age groups in their own countries.

Suggested steps

1

You could ask some of your learners how they would describe themselves in terms of their stage in life. A child? A teenager? A young man/woman? An adult? Middle-aged? Don't probe too much as certain learners may feel uncomfortable if they think they are being questioned about their age; and in some cultures it may not be appropriate. Then put them in pairs to work on the first task.

Answer key

Status	Stage
a baby	infancy
a child	childhood
a kid (informal)	
an adolescent	adolescence
a teenager	in your teens

Status	Stage
an adult	in your (early) 20s, 30s
	(mid)
	(late)
	middle-aged
a pensioner	retirement/when you are retired
an elderly person	in old age

2

This will probably be a fairly brief exchange, but does provide an opportunity for immediate personalisation of some of the target vocabulary.

Option

You can obviously extend the practice in Exercise 2 by getting the learners to mingle and talk to as many people as possible. If you do, tell them to try to remember as much as possible because you are going to test them afterwards.

After about ten minutes, stop them and throw out a series of questions quite quickly. Anyone can shout out an answer unless the answer is someone in their family – that must come from someone else. For example:
Has anyone got a sister in her teens?
Has anyone got a mother in her early fifties?
Has anyone got a father who is retired?
Has anyone got a son or daughter who is still a baby?

3

The meaning of some of these expressions is fairly transparent, e.g. *have a baby* (but possibly different in the learners' first language); other expressions may require some explanation, e.g. *take up gardening, take out insurance*, and *settle down*. See the Language Point below.

When you are happy that the group understands these expressions, organise the practice task. Go through the examples first and ask the group which one they would agree with. Then create small groups and let them discuss the other expressions. Monitor their discussion and conduct feedback at the end, giving both positive feedback and some error correction if you think it is important.

4 🔲

Ask the learners in pairs to try to predict the concerns of someone in their 20s, 40s and 60s. Get some brief feedback then play the recording. When you go through the answers, elicit also some reactions from the group. Are they surprised by any of the comments? The tapescript is on page 147.

Answer key

Speaker 1:
David (a young man) is concerned about finding a girlfriend, getting a car and a job, and the fact that there are always wars being fought somewhere in the world.
Speaker 2:
Judy (a middle-aged woman) is concerned mostly about her children's education, and worried about the advice she gives them. She is also more aware of death (after the death of her own father two years ago), and the fact that she is becoming the senior member of the family.
Speaker 3:
Walter (near retirement) is thinking about how he is going to spend his retirement and the rest of his life. He is also preoccupied with how the world has changed and how life is different for young people. He thinks most people of his age are preoccupied with the past to some extent.

5

Multinational groups can talk about people in general in their countries and so compare the concerns of people

of the same age from different countries. With a monolingual group, the discussion will need to focus on their own concerns to see whether people of the same age from the same country share the same concerns. If there are different answers in the monolingual group, you could open up the discussion to the whole class for them to decide on the concerns which they believe are the most typical and most common.

If the group seem interested in the concerns of people at different ages, you could extend it into a small project using Worksheet 9 on page 122. With learners in an English-speaking country this will provide speaking practice outside the classroom; with groups in their own country, this will mean the research is probably in the L1, but the feedback in class will be in English.

QUICK NOTES

This went well:

....

....

There was a problem with:

....

....

Things to think about:

....

....

RITES OF PASSAGE: THE FACTS

Introduction

Following a brief vocabulary activity on items related to birth, marriage and death, the learners compare laws in Britain with laws in their own country. Language of obligation, permission and prohibition is embedded in this comparison and then highlighted for analysis and further practice through a personalised activity.

If you are working outside of Europe, you should look through the lesson carefully as there may be concepts which your learners may not be familiar with.

Suggested steps

1

Most of the words in italics are clear and unambiguous, so the learners should be able to retrieve the meaning from dictionaries. You may, however, wish to explain or omit any words which would not translate meaningfully because they are not part of the culture you work in, e.g. *baptism* or *burial* or *cremation*.

At the end, check the meanings carefully as these words all appear in the next exercise and will cause problems if they are not understood.

Answer key

Possible answers
1. You record the event in a document and make it official.
2. As a baby or young child.
3. You get married, or you register a birth or a death.
4. The woman and man who are getting married.
5. The family of the woman getting married.
6. A will is an official document which states what should happen to a person's money and property after they die. People therefore make a will to ensure their money and property are disposed of according to their wishes.
7. In a religious building or crematorium.
8. *Burial* means the body is laid under the ground in a coffin; *cremation* means the body is burned. The ashes from the cremation may be kept, buried or scattered.

2

Go through the three possible answers to the example question, then let the learners answer the rest of the questions. If you feel that some learners will not know a number of the answers, put them in pairs or small groups to discuss their answers from the beginning.

Option

In a multilingual group, you could put any learners from the same country together to answer the questions; then mix the groups for comparison and discussion afterwards.

3

This is a fairly straightforward task but it should assist analysis by bringing all the expressions together in one table. Check the answers, paying special attention to *supposed to / expected to*, as this will probably be new for most learners and it is also quite a difficult concept. The *Grammar Reference* in the Class Book gives further examples which you could include at this point, and also mentions the fact that *supposed to* can imply that a rule is not observed: *You're not supposed to smoke in here* often means that the speaker knows that some people do smoke in here. *You're not allowed to smoke in here* would not imply any transgression of the rules.

Answer key

You're obliged to (do it)
You don't have to (do it)
You're allowed to (do it)
You're not allowed to (do it)
You're expected to (do it)

4

The learners may have a lot or a little to contribute here. If it is clearly the latter, you could open up the theme and allow them to write about any laws or customs in their country, ranging from rules to be observed in the classroom to laws governing employment or motoring. Let the learners compare with a partner or in groups and conduct feedback to check on both the content and language use.

5

This is a much freer activity to finish the lesson, and again it may provoke a lot of discussion or very little. Your only concern is the latter, so it is always advisable to have an activity ready if the discussion soon dries up. In this instance you could switch to one of the exercises in the Personal Study Workbook recommended below.

Personal Study Workbook

3: Birth, marriage and death: vocabulary
4: You are obliged to: obligation, permission and prohibition
5: Same or different?: pronunciation
6: Minimum ages: reading
10: Visual dictionary

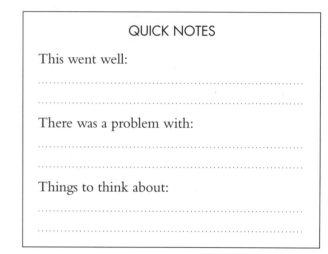

```
QUICK NOTES

This went well:
..............................................
..............................................

There was a problem with:
..............................................
..............................................

Things to think about:
..............................................
..............................................
```

WEDDINGS AROUND THE WORLD

Introduction

The learners read different texts about wedding customs and then exchange information in order to complete the comprehension task on the reading. This is followed by a brief focus on the present simple passive, which appears throughout the texts, and then further controlled practice. The lesson then returns to the theme of weddings with an exchange of opinions about the weddings they have read about and weddings in their own culture.

Suggested steps

1

Divide up the group. If you don't have a class that is divisible by four, you can give stronger members of the group two texts to read. Try to ensure that the learners focus on their own text, and give individuals help where necessary. When everyone has finished, direct them to the questions and make it clear that different learners will have the information to answer different questions, and that it is only their combined knowledge that will enable them to answer all the questions. So, if there are any questions that cannot be answered, it then becomes the responsibility of the group to go back to the relevant text and read it again to find the answer. Check answers at the end but keep the learners in their groups ready for the next exercise.

Answer key

1. false   2. true   3. true   4. false   5. false

2

Now let the learners chat more freely about their texts, adding further facts they have learned. The task of finding customs that appear in two different weddings gives them a goal, but the main aim is simply to talk and exchange information. At the end, give the learners feedback on how well they have explained their texts and add further input that might have helped them in their explanations.

Answer key

A canopy is used at a Jewish and Hindu wedding.
Small amounts of alcohol are drunk during a Japanese and Jewish wedding.
A meal follows a Muslim and Hindu wedding.
The bride wears white at a Muslim wedding and may wear white at a Hindu wedding.

3

You could write the two example sentences on the board and elicit from the learners the name of the tense, how it is formed and why it is used. You can also point out that we often omit the agent (the person or thing that does the action, or causes what happens) from a passive sentence if the agent is either known to both speaker and listener, or is unimportant. (In the case of the examples, the agent is clearly known in the first example and possibly known in the second, although you could also argue that the agent is not really important here – just the result.) The learners can then decide for themselves in the practice exercise if they need to repeat the agent at the end of the clause or sentence, or whether they can omit it.

Answer key

At a Sikh wedding reception, poems and speeches *are composed* in honour of the couple; and bank notes *are placed* in the couple's hands to ensure future prosperity.
In China astrological charts *are consulted* by the couple to fix the best time for the wedding. If the couple miss that date, they may have to wait years for another. Red *is* traditionally *worn* by the bride, but white is becoming more common.
In parts of Africa, the bride *is expected* to cry before the ceremony; and it *is thought* that the more the bride cries, the happier she will be in her future life.

Option

If you want additional reinforcement of the present simple passive, you could ask the group to go back to the texts and underline all the examples of the structure

they can find, before moving on to the practice stage in Exercise 3.

4

You may like to consider the most attractive customs from different points of view: the bride's point of view; the groom's point of view; the guests' point of view. However, if Exercise 2 produced a lot of discussion, you may feel you have exhausted the texts. In this case, move on to Exercise 5.

5

This final exercise is an opportunity for the learners to talk about their own cultures, but it also recycles the language of obligation, permission and prohibition, which runs throughout the unit. By this stage we hope that much of this language will have been assimilated, but you could still draw the learners' attention to it before the group activity. During the discussion monitor the ideas and use of language.

Option

As it stands, the final exercise might not produce much discussion with a monolingual group. You could, however, change the focus slightly and ask the learners to discuss different questions. For example:
1. What was the last wedding you went to? What was it like?
2. Have you been to two weddings in your own country which have been completely different? If so, describe how they were different.
3. Are there any wedding traditions in your country which seem to be disappearing?

Personal Study Workbook

1: Sentence transformations: passives
2: Countries and nationalities: vocabulary
7: Wedding preparations: listening
8: Sorry, we've changed our minds!: writing
9: Speaking partners

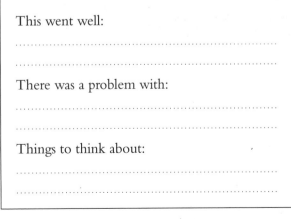

QUICK NOTES

This went well:
....
....

There was a problem with:
....
....

Things to think about:
....
....

REVIEW OF UNIT 7

1

This activity is repeated in various parts of the book, so your learners may be familiar with it by now. If not, explain the rules and show the examples before putting them in groups.

2

Even with the examples, it may still be wise to do the first one with the group. For example, ask them which introduction they need – *the thing* or *the person*. Having elicited *the thing*, now ask for suggestions using either *(the) most* or *(the) least*. When you are absolutely sure they understand, let them finish the task on their own before comparing in groups. Let the whole class listen to some of the answers at the end.

REVIEW OF UNIT 8

1

Instead of going through the example in the book, you could get your learners to do it as a group. Split the class in half, and then ask one half to write down four or five advantages of living alone, while the other half thinks of four or five disadvantages. When they have finished, write their ideas on the board, then tell them to compare their ideas with those in the book. For the rest of the exercise follow the instructions in the Class Book, and move round and help the learners wherever they need it.

2

Follow the instructions in the Class Book.

Answer key

Mostly to do with work:
receiving sickness pay
having job security
getting paid holidays
consulting colleagues
To do with home and work:
giving someone orders
sharing problems with someone
managing finances
making appointments
making cutbacks
reaching agreements
solving problems

QUICK NOTES

This went well:

....

There was a problem with:

....

....

Things to think about:

....

....

PHONAHOLICS

CONTENTS

Language focus:		*used to do* for past habits; *would* for past habits (receptively only) what to say on the telephone
Vocabulary:		telephoning hobbies and interests phrasal verbs synonyms
Skills:	Speaking:	discussing reasons for phoning telephone questionnaire role play: phone conversations
	Listening:	telephone conversations
	Reading:	newspaper text questionnaire about phoning
	Writing:	advantages and disadvantages confessions

DO YOU LIKE TELEPHONES?

Introduction

The lesson begins with a simple speaking activity to introduce the theme of the unit. The learners then complete and discuss a questionnaire on their use of the phone; the questionnaire contains useful phone vocabulary. The final activity provides practice in writing about advantages and disadvantages, and allows for further discussion.

Suggested steps

1

You could begin by telling the learners the topic of the unit and by talking briefly about any calls *you* have made in the last three days. Then ask the learners to do the same activity in groups of three or four. If necessary, remind them that they needn't mention any calls they wish to keep private. At the end, bring the class together to find out the most common reason for phoning.

2

Before the learners discuss the questionnaire, give them time to read and check the meaning of any new words in dictionaries and with each other, or pre-teach / discuss together items they don't know. You will probably need to deal with the vocabulary of telephone services in Question 2 (*telephone directory* = public phone book; *Directory Enquiries* is an operator service for phone numbers; *reversed charge calls* = the receiver pays for the

call, called *collect calls* in the US). Use the illustrations to help with the meaning of other items, and check that the learners can pronounce items such as *dial*, *directory*, *enquiries* and *mobile*.

Give the learners a few minutes to complete the questionnaire alone, then discuss their answers in groups. Monitor and note any points for feedback at the end. With multilingual groups you will need to decide whether they should talk about telephoning in their own country, or in the country where they are studying.

Conduct class feedback after group work, encouraging the learners to raise any interesting differences of experience or opinion. Then deal with any points you noted while monitoring.

3

This continues the theme with a set of phrasal verbs often connected with phoning, but also highlights a common feature of discourse, namely the use of (partial) synonyms to confirm what someone has said. This is illustrated in the example, but you could do one more together with the group before they complete the task individually. You could then go over their answers and put them in pairs for some quick drilling of the two-line dialogues.

Answer key

1. He hung up on you!
2. You put it off, you mean?
3. Oh, you got cut off.
4. You mean you woke him up.

5. You couldn't get through, then?
6. So the operator puts you through.
7. Yes, it's very annoying when you have to hang on like that.

4

You could ask pairs to think through each call very carefully so that their dialogue explains the context clearly. For example, in the first conversation, it would explain:
– who the person was calling;
– why they were calling;
– why the other person might have hung up on them;
– what they are going to do about it.

An alternative would be for the pairs to continue the conversations as if they both knew what the conversation was about, but without actually spelling it out. Then, the other pair would have to listen and guess what it was about.

5

This may provoke a lot of reaction or very little. If it is the latter and you have time on your hands, you could use the following option.

Option

List all new vocabulary items on the board, perhaps by asking the learners to look back and say which words were new. Then give simple definitions/explanations of words, and elicit the word you are describing.

Example: TEACHER: *This is the phone service you use if you want to get up early in the morning.*
LEARNER: *Wake up call.*

Then after a few examples, get the learners to continue the same activity in pairs.

Personal Study Workbook

3: Cheque book and book shop: compounds
5: Making excuses on the phone: reading

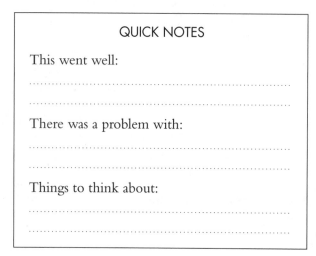

QUICK NOTES

This went well:

....

....

There was a problem with:

....

....

Things to think about:

....

....

Introduction

In this lesson, the learners are introduced to a range of useful phrases for use on the phone, and they listen to a number of phone calls which include some of these items. They also focus on appropriacy and predict the end of the calls. Finally, the learners practise the language through role play.

Suggested steps

1

You could begin by drawing three columns on the board: *caller*, *person receiving the call* and *operator/receptionist*. Check that the learners understand these, then ask them to tell you one or two phrases in Exercise 1 that these people might use in a phone conversation. Follow the instructions in the Class Book.

Answer key

Speaking.	person receiving the call
Is that Joanne?	caller or receiver
It's Nigel.	caller (possibly receiver)
Who's calling?	operator/receptionist, possibly receiver
Could you give him a message?	caller
Hold the line, please.	operator/receptionist
Is that you, Jo?	caller or receiver
Shall I get him to ring you?	operator/receptionist or receiver
Do you know when they'll be back?	caller
I'll put you through.	operator/receptionist
Hang on a minute.	caller/receiver (too informal for an operator or receptionist)
Who shall I say is calling?	operator/receptionist
Thanks for ringing.	receiver
Could I speak to Mr Roberts, please?	caller

2 ▭

Ask the learners to look at the table and follow the instructions. Play the beginnings of the three conversations (i.e. not the later recordings with the end of the conversation on them), then go over the answers with the group. The tapescript is on page 148.

Answer key

	Relationship	Language	Reason for call
1.	patient/receptionist	formal	to make an appointment
2.	caller/receptionist	formal	to speak to someone in the company
3.	friends	informal	to ask a favour

Play the recording a second time and ask the learners to tick the phrases they hear from Exercise 1.

52

Answer key

The speakers use the following phrases:
Is that Joanne?
It's Nigel.
Shall I get him to ring you?
Who shall I say is calling?
Could I speak to Mr Roberts, please?

3

Discuss possible continuations of the first call together, making it clear that they have to predict the outcome of the conversation, not the actual dialogue. Then ask the learners to predict the endings of the other two conversations with a partner. Elicit these from the group and put them on the board.

4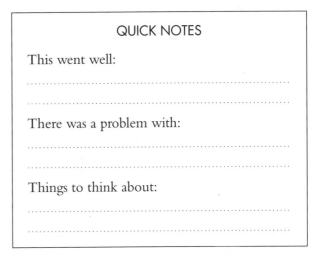

Play the second part of the three conversations to see who predicted the ending accurately. The tapescript is on page 148.

Answer key

1. The caller accepts an appointment for that afternoon with another doctor.
2. The caller asks if there is anyone else in the Marketing Department. She is put through to the secretary.
3. The friend refuses to lend the car as she needs it (she is going away for the weekend). The caller isn't upset.

5

Ask the learners to read the Telephone tips and underline the most useful advice. Clarify any problems of understanding, then put the learners in pairs, and give them a role card each (A and B, or C and D or E and F). The role cards are on Worksheet 10A on page 123. Tell them not to look at each other's cards. Give them time to think again about the advice in the Telephone tips and the language they have learnt so far. Let them do the role play, and monitor and note any problems of communication. To simulate a phone conversation, it is best if the learners are not actually looking at each other, so place them back to back, or with one learner talking over the other's shoulder.

As there are several role cards, you could give pairs new ones as they finish.

If appropriate, tape or video some of the conversations, or ask a pair to perform in front of the class. At the end, do feedback on the role play – what was the outcome in each situation? Deal with any language points that arose while you were monitoring.

Option

As a revision activity in the next lesson, the learners could write a pair of role cards similar to the ones above; swap them with another pair's cards, and perform each other's role plays.

We are grateful to Jackie Gresham for the Telephone tips in this lesson.

Personal Study Workbook

1: Telephone conversations: vocabulary
6: Half a conversation: listening
8: Speaking partners

QUICK NOTES

This went well:

....

....

There was a problem with:

....

....

Things to think about:

....

....

ARE YOU A PHONE ADDICT?

Introduction

After an initial vocabulary activity which deals with some items from the text, the learners read a text about a phone addict. The text is then exploited for language: *used to do* to talk about past habits. The language point is dealt with analytically, and the learners are then asked to explore the text to discover different ways in which past habits are expressed. Finally, the learners practise *used to do* in a controlled activity.

Suggested steps

1

Ask the learners to do the matching activity individually or in pairs, then check the answers together.

Answer key

deteriorate – get worse
hostile – unfriendly/aggressive
chat – conversation
dismiss – sack
install – fit
harmless – safe / not damaging

2

Lead into the reading activity by checking that the group understand *addict*; ask what kind of addictions people usually have (alcohol, tobacco, gambling, drugs, chocolate, coffee, TV, computer games, etc.). These will depend on the culture of your learners, so adapt accordingly. Find out if they know anyone who is always on the telephone, and ask them to describe a phone addict's behaviour (which should make the reading task easier).

Tell the learners to read the text and see if they are like the man in the article. There is a lot of new vocabulary, so encourage the learners to read for gist, and not to get too concerned with unknown items. If you like, you could tell them to choose one or two items to look up afterwards, but in our experience, this can be a very time-consuming business. Our advice would be to deal with only a few useful items, and to encourage the learners to look up others at home.

3

Either read the explanation and examples of *used to do* together and answer any questions, or choose your own examples and write them on the board. Highlight the form of the structure (*used to* + verb; *didn't use to* + verb).

Work through two or three examples of the exercise in which *used to do* can be substituted.

In feedback, ask the learners to *produce* sentences with *used to do* where transformations can be made.

Answer key

Phrases where *used to do* can be used:
I was spending all my lunchtime …
I would disappear …
I would ring someone …
I was phoning people …
I often rang people.

> **Language Point: used to *and* would**
>
> *Would* is interchangeable with *used to* where dynamic verbs are used:
> *I used to jump out of bed in the mornings.*
> *I would jump out of bed in the mornings.*
>
> However, *would* cannot be used in place of *used to do* with stative verbs:
> *He used to be fat.*
> ~~*He would be fat.*~~
> *He used to have a boat.*
> ~~*He would have a boat.*~~
>
> This lesson focuses on *would* for past habit receptively, so it should not be necessary to draw your learners' attention to this.

Option

You may wish to elicit the learners' own examples of the structure to check understanding. Ask them about things they used to do at school, or possessions they no longer have, or food/drink they used to dislike as a child. Check constantly that they are expressing meaning accurately, perhaps through questioning:

Example: LEARNER: I used to have a gold watch.
TEACHER: Have you got it now? / Have you still got it?
LEARNER: Yes.

(This learner hasn't grasped the concept, so you will need to re-clarify it, through explanation, translation or further examples.)

4

Work through the example about TV addicts, then ask pairs to choose one of the other addictions, or one of their own if they prefer. Encourage humorous examples. Monitor pair work, and at the end, conduct feedback on their 'confessions' as a group. Correct errors of form or meaning.

Option

You could get the learners to turn their ideas into posters, like this:
COMPUTER ADDICTS ANONYMOUS
We used to stay in all day, playing computer games.
We used to eat in front of the computer.
We used to get up two hours early to use our
  computers.
BUT THEN …
We discovered English lessons.
(And now we're English addicts …)

After the final activity (or instead of it if you feel this final activity is not suitable for your group), you could do Worksheet 10B on page 123, which revises a number of verb + noun collocations from the unit.

Answer key for Worksheet 10B

1. Do you play chess?
2. Do you ever do crosswords?
3. Do you usually leave a message on an answerphone?
4. Do you often dial the wrong number?
5. Do you ever make reversed charge calls?
6. Do you often ask a favour of an old friend?
7. Do you sometimes sack employees?
8. Do you ever use the phone late at night?
9. Do you ever wear make-up?
10. Do you ever jump out of bed in the morning?

Personal Study Workbook

2: It used to be Carthage: *used to*
4: Harmless inventions: word building
7: Don't forget to call the office: writing messages

QUICK NOTES

This went well:
....
....

There was a problem with:
....
....

Things to think about:
....
....

REVIEW OF UNIT 8

1

Follow the instructions in the Class Book. If you do not have access to a number of monolingual dictionaries, write down the definitions from several before you go to class, and then put them on the board or OHP for the learners to look at.

Answer key

1. ... they are ill and cannot go to work.
2. ... you can vary the time when you start and finish.
3. ... you don't go to work for one day.
4. ... you tell someone what to do.
5. ... don't have enough of something.
6. ... know that you are very unlikely to lose your job / it is very improbable that you will lose your job.

2 ▭

Do two or three examples with the group. Then they can finish the task individually, using dictionaries to help them.

Play the recording and check answers, and do some drilling round the class. Give the learners a minute to themselves to repeat words at their own pace. Move round and monitor their pronunciation while they do this.

Finally, put them in pairs to create the sentences and listen to some examples round the class when they have finished.

Answer key

company	appointment
organise	collect
orders	solution
sickness	involve
colleague	effective
difficult	advantage
positive	consult
training	agreement
cutbacks	employed
manager	discuss
flexible	financial
budget	accept

REVIEW OF UNIT 9

1

Set a time limit for the groups to answer the questions, e.g. two or three minutes. Then elicit answers but do not confirm or reject any at this stage. Finally, give them two minutes to go through Unit 9 to find out if they were right.

Answer key

1. Jewish
2. China
3. a Muslim wedding
4. Africa
5. Sikh
6. a Jewish couple

2

This has more mileage with a multinational group, but even in a monolingual group there are often disagreements about the laws of the country. Be prepared for this discussion to last a long time if you have learners from different countries.

QUICK NOTES

This went well:

....
....

There was a problem with:

....
....

Things to think about:

....
....

GOODS AND SERVICES

CONTENTS

Language focus: *if* sentences with *will, may* and *might*
                  to have something done

Vocabulary: clothes
                  electrical appliances and consumer goods
                  word building: *-able* and *-ible*

Skills: Speaking: features of consumer products
                       shopping customs around the world
                       talking about services
                       role play: selling goods
          Listening: selling goods
          Reading: a text about shopping customs
                       different advertisements

A HARD SELL

Introduction

This lesson revises the use of conditional sentences
through a speaking activity, and introduces and elicits a
range of vocabulary to do with consumer products. The
learners go on to discuss the benefits of features of
various goods, an activity which should generate a good
deal of useful vocabulary.

Suggested steps

1

You could begin by describing something that you
bought recently where the sales assistant tried to sell you
a related item, and see if the learners can think of any
similar experiences before they open their books and do
the activity. Otherwise, use the examples in the Class
Book.

Highlight the form of the conditional in the examples:
If + present simple, *will/may/might* + verb

See if the learners can add any other related goods for
the cassette recorder, using the pictures. Then check that
they understand the vocabulary in the list before they
begin to work in groups.

Conduct feedback afterwards, eliciting their ideas and
writing them on the board. To ensure practice of the
structure, ask for full sentences as answers. Check that
other learners understand new items which arise and can
pronounce them.

Answer key

Possible answers
a torch: batteries
a man's shirt: tie
a woman's handbag: gloves, purse, possibly shoes
a camera: flash, films, extra filters or lenses, carrying case
a table lamp: light bulb, plug, lampshade
a bicycle: puncture repair kit, cycling gloves, helmet,
   pump, bell
a home computer: software, computer games, blank
   disks, paper for the printer
an expensive ballpoint pen: refill
a pair of shoes: shoe polish, shoe trees, tights, socks,
   handbag
a washing machine: insurance, tumble drier

Option

At the end of this activity, you could give the learners
two minutes to study the words, then test each other.
Demonstrate like this:
TEACHER: *If you buy a camera, what will they try to sell you?*
LEARNER: *A film, flash, filters,* etc.

Then tell the learners to carry on testing each other in
pairs, one with their book open, and one with their
book shut. Clean the board before they start.

2

Clarify the meaning of *benefit* using the example in the
table, then elicit the benefits of the other three features
of the jeans. The learners will be able to use the present
simple and *will* (prediction) in their answers, although
this context would also allow the present simple in both
clauses as some of these benefits may be regarded as an
inevitable consequence of the particular feature of the
jeans.

Before they work with a partner on the benefits in the rest of the table, check that they understand the vocabulary relating to the car radio/cassette.

Answer key

Possible answers
Levi jeans:
dark grey: they will never look dirty; grey goes with a lot of other colours; it is fashionable
loose fit: they are comfortable (and fashionable)
pre-shrunk: they won't shrink when you wash them
Car radio/cassette:
portable: less easy for people to steal (because you can take it with you or lock it in the boot when you leave the car)
10 station memory: easier to find a channel you like listening to
4 speakers: the sound quality will be very good, especially for music and passengers in the front and back of the car will be able to hear equally well
12 month guarantee: if it goes wrong, it will be repaired free for a year.

3

Put the learners in groups and ask them to choose a product or decide on one of their own, and draw up a list of features and benefits. Ideally, they will need about three or four features for their product.

Option

If you have access to authentic advertisements for these goods or other similar ones, you could give them to the learners as a stimulus. In a monolingual situation, you could even give them advertisements in their own language as a source of ideas.

4

Follow the instructions in the Class Book.

Personal Study Workbook

1: If you don't keep the guarantee …: *if* sentences
5: Legal rights: reading
9: Visual dictionary

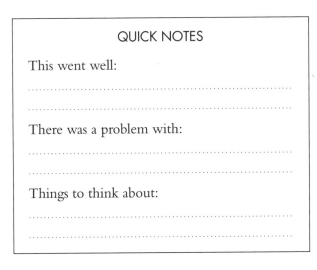

QUICK NOTES

This went well:

....

....

There was a problem with:

....

....

Things to think about:

....

....

Introduction

In this lesson, the learners read and discuss a text which raises issues to do with shopping customs in different cultures, and incidentally learn some useful lexical items. The text contains some examples of the target language structure for this lesson: causative *have*. The structure is dealt with analytically and then practised through personalised activities.

Suggested steps

1

Ask the learners to look at the picture to say what is happening; if necessary feed in key vocabulary, e.g. *to shorten* and *fabric. Gift wrap, to wrap something up* and *deliver* are also useful items to pre-teach. Then tell them to read the first four lines of the text, and to decide which actions would be unacceptable or unusual in their country. Discuss their answers as a class. This will allow you to check that they have understood the aim of the reading exercise. Tell them to continue reading the text alone, underlining any unusual behaviour.

When they have finished reading, put them in small groups to discuss their answers. With a multilingual group, there should be a fair range of differences in what is considered acceptable or usual. Even within a monolingual group, there may be differences of opinion.

Conduct a whole-class feedback on the exercise, in which the learners can mention the most crucial cultural differences.

2

Follow the instructions in the Class Book. If you wish, the learners can practise the construction in the table orally in a drill (*You can/can't have a dress made*, etc.).

You may also wish to contrast the structure with the active form by writing two sentences on the board and asking the learners to describe the difference in meaning between them:
She made the dress.
She had the dress made.

Alternatively, the learners could translate the structures, or you can check by questioning:
Did she make the dress herself?
Did someone make it for her?
Did she pay them to do it?

When you feel they have grasped the concept, go on to the practice activity. Make sure before the pair work that the learners are practising whole sentences, and not just pointing and saying *yes* or *no*!

Conduct feedback on the practice activity, including error correction.

3

You could elicit one or two examples, then let groups work on the exercise using dictionaries to check new vocabulary. At the end, do feedback by eliciting their answers and putting them on the board, or asking the representatives from the groups to write up their lists on the board.

Answer key

1. *a hairdresser's:* you can have your hair washed, cut, dried, permed, tinted, set, etc. You can have your nails manicured, eyebrows dyed or plucked, etc.
2. *a garage:* you can have your car serviced, the oil changed, the car repaired, the tyres changed, the car washed/cleaned, etc.
3. *a doctor's surgery:* you can have your blood pressure checked, your temperature taken, your eyes/ears tested, your cholesterol level checked, your heart monitored, your blood tested, etc.

Option

You can integrate practice of this structure in a communicative game. Put the learners in pairs, and tell them to write down ten questions they want to ask you about your last visit to the hairdresser's/barber's. (Women teachers may be at an advantage here.)

Examples: *When did you last go?*
Did you have your hair washed and cut?
Did it cost a lot?
Did you have your usual hairdresser or a different one?
etc.

Monitor while they are writing their questions and correct as necessary.

Call the class together and tell them to ask their questions and answer them. They must not repeat a question asked by someone else. Then tell them to ask their questions to a new partner.

Personal Study Workbook

4: Getting things done: pronunciation
6: Displaying the goods: listening

```
                    QUICK NOTES

This went well:

.........................................................

.........................................................

There was a problem with:

.........................................................

.........................................................

Things to think about:

.........................................................

.........................................................
```

Introduction

This lesson introduces a lexical set of properties products may have, and focuses on word building. The learners are asked to paraphrase items (a useful skill for them if they do not know particular words). They then read advertisements which include some of the items, and listen to people trying to sell the products. The lesson ends with a free speaking activity in which the learners try to 'sell' each other some unusual goods.

Suggested steps

1

Use the pictures at the beginning of the lesson as suggested.

Answer key

If something is *portable* it means you can carry it.

Work together on a couple of the long explanations. If your learners speak a language which does not have similar *-able/-ible* suffixes, you will probably wish to show what the ending means: in this case, it means that it can be done (can be washed, can be locked, etc.). The learners will benefit from dictionaries in this activity.

Answer key

disposable: can be thrown away
inflatable: can be inflated, filled with air, blown up
washable: can be washed
reversible: can be turned inside out
unbreakable: cannot be broken
edible: can be eaten
adjustable: can be adjusted
lockable: can be locked
detachable: can be removed or taken off

After feedback on the activity, ask the learners to think about the word stress rule, and if they are having problems, say the items for them so that they can work it out. Provide pronunciation practice either through drilling or in pairs.

Answer key

Words ending in *-able* or *-ible* are usually stressed on the syllable before the suffix.
Examples: *disposable, inflatable, washable*
Note: This rule operates when *-able* or *-ible* are attached to a verb, as in the items in the exercise. It is not the case when these suffixes are attached to nouns such as *comfortable* (comfort) or *miserable* (misery). In this case, the meaning of the suffix is different.

2

Ask the learners to use the words from Exercise 1 to describe the pictures. They could do this in pairs, followed by class feedback. Correct any errors of pronunciation.

Answer key

1. unbreakable   2. reversible   3. washable
4. disposable   5. inflatable   6. detachable   7. lockable
8. adjustable   9. edible

3

This requires the learners to scan the texts quickly, so you may wish to set a time limit, e.g. one minute, to encourage this. Then proceed as suggested in the Class Book, and follow up with a class feedback if you like.

4

The learners may wish to use dictionaries, since the questions require a more intensive reading of the text. Go over the answers together at the end.

Answer key

1. The socks are odourless so you can take your shoes off in public and not upset anyone.
2. The suits are very cheap (£25 for 12) and they can be lightweight or tweed (a warm material).
3. The encyclopedias are easy to carry around with you.
4. The trousers are reversible and suitable for men or boys.

5 ▭▭ ▭▭

Play the appropriate recording. The tapescript is on page 148.

Answer key

Version 1:
The speaker is selling the disposable suits. He emphasises that the buyer will save money on cleaning bills, and implies that the trousers are very cheap. However, the buyer does not seem interested.

Version 2:
The speaker is trying to sell the odourless socks. She says they are good after aerobics (exercise) class, you can buy them in different colours to go with what you are wearing, and they are made of natural fibres. The buyer seems interested.

6

Allow the learners a little time to read their own advertisement, check any new words and think about how to sell the item. To this end, you could put the learners in pairs who will be selling the same items to work out their strategy. Then put them with new partners who have a different product, and let them do the role play. Monitor and make a note of any points (linguistic or otherwise) you wish to deal with later.

At the end, either have feedback on the ways they sold their products or ask one or two pairs to act out their role play for the class. Then give the learners feedback on their language.

Option

As a vocabulary round up to the unit and for speaking practice, you could use Worksheet 11 on page 124.

Personal Study Workbook

2: Words ending *-able* or *-ible*: suffixes
3: Product features: vocabulary
7: A letter of complaint: writing
8: Speaking partners

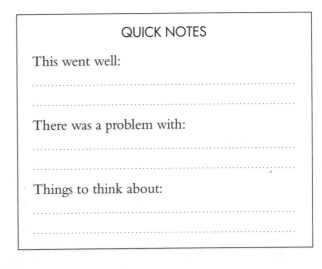

```
QUICK NOTES

This went well:
.................................................
.................................................

There was a problem with:
.................................................
.................................................

Things to think about:
.................................................
.................................................
```

REVIEW AND DEVELOPMENT

REVIEW OF UNIT 9

1

You could do this with the learners working on their own, or you could put them in groups. If so, ask them to think about their island first. Where is it? How big is it? What's it called? Once they have got involved in defining the type of place it is, the laws and customs should start to emerge quite naturally. Monitor the discussion and make notes on their ideas and language, and then at the end you can redistribute the groups so they can explain their rules to others. Give them some positive feedback at the end plus any new input that might have come out of discussion with one of the groups, and any important error correction.

2 ▭▭

This is not only a check on their understanding of the items, but in using dictionaries, the learners should also become more aware of the type of information dictionaries include, i.e. information about style and usage. Play the recording at the end for them to check their answers.

Answer key

See the tapescript on page 149.

REVIEW OF UNIT 10

1

Go through the examples in the Class Book and possibly elicit one or two examples from the class. Then put them in groups. We have found that this activity can reveal some very funny habits and can be great fun.

2

Telephone role plays in the classroom are inevitably rather contrived, but if you can create an information gap and get the learners sitting back to back, they can still provide useful practice and the learners do seem to enjoy them. Make sure the learners do not read their partner's role card, and give them quite a lot of time to think about the situation and what they are going to say. Once again, we would stress the value of rehearsal here, so do encourage the learners to talk themselves mentally through possible questions and replies, and rehearse utterances they know they are likely to use. You might want to refer them back to the *Telephone tips* on page 69 of the Class Book.

If possible, record some of the conversations for discussion and feedback.

```
QUICK NOTES

This went well:

.........................................................
.........................................................

There was a problem with:

.........................................................
.........................................................

Things to think about:

.........................................................
.........................................................
```

BARE NECESSITIES

CONTENTS

Language focus:	describing degrees of need	
	frequency and degree adverbs	
	qualifying adjectives	
	numbers and measurements	
Vocabulary:	climate and geography	
	toiletries	
	personal belongings	
Skills:	Speaking:	where people store personal belongings
		staying in an igloo hotel
		necessary items for a long flight
		role play: describing a terrible flight
	Listening:	people talking about personal belongings and whether they really need them
		items for your comfort on long flights
	Reading:	a text about an igloo hotel
	Writing:	a note for a noticeboard

I COULD MANAGE WITHOUT IT

Introduction

The lesson centres around the theme of *need*: Do we really need all the personal possessions we seem to accumulate? It opens with a discussion about different belongings and whether they would be needed and used in different cultures. This is followed by more discussion about where people keep things in their homes, before listening to native speakers talking about the same subject. Further personalised speaking activities conclude a free-speaking lesson.

Suggested steps

1

Get the learners to match the words and the items shown in the picture and then put the class into small groups for the first speaking activity. Conduct a short feedback.

With a monolingual class you will have a representative group, so you could simply ask them whether they possess the items in the list, and if so, do they use them regularly. And you may also wish to add some more items of your own if you feel they will promote more discussion than some of the ones we have included. First check the meaning of the frequency adverbs in the rubric (*regularly, occasionally, rarely*); add others if you wish, e.g. *hardly ever*; and also check that the class know about the position of frequency adverbs. See the Language Point below.

Language Point: frequency adverbs

These adverbs usually go directly before the main verb:
He occasionally wears cuff links.
We rarely use our barbecue.
I have never owned a sleeping bag.

The exception to this rule is that frequency adverbs follow the verb *to be*:
He is occasionally late for class.
They are hardly ever at home.

Some frequency adverbs can also take an initial position in the sentence:
Sometimes we go and visit them.
Occasionally I see her in the high street.

And some adverbs can also take a final position in the sentence:
I see her occasionally.
We go there regularly.

Answer key

A barbecue is used for barbecues in the summer.
Christmas decorations are used at Christmas.
Candles might be used for a party, a candlelit dinner (they provide a nice atmosphere), or in emergency if there is a power cut.
A sleeping bag is used for camping.
Cuff links are needed on certain shirts, often for formal occasions.
A torch is needed to see into dark places, usually where there is no electricity.
A beach umbrella is used on the beach in the summer to provide shade or protection from the sun.

Mosquito spray is used to protect the skin from mosquitoes in summer.
An electric fan is used to cool a hot room in summer.
A trunk is used for storing things, and occasionally when you want to send a lot of belongings somewhere.

2

Pre-teach the new vocabulary, e.g. *cellar* and *basement*, then put the learners in pairs to exchange ideas.

Option

If you think your group will find the listening task (Exercise 3) very challenging, you could ask them first to brainstorm the items they think the speakers are likely to talk about. Feed in vocabulary to help them with items they cannot express in English, and put them all on the board. With luck and guidance from you, they will have predicted many of the words they are now likely to hear on the recording.

3

Check that the learners know the phrases *to manage without something* and *to get rid of (somebody* or *something)*. This latter expression is common in English and it does not always translate very easily into other languages, so give several examples:
We don't need that chair in the corner. Let's get rid of it.
The club would like to get rid of their existing manager.
We'll have to get rid of these mosquitoes before we go to bed.

Choose the appropriate version of the recording and play it. Let the learners compare in pairs before you go through the answers with the whole group. You will probably need to play the recording a second or third time, or let the learners listen with the tapescript on page 149.

Answer key

Version 1:
Speaker 1 wants to keep the beach stuff, e.g. buckets and spades, and beach umbrella; and also the Christmas decorations. He could manage without some of the toys. He doesn't want to get rid of anything.

Speaker 2 wants to keep the football magazines and the tennis racket. He could manage without/get rid of the old clothes.

Version 2:
Speaker 1 wants to keep the bike and the cases of wine. She could manage without the picture frames and she would like to get rid of the hi-fi and speakers. She already gets rid of the newspapers on a regular basis.

Speaker 2 wants to keep the family heirlooms, the photographs, the sports equipment, the foldaway bed and the sleeping bag. He could manage without the lampshades and the curtains, and he would like to get rid of some old college notes and books.

4

The listening has already provided a model for this activity, so you can put the class into groups to talk about the things they keep in store. During the discussion you will almost certainly need to help with items of vocabulary, and you can also make notes on their use of language. During feedback, point out good examples of language use along with important errors for correction. If possible, see if the learners can correct their own errors.

5

This activity is based on an old television programme called *Swapshop*. Illustrate the meaning of *swap* and see if your learners did this with their possessions as children or whether they still do it now. The activity provides some writing practice, a change of focus, and can be great fun. You could even invite learners from other classes to add to the display, and if it works well, try to encourage more wall displays during the course.

Personal Study Workbook

1: Frequency and degree: adverbs
5: Handbag secrets: reading
9: Visual dictionary

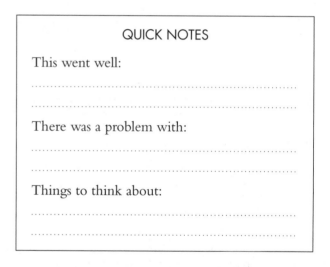

QUICK NOTES

This went well:
....
....

There was a problem with:
....
....

Things to think about:
....
....

ICE BREAKS

Introduction

A range of vocabulary items is presented with the help of a mind map, and for some learners this type of visual representation of items on a page can be a very effective learning aid. The lesson then continues with an intriguing text about a hotel built from snow, and it is exploited both for discussion and the presentation of various numbers and measurements used in English. This language is then extended and practised through a general knowledge quiz.

Suggested steps

1

Let the learners try to complete the mind map on their own, and then they can compare with a partner before you go through them with the class. When you do, check the pronunciation of *flood* and *blizzard*.

Answer key

1. pond   2. stream   3. sleet   4. drizzle   5. flood
6. lightning   7. typhoon   8. melt   9. boil

Many learners find mind maps a very effective aid in remembering vocabulary and the learners should be encouraged to personalise the map in any way they find helpful, e.g. with their own words, symbols and pictures. Ask the group if they already use mind maps or will now consider using them in the future. If there is a fairly positive response, you could provide immediate practice with Worksheet 12 on page 124.

Option

If you have used Worksheet 12, you may not have enough time to move on to the reading text in this lesson. If this is the case, and you just find yourself with ten or fifteen minutes left of the lesson, you could finish by returning to the original mind map. Ask the learners in pairs to divide the map into words normally associated with a hot climate and words normally associated with a cold climate. They can, of course, put certain words in both lists. Then they can compare with another pair. They should also be encouraged to add their own words as well.

2

Ask the class if they know what an igloo is, then put them in pairs and introduce the task. Answering the questions requires an understanding of vocabulary that may be new, e.g. *chilly* and *pretty* (meaning *very*), but let the learners find the meaning for themselves using dictionaries. You could do the first question together as *melt* has just been introduced. At the end, conduct a feedback and write examples of the advantages and disadvantages on the board; this may provoke discussion and may also be useful when the learners read the text.

3

Ask the learners to read the text on their own and underline/highlight the key points which answer the pre-set question. At the end they can compare with a partner. Check the answers and then you could invite discussion with the whole class on whether they would like to stay in such a hotel.

Answer key

1. It is a novelty, i.e. something new.
2. He can always look forward to building a bigger and more beautiful hotel the following year.
3. It is good practice for survival training.
4. You can fit lots of people in very easily.
5. Snow is a good insulator so people feel warm despite the cold.
Although Nils Bergqvist does not actually say this, the text also suggests a further advantage:
6. The raw material (snow) is very cheap.

4

See how many numbers and measurements your learners can find in the text, and set a time limit, e.g. one minute or ninety seconds, to add a little spice to the activity.

Answer key

two weeks   1991   200 square metres   six workmen
eight weeks   1,000 tons   100% snow   £25–30 a night
0 degrees centigrade   two metres thick   800 people
10 rooms   three metres wide by two metres long
four at one time

Highlight new vocabulary items and constructions in some of the key measurements: 3 metres **by** 2 metres; 0 **degrees** centigrade; 200 **square** metres, 100 **per cent**; and the use of adjectives, e.g. two metres **thick**, three metres **long**, four centimetres **wide**.
Note: A ton is equal to approximately 1,000 kilos.

5

Give each pair ten minutes to answer the questions and think up their own questions. They can then exchange books with another pair to check answers and answer each other's questions. If you have any time left over, get the pairs to think up more questions for the whole group to answer.

Answer key

1. 50 metres long by 25 metres wide; 1 metre deep
2. 10 metres; 24 hours
3. 100
4. approx. 300 square metres
5. 1 mm
6. 70%
7. 25 cm
8. 500

Personal Study Workbook

4: My heart beats: noun + verb and verb + noun collocation
6: Living in basic conditions: listening
8: Speaking partners

QUICK NOTES

This went well:

....

....

There was a problem with:

....

....

Things to think about:

....

....

Introduction

The learners have to consider the value of the various items which airlines provide for our comfort. The main language point – the use of *very* and *absolutely* before adjectives – arises naturally out of this, as does a large lexical set comprising both adjectives and consumer goods. Several speaking activities provide practice of the new items and opportunities for personal views, and a short listening activity brings the lesson to an end.

Suggested steps

1

Ask the class if they have experienced a long night flight. If so, can they remember what the airline provided them with for their comfort. Elicit answers and feed in vocabulary where necessary. Then use the picture to help explain any other new items, and ask them to grade the items using the five phrases in the box. Afterwards put them in groups to compare answers.

2 and 3

It may be more effective to copy these phrases onto the board or use an OHP if one is available. Give each pair a minute or so to try to work out the difference between *very* and *absolutely* and then elicit the answer if possible. Consolidate understanding by testing them on the first two or three adjectives from Exercise 3, and then put them back into pairs to finish the activity, using dictionaries if necessary to look up the meaning of any new items, e.g. *furious* or *dreadful*. Check answers and pronunciation.

Answer key

Exercise 2:
See the Grammar Reference in the Class Book on page 165.

Exercise 3:

very hot	absolutely exhausted
very bad	absolutely dreadful
absolutely boiling	very tired
absolutely furious	absolutely unbelievable
very angry	absolutely useless

Option

If necessary, you can consolidate understanding of the adjectives with this short speaking activity. Give a stimulus using a 'scale' adjective, and get a learner to reply using the correct 'limit' adjective. For example:
A: *Was it very big?*
B: *Yes, it was (absolutely) enormous.*
A: *Was it very hot?*
B: *Yes, it was (absolutely) boiling.*

Do several examples with different learners, then put them in pairs to practise using the other adjectives. First explain the following language point.

Language Point: unbelievable *and* useless

The only problems might be with *unbelievable* and *useless*, so you could give them examples to show how they are used with 'scale' adjectives:
A: *Were the instructions very useful?*
B: *No, they were (absolutely) useless.*
A: *Were the results surprising?*
B: *Yes, they were (absolutely) unbelievable.*

If your learners wish to use *surprised* and not *surprising* (to refer to the effect that something has on us), it would be accompanied by the following limit adjectives:
A: *Were you very surprised?*
B: *Yes, I was (absolutely) amazed/astonished.*

4

You could instruct the pairs to talk about the situation and then rehearse it; or you could make it a more controlled activity by asking the learners to write their dialogues. You can also vary the degree of freedom by the extent to which you instruct them to use the target lexis. If you want to ensure the target vocabulary appears, you could tell each pair they must include a certain number of items in their dialogue, e.g. six; or you could simply encourage them to use the adjectives but without forcing them to use anything in particular.

Move round and monitor the pairs, giving help where necessary. When you judge they are well prepared, put pairs together to listen to each other's dialogues.

5 ⬚⬚

This brings the lesson full circle by returning to the theme of items that airlines provide for the comfort of their passengers. Play the recording once, let the learners compare, and then discuss the answers with the group. The tapescript is on page 150.

Answer key

1. Toiletries such as dental floss, toothpicks and make-up remover.
2. Zone oils: special moisturisers for dry, tired skin.
3. Osmotherapy wipes: tissues with a relaxing aroma designed to combat fear of flying.
4. A bag which opens out to become a small case with a handle for documents.
5. Items with special value in certain parts of the world, e.g. sunblock for passengers travelling from a cold climate to a hot climate.

Personal Study Workbook

2: Absolutely: adjectives
3: Dental floss and dental surgeon: compounds
7: Make it more interesting: writing

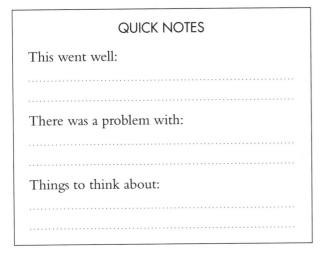

REVIEW AND DEVELOPMENT

REVIEW OF UNIT 10

1

Explain that the learners are not being asked to write down what is said in each phone call (in the first call nothing is said). The task is to explain what *happens*, e.g. the caller gets a wrong number, the caller has to leave a message, etc. Play the recording once, pausing after each call so that the learners have time to write down their answers. The tapescript is on page 150.

Answer key

1. The line is engaged.
2. The caller gets a wrong number.
3. The person receiving the call does not want to speak to the caller.
4. It is an overseas call and the speaker gets cut off.
5. The caller wants to speak to Tony, who is out. He leaves a message for Tony to ring back.
6. This is a business call. The caller wants to make an appointment with Mr Macgregor. He does so for 2 pm on Wednesday.

2

Point out that examples of the two sounds do not only occur on the letter *i*. Play the recording when the group has finished and go over any problem words before the learners practise their pronunciation in pairs.

Answer key

/ɪ/	/aɪ/
add<u>i</u>ct	host<u>i</u>le★
mess<u>age</u>	mob<u>i</u>le★
min<u>u</u>te	supervisor
bus<u>i</u>ness	d<u>i</u>al
prom<u>i</u>se	d<u>i</u>alogue
aggress<u>i</u>ve	exerc<u>i</u>se
antic<u>i</u>pate	tr<u>i</u>ed

★ hostile is pronounced /hɑːstəl/ and mobile /məʊbəl/ in American English.

REVIEW OF UNIT 11

1

Give the learners the example in the Class Book from Unit 11, then do the first example of this new exercise with the class. After that, put them in pairs for the activity, then go through the answers.

Answer key

1. typewriter
2. pen
3. bicycle
4. women's shoes
5. radio, walkman, torch, etc.
6. shirt
7. handbag
8. word processor and printer
9. lamp
10. camera

2

Most of these activities are things that people have done for them, but we have included an example of an active construction for learners who may do some of these things themselves.

While your learners are completing the activity, move round and monitor their answers carefully, paying attention to both the noun + verb collocations and correct use of tenses. If you notice lots of errors, go through the sentences before the group activity.

Answer key

Possible answers

I have my eyes tested once a year.
I have the house painted every five years.
I'm having the curtains cleaned next week.
I had a film developed yesterday.
I've had my watch repaired this year.
I haven't had my hair cut for six weeks.
I had central heating installed two years ago.
I have my car serviced every six months.

13

WHO IS REALLY ON TRIAL?

```
┌─────────────────────────────────────────────────────────────┐
│                         CONTENTS                             │
│                                                              │
│   Language focus:   if sentences with would and might        │
│                     defining relative clauses (2)            │
│                     link words: similarities and differences │
│                                                              │
│     Vocabulary:     law and the legal system                 │
│                     crime                                    │
│                                                              │
│         Skills:     Speaking:  ways to produce more effective policing │
│                                protecting one's home from burglary     │
│                                predictions about prison life           │
│                                pros and cons of the jury system        │
│                     Listening: an ex-prisoner describes prison life    │
│                                advice on protecting your home          │
│                     Reading:   a jigsaw text on the advantages and     │
│                                disadvantages of the jury system        │
│                     Writing:   making a poster on ways to beat crime   │
│                                                              │
└─────────────────────────────────────────────────────────────┘
```

CRIME PREVENTION

Introduction

The first activity introduces crime vocabulary the learners will need for the rest of the lesson, which is largely built around the presentation and practice of *if* sentences with *would* and *might*. The issue remains crime prevention, and at the end of the lesson the learners have an opportunity to express their own views on the subject using the target structures and lexis from the lesson.

Suggested steps

1

One potential problem with groups, and particularly multilingual groups, is that they come to class knowing different things: a word that is new to half the class might be known by the other half, and so on. When this happens teachers may be loath to spend too long on lexical items for fear that some learners may get bored if they already know them. One way round this situation is the framework provided for the first exercise. The learners will be able to see quite clearly who knows a certain lexical item, so they can then ask that person for help. In other words, there is no reason for any learner to remain unoccupied: if they aren't learning, they're teaching.

Follow the instructions in the Class Book and listen very carefully to the explanations provided by members of the group, not only to check that they are accurate, but also to feed in vocabulary that may be very useful in helping to define other items, e.g. *it's a type of ...*; *it's what you get when ...*; and so on.

2

Exercise 1 includes all the potentially difficult lexis in the reading text, so you can now go straight into the text and allow the learners to compare their responses with a partner afterwards. Keep the feedback brief as there will be an opportunity for the learners to expand on their views later in the lesson.

3

You could put the questions on the board while the group are working on their own. As you elicit answers from them you can then put the answers on the board and highlight/clarify any problems. The major one might be question 4. See the Language Point below.

> **Language Point: if sentences with would**
>
> These sentences are often used to talk about hypothetical situations, but can also be used to describe situations that exist. In this case, the difference between *if + will* and *if + would* is in the likelihood of something existing. Compare:
> *If he loses his gloves, I'll be very angry.*
> and
> *If he lost his gloves, I'd be very angry.*
>
> In the second sentence the speaker has used *if + would* to signal that he/she thinks it is unlikely that the person will lose his gloves.
>
> Inevitably there are situations where the two constructions overlap and both may be possible.

Answer key

1. past simple
2. *would* or *might* + verb
3. crime now and in the future
4. situations that are imagined

4

Give the learners a few minutes to amend some of the original sentences and move round to help where necessary. Then put them in small groups to discuss their answers. When you feel the conversation is flagging, move on to the final activity.

5

Allow about five minutes for the learners to complete these new sentences, then put them back into their groups for discussion. If you were not happy with the way the group interacted in the previous activity, change them round a bit to see how different combinations work. If time permits, give some positive feedback on the discussion and some error correction and/or new language that might have helped them in their discussion.

Personal Study Workbook

1: We wouldn't get wet because …: *if* sentences
3: The sound of money: pronunciation

```
             QUICK NOTES

This went well:

...............................................................
...............................................................

There was a problem with:

...............................................................
...............................................................

Things to think about:

...............................................................
...............................................................
```

ADVICE FROM SOMEONE WHO KNOWS

Introduction

The lesson provides practice in the use of link words and phrases to compare and contrast different institutions – prison, hospital, the army and boarding school. Much of the lesson, however, revolves around two genuine listening texts spoken by a man who spent about 15 years in prison. He describes life in prison, and what people can do to protect their homes from thieves. The learners have several opportunities to predict some of his comments and respond to his advice.

Suggested steps

1

You could ask if any members of the class have ever visited a prison, and if so, what was their impression of it. From this, ask others, in groups, to note down their impressions of what prison life must be like for most prisoners. With a multicultural group this might produce a very wide mix of impressions. If so, you could ask what these different impressions are based on.

2 ▭

Introduce the listening. The speaker spent about 15 years in prison, so he is well-qualified to comment on prison life. He is now reformed and spends most of his time talking to both schoolchildren and adults about his experience and also the need for changes in the penal system. Play the recording once and then elicit answers to the questions. If this presents no problems, you could then invite responses to the speaker. Is there anything that is particularly surprising? Is there anything he describes which would be radically different in their country? etc. The tapescript is on page 150.

Answer key

1. false (He spent about 15 years in prison.)
2. true
3. true
4. true
5. false (They work.)
6. false (They get two visits per month.)

3

You could ask if any members of the class have attended boarding school, been in the army or been in hospital as a patient. Elicit a few responses on what it was like, and then look at the example sentences illustrating the link words and phrases (1, 3, 5). Check that they understand the links by referring to the information in the clauses. For example, in sentence 1, is the routine the same or different in the two clauses? (It's different, or contrasting information, so *whereas* is used.)

Then ask the group to complete the rest of the sentences individually. When everyone has finished, put the learners in pairs to compare answers and try to think up more similarities and differences.

Option

If you have at least two or three people who have experienced boarding school and/or hospital and/or the army, you could ask them to sit at the front of the class when everyone has finished writing their sentences in Exercise 3. Other class members can then read out their sentences, and the learners at the front of the class can say if they agree with them.

4 ▭

Now play the second listening extract in which John talks about protecting the home from burglars. Play the recording once and let the learners compare answers. The tapescript is on page 151.

Answer key

1. Leave lights on in your house.
2. Don't leave doors unlocked.
3. Fit an alarm.
4. Get a dog, and also put a picture of a dog on the gate.

Option

Before playing the recording you could put the learners in pairs and get them to predict the content of the listening. You could then put their ideas on the board and the group can then listen to confirm their ideas and add any new ones.

5

It is unlikely you will have time to complete this activity in the present lesson. You could give it for homework, or leave it until the next lesson.

Personal Study Workbook

4: It's similar and different: link words and phrases
5: Plants and burglars: reading
6: How to beat car theft: listening
8: Speaking partners

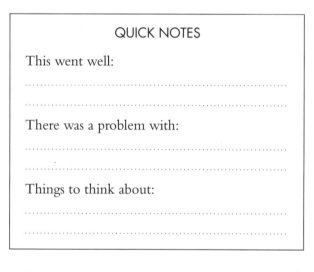

```
QUICK NOTES

This went well:

.................................................

.................................................

There was a problem with:

.................................................

.................................................

Things to think about:

.................................................

.................................................
```

THE JURY SYSTEM ON TRIAL

Introduction

Judicial systems vary from country to country. If you work in a country where the learners may not be familiar with the jury system, you may choose to omit this lesson. (You might like to try Worksheet 13 on page 125 instead. If so, see *Suggested steps for Worksheet 13* at the end of this lesson.) However, the lesson does provide an opportunity for the learners to talk about the justice system in their own country, and the lexical area may be very relevant to some of your learners. The principal arguments are contained in a jigsaw reading, and there is also practice with defining relative clauses.

Suggested steps

1

Use the pictures to elicit the target items.

2

Introduce the concept of the jury system and then divide the class into groups. If you have any lawyers, law students or just learners who are well informed about the legal system in their country, try to ensure there is one in each group; they can act as teachers/informers if the rest of the group are not very sure of the system in their own country. In our experience, class members who are not well informed are often very keen to find out more about their own legal system as well as the system used elsewhere.

3

Divide the class into pairs and direct one partner in each pair to the text on page 90 of the Class Book while the other reads the text on page 172. Give everyone time to read and digest the information in their texts, and be prepared to move round and help the learners with new lexis. When they have finished, put the pairs together to complete the table on the advantages and disadvantages. A pair can then compare with others before you check answers and clarify any problems in the text.

Answer key

Advantages:
1. Being judged by one's peers seems the fairest way.
2. Twelve people should provide a balanced judgement.
3. It gives people a sense of responsibility – they are contributing to society.
4. People believe it is the best system and it is important that they have faith in their system of justice.
5. Nobody has come up with a better idea.
Disadvantages:
1. Some jurors don't take it seriously.
2. Conditions for jurors are often very poor.
3. Some jurors may not have the education to understand complex trials.
4. It is a very expensive system.

Option

After each pair has completed the table, an alternative way of checking is for partner A to read partner B's text and vice versa. They can then decide if their partner has extracted all the information from their text and expressed it accurately.

4

Follow the instructions in the Class Book for the vocabulary exercise, and try to ensure a brisk pace in the practice phase.

Answer key

1. b   2. a   3. e   4. c   5. f   6. d

5

Elicit answers from the class for the first part of the activity, and then do the first one together. For example: *A criminal is a person who commits a crime.* Then let them finish the task and compare in groups.

Answer key

Who is used for talking about people, *which* for things and *where* for places.

Suggested steps for Worksheet 13

Divide the class into groups of four, and then subdivide each group into two pairs. The first pair should read situations 1 and 2 on the worksheet; the second pair should read situations 3 and 4 on the worksheet. Their task is this: one person in each pair must add additional information which supports and justifies the action taken by the police; their partner must think of additional information which supports the person who suffers damage or injury. When the group is ready, the first pair put their case for each party in the two situations, and the second pair must then decide if the police action was reasonable or unreasonable. Repeat the procedure for situations 3 and 4 with the second pair.

Give each pair time to read through their situations, and explain any new vocabulary, e.g. *siren*. You may also need to give one or two examples of additional information to illustrate what they have to do. For example, in situation 1, the boy may be known to the policeman as a youth who has a criminal record; on the other hand, the boy may simply be in a hurry to get home because it is about to rain.

Give each pair time to prepare their case, and move round and help the learners where necessary.

Personal Study Workbook

2: It's the place where you …: relative clauses
7: That's the woman who …: writing

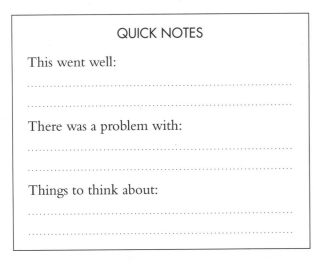

```
QUICK NOTES

This went well:
.................................................
.................................................

There was a problem with:
.................................................
.................................................

Things to think about:
.................................................
.................................................
```

REVIEW AND DEVELOPMENT

REVIEW OF UNIT 11

1

Follow the instructions in the Class Book.

Answer key

1. If birds didn't have wings, they wouldn't be able to fly.

2. I would be very unhappy if I didn't have so many friends.
3. If it is (or were) cold again tomorrow, we'll (or would) have to stay at home.
4. If we don't leave now, we'll miss the beginning of the film.
5. I will (or would) be very surprised if you don't (or didn't) like the film.
6. I would see him tomorrow if I were here, but in fact I'll be in Germany.
7. I'll take you out for dinner this evening if you like.
8. If I go (or went) to Switzerland, will (or would) I need a raincoat?

2 ▭

Follow the instructions in the Class Book. The tapescript is on page 151.

REVIEW OF UNIT 12

1

If you do not have a board in your classroom, include something else from the room that you can measure. (Even if you do have a board, you may still wish to include additional questions.) Here are some further possibilities:
– the length and width of a rug or carpet
– the length, width and height of a table or tables
– the thickness of a dictionary
– the length, width and height of a bookcase
etc.

Follow the instructions in the Class Book for the procedure.

2

Check that the learners can identify all the things in the pictures before moving on to the second part of the exercise, which might generate more discussion if it were done in small groups rather than pairs.

Answer key

1. a collection of sea shells 2. a picture frame
3. a chair 4. a bird in a cage 5. a pair of slippers
6. a clothes brush

```
QUICK NOTES

This went well:
.................................................
.................................................

There was a problem with:
.................................................
.................................................

Things to think about:
.................................................
.................................................
```

TALL STORIES, SHORT STORIES

CONTENTS

Language focus:	past perfect simple making excuses and reassuring expressing purpose, reason and result	
Vocabulary:	the countryside transport action verbs	
Skills:	Speaking:	discussing events in an unlikely story opinions about the use of computers role play: being late and making excuses
	Listening:	a short story people explaining why they were late
	Reading:	a text about computer stories the beginning of a short story
	Writing:	a short story reasons for being late

THE FACE ON THE WALL

Introduction

The main focus here is the presentation and controlled practice of the past perfect simple. But first, the learners listen to an intriguing short story which is explored through a range of tasks involving prediction, detailed comprehension and discussion.

Suggested steps

1

The best introduction would probably be if you could go into class and tell a short story which is clearly also a 'tall' story. Tell the class that it is both a short story and a tall story and see if they can explain this seeming contradiction. If you have no stories up your sleeve, just follow the instructions in the Class Book.

2 ▭

Use the picture to try to elicit the meaning of *patch of damp* or simply explain it to the group. Ask the group to read the first passage of the story and ask one or two questions to test their understanding. For example:
What was unusual about the patch of damp on the wall?
What did the man start to believe after a while?
Why did the man look at people in the street all the time?

Ask the learners if they would like to find out the next part of the story; if you like, ask them for predictions about what happens. Then play the recording. The tapescript is on page 151.

3

See if your learners can now correct the sentences. When they have finished, let them compare with a partner and then find out what they think the errors are. Don't give the correct answers at this point. If there is any disagreement, play the recording again and see if the group can resolve their differences.

Answer key

1. He followed him to a *railway* station not a coach station.
2. He asked the man for his card *on the boat*, not in Boulogne.
3. He came from *America*, not Australia.
4. His parents had lived in *London*, not France.
5. He noticed it when he *woke up in the morning*, not when he went to sleep.
6. Mr Wall had been in a *motor* accident, not a train accident.
7. The face *disappeared*, not got darker.
8. Mr Wall *had died*, not left hospital.

4 ▭

Tell the group that they are now going to listen to the end of the story in which the storyteller explains that there are three extraordinary things about the story. Put the class into pairs and ask them to say what they are. Put all their ideas on the board and then play the recording to see which pair, if any, predicted all three things. The tapescript is on page 151.

Answer key

The three extraordinary things are:
1. that damp patches on a wall could look like a man;
2. that the man's name should be the same as the street where it appeared;
3. that he invented the whole story just half an hour before.

Option

If you have a particularly lively or imaginative class, and they have enjoyed the short story they have been listening to, you might ask them if they know any stories which are remarkable or hard to believe. Tell them not to disclose whether they are true or not. If you have some volunteers, put the rest of the class into listening groups and let each member with a story circulate and tell their story to each group in turn. At the end, ask the groups who listened whether they think the stories were true or not, giving their reasons. The storytellers can then disclose the truth.

5

If possible, put the example sentences and time line on the board or OHP so that you have the attention of the whole class focused in one place rather than ten or twenty heads all buried in books.

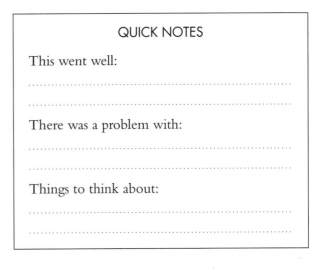

Explain this use of the past perfect, highlight the form, and give one or two further examples. For example, ask them to explain the use of tenses in these two sentences:

I could see the receptionist, but when I went in and rang the bell she had disappeared.

I could see the receptionist, but when I went in and rang the bell she disappeared.

Now give them the short text to further test and consolidate their understanding. Check with the whole class.

Answer key

… the milk and eggs he **had** bought …
… they **had** collected plenty of wood …

6

Go through the example clearly before they work on the rest of the sentences in pairs. At the end, listen to the different answers and ask the group if they approve of each other's explanations.

Answer key

Possible answers
1. … because he had missed the last bus.
   … because he was tired.
2. … because she had had a terrible argument with her boss.
   … because she was pregnant.
3. … because he hadn't worked hard enough.
   … because he was no good at maths.

4. … because the chef had put too much salt in it.
   … because it was cold and greasy.

Personal Study Workbook

1: When they had left …: past perfect simple and past simple
5: I never forget a face (I): reading
6: I never forget a face (II): listening

QUICK NOTES

This went well:
....
....

There was a problem with:
....
....

Things to think about:
....
....

CAN COMPUTERS TELL STORIES?

Introduction

The lesson provides practice in using different types of clause (purpose, reason and result), and also expands vocabulary through the development of a range of noun + verb collocations. These linguistic aims are realised through simple storytelling and a text about computer programs which develop plots for children's stories.

Suggested steps

1

Help the learners with any items of vocabulary in the picture, and then put them in pairs to write their very short story (it can be as close to the original picture as they wish). Listen to some examples.

2

When you have heard a number of examples from the first exercise, let them read the text and answer the questions below. Conduct a brief feedback and discuss any problems arising from the text.

Answer key

1. false   2. true   3. true   4. true

The discussion need not confine itself to this particular computer activity.

Option

You could broaden this discussion to include the general advantages and disadvantages of computers for the education of children today. This discussion could take the form of a brainstorming session in small groups before coming together as a class. If you have a group with a wide age range, the discussion could focus on the difference between education now and ten or twenty years ago. How have computers influenced education? Are these influences all positive? How do older class members feel about the absence of computers in their education?

3

You may decide to pre-teach the new vocabulary yourself using pictures, mime and explanation, and also provide additional examples to illustrate the different clauses, i.e. of purpose, reason and result. Starting with the example, this might be:

*The children dived into the lake **and** swam to the other side.* (result)

*The children dived into the lake **(in order) to** save the young girl from drowning.* (purpose)

*The children dived into the lake **because** a man was chasing them.* (reason)

While the pairs work on their sentences, move round and help where necessary. At the end, listen to a sample of the sentences. The group can decide on the most amusing, imaginative, bizarre, etc.

Answer key

Possible answers

The pilot landed on the lawn to prevent an accident.
The soldier crept through the bushes because he didn't want to be seen.
The sparrow hopped along the path to pick up the crumbs.
The motorbike skidded into the fence but the rider was unhurt.
The helicopter crashed into the cliff and fell into the sea.
The horse galloped through the woods and disappeared.

4

This gives the learners an opportunity to expand their vocabulary around specific subjects. Ask them which subjects from the list they would like to choose, and then create pairs accordingly, i.e. pairs interested in the same subjects. You will be called upon to help them express ideas, so move round as freely as possible. Here are just some of the likely collocations they may wish to produce:

The horse/fell/fence	The pilot flew
The horse/bolted/stable	The helicopter took off
The horse/trotted/gate	The helicopter circled
The soldier marched	The sparrow flew
The children ran	The children whispered
The motorbike accelerated	The motorbike was stolen

5

If the group have been very creative in the previous exercise, you may have to give this activity for homework. If there is enough time in class, remind the group of the simple formula of the computer story as a possible model. Listen to as many stories as you can.

Personal Study Workbook

3: What could it be?: vocabulary
7: Film synopsis: writing
8: Speaking partners
9: Visual dictionary

QUICK NOTES

This went well:

....

....

There was a problem with:

....

....

Things to think about:

....

....

EXCUSES, EXCUSES

Introduction

The learners focus on common chunks of language which are often needed to explain why people are late, and these expressions are practised through personalised activities in which the learners exchange their own reasons for being late and the frequency with which they need to make excuses. Common ways of responding to excuses are also practised in the lesson, and there is a listening passage in which native speakers tell their own unlikely stories about being late (continuing the theme of tall stories).

Suggested steps

1 ▢▢ ▢▢

You could obviously start by telling your own story about why you were late on a particular occasion, or just introduce the stories on the recording. Choose the appropriate version and play it. Let the learners compare their answers, then play the recording a second time if they had difficulty, or check the answers. The tapescript is on page 152.

Answer key

Version 1:
Speaker 1
1. He was going to a football match.
2. The alarm didn't go off, then he forgot his football things.
3. He got to the game just as it was finishing.
4. The story is true.

Speaker 2
1. She was on her way to a date.
2. Her train was late and then she had to go back home for her money.
3. She was 45 minutes late.
4. The story is false.

Version 2:
Speaker 1
1. He was on his way to a job interview.
2. The train was late.
3. He had the interview on the way to the airport and didn't get the job.
4. The story is true.

Speaker 2
1. He was waiting for a bus on his way to his first day at work.
2. He was taken to the police station for questioning.
3. He took the policemen with him to his workplace to explain what had happened.
4. The story is true.

2

You will probably be able to elicit the meaning of many items of vocabulary here; explain any you can't. See how many excuses the class can remember from Exercise 1, and if they can't remember much at all, play the recording one more time.

Put the learners in pairs to think up more excuses, then let them compare with other pairs. At the end, put their suggestions on the board and highlight any useful new words or phrases that emerge.

Answer key

The excuses used in Exercise 1 are:
– my alarm clock didn't go off
– I realised I'd left my money at home

3

Now divide the learners into groups and encourage them to explain why certain things seem to happen to them. And are these excuses the truth, or are they a cover-up for other reasons for being late? Monitor the groups while they are talking and make a note of useful language for discussion and feedback.

4

These little phrases are unlikely to be new, but they are often used incorrectly, or simply not used in situations where native speakers would deem them essential for polite reassurance. In other words, if your learners cannot use these phrases freely and appropriately, they may appear rude or abrupt to some native speakers of English. This, of course, may not apply if they are using their English with other non-native speakers of the language.

Answer key

Most of these phrases can be used to reassure the person who is apologising, and often we use two of them in one utterance. For example:

A: *I'm sorry I'm late but I missed the bus.*
B: *That's all right. Don't worry.* or *Never mind. It's not important. It doesn't matter.*

Phrases we don't use here are: *I don't mind*; *I don't care*; *Nothing*. The first two of these can express no preference. For example:

A: *Would you like to go out?*
B: *I don't mind. (I don't care.)*

You have to be careful with the second of these phrases as it can also be used to express indifference:

A: *He lost all his money.*
B: *I don't care. (= I have no sympathy. It means nothing to me.)*

The word *nothing* is sometimes used by learners in these situations and is a translation error.

5

By asking the learners to write their own situations to act out, they have an opportunity to prepare situations that may be familiar or relevant to them. It can also be more fun. However, you may need to move round and monitor their situations to ensure they are practical and sensible. Also check that their handwriting is legible.

If you wish to have a break from these functional exchanges and also explore the cross-cultural differences involved in these inter-personal matters, try Worksheet 14 on page 125 in this lesson or the next.

Personal Study Workbook

2: Excuses, excuses: functional language and transport vocabulary
4: Find the right word: word building

> ### QUICK NOTES
>
> This went well:
> ....
> ....
>
> There was a problem with:
> ....
> ....
>
> Things to think about:
> ....
> ....

REVIEW OF UNIT 12

1 ⊂⊃

Follow the instructions in the Class Book and check the learners' sentences before playing the recording. As much as anything, the learners have to recognise that the correct intonation pattern here is an acknowledgement of the emotion being expressed. Some learners produce very flat intonation because they are preoccupied with their search for the right grammar and vocabulary, and they tend to forget the reason for the utterance in the first place, which may be joy, anger, frustration, excitement and so on. The tapescript is on page 152.

2

You can either tell your learners to look through the unit before they see the questions; or they can read through the questions then look through the unit. In other words, in the second instance, they know what they are looking for.

REVIEW OF UNIT 13

1

Follow the instructions in the Class Book.

Answer key

Crime against people	*Crime against property*
murder – murderer	burglary – burglar
robbery – robber	robbery – robber
blackmail – blackmailer	shoplifting – shoplifter
kidnapping – kidnapper	arson – arsonist
	vandalism – vandal
	smuggling – smuggler
	hijacking – hijacker

Option

If you would like further practice of this lexical area, you could ask the learners in pairs to make a list of the likely targets in each of these crimes. For example:
What do people usually smuggle?
Who do kidnappers usually kidnap?
What buildings do arsonists usually set fire to?
What property do vandals usually destroy?
etc.

2

This type of questionnaire has become a common feature of English language books. Nevertheless, they remain popular and do provide intensive practice of *if* sentences. Follow the instructions in the Class Book.

QUICK NOTES

This went well:
....
....

There was a problem with:
....
....

Things to think about:
....
....

15

LOVE THY NEIGHBOUR

CONTENTS

Language focus: verb patterns
present perfect simple and continuous

Vocabulary: guessing words in context
reporting verbs
relationships

Skills: Speaking: assessing acts of kindness of others
inventing your own acts of kindness
problem solving: grammar rules
describing groups you belong to

Listening: an explanation of grammar rules
positive and negative features of
different groups

Reading: a text about unusual acts of kindness
texts about noise problems

Writing: sentence building using different verb
patterns

ACTS OF RANDOM KINDNESS

Introduction

The learners spend much of the lesson reading, responding to and interpreting a text, which is also exploited for the development of the skill of contextual guesswork. In the second half of the lesson there is an analysis of different constructions which may follow important reporting verbs, and these different verbs and verb patterns are practised in a personalised activity which draws upon the ideas earlier explored in the reading text.

Suggested steps

1

Ask the class if they consider themselves to be model citizens – kind, polite, thoughtful towards others and so on. Following this introduction, which usually prompts a few humorous responses, you can set up the small groups for the warm-up activity, checking first if there are any words they don't understand. At the end conduct a brief feedback and then introduce the text.

2

Explain the word *random* (a *random act* is one without any obvious logic or rational explanation), then your group can read the text. As there is a later activity on contextual guesswork, don't explain any vocabulary items in the text and also ask them not to use their

dictionaries on this occasion. At the end, let them exchange opinions with a partner or in groups, but keep it brief as there will be a further opportunity for the learners to respond to the specific suggestions in the text.

3

Some words in a text are not guessable, and it can be very frustrating for the learners to be asked to guess the meaning of a word which simply isn't elucidated by the text. With these words though, there are clues in the text which should guide them towards the meaning and it is important that the learners do try to make use of various strategies to help them. For example, new words may be synonyms of other words already used in order to avoid repetition (this explains *craze*, a paraphrase of *trend*). It may also help for the learner to cover the unknown word and try to think of a meaning which makes sense in that space (this may help to explain *packed*). In many cases though, other words in the sentence clearly point to the meaning (*address book* and *greetings card* clearly suggest that *chum* must be either a friend, relative, or business contact).

At the end of the activity, get the learners to try to explain how they arrived at their answers. You can, of course, repeat this activity with any reading text during the course, but do choose words that can be retrieved from the text.

Answer key

craze = fashionable activity/trend
running out = finishing (having no coins in this case)
packed with = full of
praising = saying positive things
chum = friend (informal)
row = line of seats (in a cinema, plane, church, etc.)

4

This activity could last five minutes or twenty-five minutes. If the groups are very engaged in discussion, you may decide to leave the analysis of verb patterns until the next lesson. During the discussion move round and monitor the groups and note down any points for praise or correction. If you decide to postpone the verb patterns until later, you could have a much lengthier feedback on both language and ideas at the end of the group discussion.

5

The initial activity is a first step at processing the meaning of any new verbs, but you will have to consolidate some of them with a fuller explanation when you check the answers. See the Language Point below.

> **Language Point: accuse vs. blame**
>
> These verbs are often confused as some languages may translate both with a single verb. If you *accuse* somebody, you think they are guilty of an action which is wrong or illegal. If you *blame* somebody, you are saying that they have overall responsibility for the action. For example:
> *She accused the boy of stealing, but she blamed the boy's parents because they never disciplined him.*
> *She accused the man of driving through a red light and blamed him for the accident.*

Answer key

Positive	Negative
promise	prevent
thank	make somebody do
let somebody do something	something
offer	threaten
help somebody	blame
agree	refuse
congratulate	accuse
praise	

Let is the one verb which could arguably appear in both lists.

6

Encourage humorous examples here and listen to as many examples as you have time for, checking each time that they have used the correct constructions with each verb.

Option

If this proves popular, and the lesson has already spilled over into a second lesson, you could add a further activity in which the learners invent acts of classroom unpleasantness using the negative verbs. You could give one or two examples from the teacher's perspective:
– refuse to mark homework
– accuse the learners of stealing books if any go missing
– threaten to fine learners who make grammatical mistakes

Personal Study Workbook

2: You promised to help: verb patterns
3: More acts of kindness: guessing words in context
9: Visual dictionary

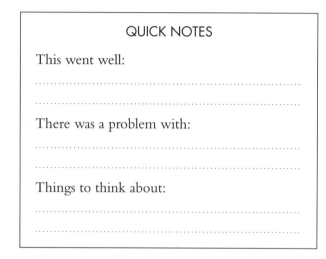

QUICK NOTES

This went well:

....

....

There was a problem with:

....

....

Things to think about:

....

....

NEIGHBOURS

Introduction

Understanding a grammar point is usually a good reason for listening, so we have decided to use it as the basis for the listening in this lesson. First the learners have to try to sort out the difference in meaning between sentences in the present perfect simple and continuous, then they listen to an explanation of the differences from a native speaker. The differences are further explored and practised, first through a maze activity and then a split reading for reformulation using the two structures. The lesson ends with a freer discussion of issues arising from the texts.

Suggested steps

1

While the pairs are working on this activity, move round and monitor the discussion. Sometimes the learners may understand a difference but lack the precise language to explain it clearly; you can help them in this situation. When they have had a go at answering the questions, conduct a feedback session and write a summary of their ideas on the board. At this stage do not confirm or reject any of their ideas.

Answer key

See the tapescript for Exercise 2 on page 152.

2 ▭

Play the recording, twice if necessary, then let the pairs compare their notes from the listening with the discussion they had before. Clarify the points from the listening and ask the learners to assess whether their original ideas covered all the points mentioned on the recording. The tapescript is on page 152.

3

Explain the maze very carefully, and emphasise that they should keep a clear record of the numbers they visit and in which order. It is important they consider each of their decisions carefully, so stress this is not a race. Do the first couple of stages with them as an example, then let them work in pairs. If one pair finishes ahead of the rest, you can look at their answers with them. If they have mistakes, tell them to go back and try again. When everyone has finished, go through it with the whole group.

Answer key

The correct sequence of questions is 4, 7, 6, 1, 3, 8, 5, 2, 9, 10, 11.
We are grateful to Mark Bartram and Richard Walton for the idea for this maze from their book Correction *(LTP).*

4

Read through the questions first so that the learners know exactly what they will have to explain. Then they can read their respective texts, close their books and retell the story to their partner. Try to move round the whole class to ensure they are using the two target structures correctly and have the facts correct.

5

This may be more interesting if you have learners from different cultures in your group, as the attitude to noise varies from country to country, as do the types of noise which occur. With monolingual groups, it may be more interesting to focus on the way the learners would respond in each of the situations.

Option

With a multicultural group, you could get the learners to write their own questionnaire about noise in order to uncover cultural differences. For example:
Is it common / reasonably common / rare for people to play radios:
   a) on public transport b) in the street c) in parks?
Is it very common / reasonably common / uncommon for drivers to use their car horns?
Is it very common / reasonably common / unusual for neighbours to make a lot of noise after 10 pm?
etc.

Personal Study Workbook

1: I've been waiting for ages: present perfect simple vs. continuous
4: Sounds and spelling – same or different?: pronunciation

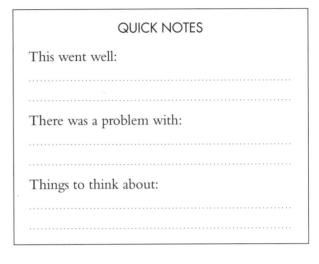

```
QUICK NOTES

This went well:
...........................................................
...........................................................

There was a problem with:
...........................................................
...........................................................

Things to think about:
...........................................................
...........................................................
```

GETTING ON IN GROUPS

Introduction

We all belong to many different groups – family, work, leisure, etc. – and this lesson explores some of the features of groups: what makes them successful, and what creates conflict? In the process, the learners learn a number of words and expressions connected with relationships; they listen to native speakers talking about groups they have belonged to; and they have several opportunities to talk about their own experiences of being in a group. Finally, they work in small groups in class to create a new group with a name and specific aims.

Suggested steps

1

Ask the learners individually to add one more example to the list, then put them in small groups to share their examples and talk about the groups they belong to. This often reveals facts about class members which were previously unknown and can stimulate a lot of interest and discussion.

2

Put the learners in pairs to complete the task with the aid of dictionaries, and clarify any problems of meaning when you check the answers at the end.

Answer key

Features of good groups:
People get on well with each other.
They are prepared to compromise.
They feel they have something in common.
They trust each other.
New members of the group fit in easily.
People are tolerant towards each other.
The atmosphere among the group is supportive.

Changed sentences:
They don't have rows at all.
They don't get on each other's nerves. / They are sensitive towards each other.
People work hard to avoid conflict.
There is no hostility in personal relationships.

3

This could be a very personal activity, but the learners can choose which group they wish to talk about and obviously edit out anything they wish to remain private. In our experience this can stimulate a lot of very engaging discussion. You are also likely to find your learners need additional language to help them express some of their ideas, so move round and be alert to these needs.

4 ▢▢ ▢▢

The listening gives the learners the opportunity to hear native speakers doing the same activity. Choose the appropriate version of the recording and let the learners exchange answers before you check with the whole class. The tapescript is on page 152.

Answer key

Version 1:
Speaker 1
Type of group: local residents' association
Positive features: none
Negative features: they had rows all the time; they got on each other's nerves; nobody trusted one another; some people tried to create conflict
Speaker 2
Type of group: people on holiday together
Positive features: they got on well; a good atmosphere; they had things in common (they wanted to be there)
Negative features: some of the group played very loud pop music

Version 2:
Speaker 1
Type of group: a brass band
Positive features: they get on well together; they are supportive towards one another; there's a good atmosphere; new members are made to feel welcome
Negative features: occasionally there is a clash of personality

Speaker 2
Type of group: a riding club
Positive features: they got on well together; they were very supportive
Negative features: new members found it difficult to fit in, and they behaved very badly to one woman in particular

5

This final exercise continues the theme of groups, but explores it in a different way and also allows for some more creative thinking. If you have had success with wall displays, you could ask each group to put their ideas on a poster and put it on the wall. At the end, people can move round and read them all – and sign up if interested.

You might also like to follow up this theme with Worksheet 15 on page 126 which explores the lexis of different groups and group members or places where they meet.

Answer key for Worksheet 15

a team of rugby players
a crowd of spectators
a congregation at a church service
a committee of representatives
the crew of a ship
a regiment of soldiers
a gang of hooligans
a board of directors
a choir of singers
an audience at a play
the staff of a school

Personal Study Workbook

5: A group of wolves: reading
6: The Living Flag: listening
7: My neighbourhood: writing
8: Speaking partners

QUICK NOTES

This went well:

....
....

There was a problem with:

....
....

Things to think about:

....
....

REVIEW OF UNIT 13

1 ▭

Ask the class if they think there is a link between criminals and ballet dancing. Tell them to think of one or two possibilities and put them on the board. Play the recording and then let the learners compare their notes with a partner. Check with the whole group and then put them in small groups for them to discuss the issues. You could ask them if they have any suggestions for activities which they consider more useful than ballet dancing. The tapescript is on page 153.

Answer key

Dancing is hard work and it can help prisoners get rid of some of their frustrations. The dance programme can also help to give prisoners more self-esteem. The scheme is not expensive.

2

You could ask the questions round the class and then put them in pairs to test each other.

Answer key

1. Burglars
2. The police
3. Victims (members of the public)
4. People who are charged with an offence / the accused
5. Barristers (a type of lawyer)
6. Witnesses
7. Juries or judges
8. Judges

For the second part of the exercise, you could put the learners in pairs to form the questions, then split each pair so they are in different groups to ask their questions.

Answer key

Possible answers
1. Who cuts hair?
2. Who acts in films and plays?
3. Who represent people in parliament?
4. Who looks after your teeth?
5. Who writes books?
6. Who repairs cars?

REVIEW OF UNIT 14

1

Give the learners time to prepare their stories and also encourage them to rehearse them, i.e. tell the whole story mentally to themselves to see whether they can actually turn ideas into coherent utterances, or tell the story to their partner as a type of 'dry run'. This can be very beneficial.

2 ▭

Follow the instructions in the Class Book. The tapescript is on page 153 and on page 174 of the Class Book.

QUICK NOTES
This went well:
....
....
There was a problem with:
....
....
Things to think about:
....
....

YES AND NO

CONTENTS

Language focus: *wish* + past simple
forming negatives
indefinite pronouns: *something, anything, nothing*
if sentences with *would* and *might*
saying *no* politely

Vocabulary: negative prefixes
negative adverbs, e.g. *rarely*

Skills: Speaking: positive and negative thinking
when can you say·*no*?
Listening: cross-cultural differences: refusing to
do things
Reading: a text about positive thinking
Writing: positive thoughts

SAYING NO POLITELY

Introduction

The language focus here is on ways of refusing things in English, but the discussion point is whether it is polite to say *no* in different situations. This may vary a great deal from culture to culture, and is the context for the listening activity. There is also an opportunity to practise conditional clauses, but with no special emphasis as the learners should now be quite familiar with these structures.

Suggested steps

1

Explain the situation to the group and elicit responses using *you could say no* or *you couldn't say no*. With learners from different countries there may be interesting cross-cultural differences, but with learners from the same country there may be little to discuss (however, don't assume this is the case without finding out first). But if, for example, everyone agrees it is acceptable to refuse the main course, you could go on to ask them if there are circumstances where they would eat something they don't actually like.

2 ▭▭ ▰▰

Play the appropriate version of the recording and pause after each speaker to allow the learners time to make notes. At the end, let them compare their notes with a partner before you go through the answers. The tapescript is on page 153.

Answer key

Version 1:
1. Lyndham is from India. He was able to say *no* when offered pork, because eating it is against his religion.
2. Gertrude is from Germany. She feels it is OK to say *no* if, for example, you are a vegetarian and are offered meat. She thinks it would be difficult if people have cooked something special for you.

Version 2:
1. Aisha is British. She thinks that the British are very polite and find it difficult to say *no*. Now, however, she is a vegetarian so she feels it is necessary to say *no* if offered meat.
2. Lorelei is American. She says that Americans are used to people saying *no* for various reasons, e.g. dieting. However, she feels it is a bit rude to say *no*.

3

The group should be familiar with these conditional clauses, but you could remind them about the use of *would* and *might* in hypothetical situations. Before putting the learners in groups, ask them to read through the six situations to check they understand them, and discuss the first situation as a group.

When most of the groups have finished their discussion, elicit responses from different groups about the situation they have chosen. Give some feedback as well on their use of language and highlight any useful new vocabulary which has arisen out of the discussion.

4

The target language in this exercise is basically transparent as far as meaning is concerned, but will probably not be part of their active vocabulary and some items may be new. *Wish* + past simple is the main focus of the third lesson, so at this stage you can just gloss the expression *I wish I could* as *I would like to but unfortunately it's not possible.* You could ask pairs to write out brief dialogues for two or three situations. If any pairs finish before the others, just ask them to do the same for two more situations. Listen to examples round the class and discuss any problems.

Answer key

There is a wide range of possible answers. Here are some suggestions:

1. That's very kind of you, but I'm afraid I'm going to the opera this evening and I have to be at the theatre by 7.30. I'm very sorry.
2. I'm terribly sorry, but my plane is boarding and I have to go.
3. I'd love to come, but I'm expecting a friend from Paris on that evening and I may have to go to the airport to pick her up.
4. I'm terribly sorry but I'm waiting for someone and they'll be here any minute.
5. I wish I could, but unfortunately I forgot to go to the bank today and I just haven't got any money on me at all. I'm terribly sorry.
6. It's a bit difficult, I'm afraid. You see, I'm expecting an important call at any minute. Could you make your call later?

Language Point: apologies

You may have noticed in the sample answers to the last exercise that several answers begin and end with an apology. This is a very common feature in both spoken and written English. You could ask your learners if the same would be common in their culture.

5

You may not have much time for this exercise. If so, you could give it for homework or begin your next lesson with it as a form of revision. You could also follow it up with Worksheet 16 on page 126, in which the learners have to try to predict whether their partner will answer *yes* or *no* to a series of questions.

Personal Study Workbook

5: When *yes* means *no* and *no* means *yes*: reading
6: Saying *no* politely: listening

NEGATIVES AND OPPOSITES!

Introduction

Using the format of a quiz to create interest, the lesson examines a number of common grammar problems all associated with negation. The lesson concludes with personalised practice of some of the points. There is much more controlled practice material in the Personal Study Workbook.

Suggested steps

1

You could begin by writing two or three questions that people have asked you today (if possible, include a question asked by one of your class). Then ask them if they know or can guess who asked you these questions and what your answer was. Tell them the right answers and whether you regret any of your answers.

Put them in pairs to do the same exercise.

2

The prospect of a quiz is usually quite motivating, so you can probably move straight into the exercise without a long introduction. Put the learners in pairs and give them a time limit to add further interest, e.g. 15 minutes. Monitor the pairs while they are working, so you will know which points require the most detailed explanation at the end.

Answer key

1.
We didn't have a very good holiday. (*We had a very bad holiday* is not grammatically wrong, but native speakers are much more likely to express the negative idea through the verb here.)
Elizabeth advised me not to take the job. *or* Elizabeth didn't advise me to take the job. (The meaning of these two possible answers may be different.)
I don't think it's raining.
I hope not.

He'll probably make an interesting speech. *or* He probably won't make a boring speech.

We didn't use to go there. *or* We never used to go there.

Language Points

1. Some learners still think the negative of *had* as a main verb is *hadn't*. This is now very unusual among native speakers, who prefer to use the auxiliary, i.e. *didn't have*.
2. When we introduce a negative idea using the verb *think*, we normally put the verb into the negative, i.e. *I don't think it is* (not *I think it isn't*).
3. Notice the normal position of *probably* with *will* and *won't*, i.e. after *will* but before *won't*.
4. *Never used to* is often used to express the negative, rather than *didn't use to*.

2.
1. anywhere   2. nothing   3. someone   4. everything
  5. anything   6. any   7 no

3.
agree – disagree
approve – disapprove
accept – refuse or reject
satisfied – dissatisfied
admit – deny
obedient – disobedient
honest – dishonest
innocent – guilty

4.
Rarely, *seldom* and *hardly ever* are similar in meaning. *Invariably* means *almost always*.

5.
Everybody **has** to arrive on time.
The second sentence is correct.
Neither of us **has** been to Italy. (But the plural verb form is common in spoken English in the structure *neither of* + noun/pronoun.)
No one **tells** him what to do.

6.
Yes, you can open it.
No, B doesn't like chocolate.

When the 15 minutes are up (you can adjust the time allowed if necessary), go through the answers. This may take some time as further explanation will be necessary on some questions. At the end tell them to add up their scores, and this will give you an indication of how much extra practice is necessary.

Option

A very useful skill to develop in class is the ability to use grammar reference books effectively. Some learners buy them but don't get into the habit of using them; others buy them but experience great difficulty in using them. If you are fortunate enough to have access to a good supply of grammar reference books, you could divide the class into groups, give each member of a group a grammar book, and get them to retrieve the answers to

the quiz. This should not be too time-consuming if each member is only made responsible for the answers to one question.

For ease of access, we would currently recommend:
Practical English Usage by Michael Swan (OUP)
Collins Cobuild English Usage (Collins)

Both these books have an alphabetical index, which makes it relatively easy for the learners to find what they are looking for.

3

Elicit one or two answers to the example from the class. Please note that amusing answers are to be encouraged, but not offensive ones. Put the learners in groups to complete the exercise, then let them exchange answers with other groups.

Personal Study Workbook

1: Find the mistakes: forming negatives
3: Agreeing with each other: *so do I / neither do I*
4: What's the opposite?: prefixes and suffixes
9: Visual dictionary

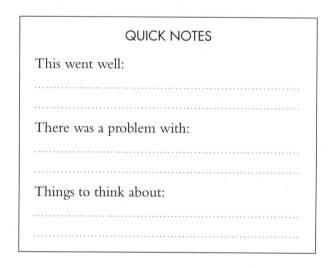

```
                QUICK NOTES

  This went well:
  ................................................................
  ................................................................

  There was a problem with:
  ................................................................
  ................................................................

  Things to think about:
  ................................................................
  ................................................................
```

POSITIVE THINKING

Introduction

There are a number of opportunities for the learners to talk about themselves and express their own opinions, but the first part of the lesson has more controlled activities to present and practise the use of *wish* + past simple to talk about situations you would like to be different.

Suggested steps

1

Get the group to look at the pictures in Exercise 1 and focus on the use of *wish* + past simple. Then ask them why the construction is used. These questions will help to focus on the concept:
Can the woman drive in picture 2?
Does she want to be able to drive?

So how does she express this desire?
And why does she use the past tense?

For most learners this concept is not difficult to grasp, and you can probably move straight into some personalised practice to consolidate their understanding. Ask different people if they have any wishes? This usually produces predictable responses:
I wish I could speak English very well.
I wish I had more money.
I wish I was/were in bed.

> ### Language Point
> *I wish I were* is often preferred in formal English for the first person singular and third person singular. In everyday spoken English *I wish I was* is quite acceptable.

If you are happy with their responses, move on to the second part of the exercise and ask the group to complete the bubbles in a suitable way. Check their answers.

Answer key

1. I wish I had my sunglasses.
2. I wish I was/were at home; I wish it was/were Friday; I wish I could leave.
3. I wish I could play the guitar like that.

2

Begin by telling the group a few of your negative thoughts. For example:
Why aren't there any letters for me?
I wish the bread shop opened earlier.
Why am I always in the slowest supermarket queue?
My cat is never happy with the food I give it.

A range of examples will help to give the group ideas and make them realise that they are not simply being invited to regurgitate sentences with *wish* + past simple. It would be nice for the learners to produce the construction naturally, but they should not feel compelled to produce it. Give them several minutes to write down examples – they need to write them down for an exercise later in the lesson – before putting them in groups to exchange their negative thoughts. Ask each group to tell the class their most common negative thoughts.

3

The class can now go on to read the text by Vera Peiffer. Elicit responses with a few questions. For example:
Have you ever had similar negative thoughts to these?
What do you think of Vera Peiffer's positive thoughts?
Can you think of other positive thoughts for these negative thoughts?

4

Now put the learners in pairs. When they have finished they can exchange answers with another pair or you can do this with the whole class.

5

The questions are just examples to stimulate discussion; the groups themselves may wish to focus on different aspects of the topic, such as the degree to which they see themselves as optimists or pessimists. If certain groups are involved in discussion while others seem rather quiet, you could try to prompt the discussion with a few additional questions that you feel may engage these particular learners.

Personal Study Workbook

2: I wish I knew …: *wish* + past simple
7: Look on the bright side: writing

> ### QUICK NOTES
>
> This went well:
> ....
> ....
>
> There was a problem with:
> ....
> ....
>
> Things to think about:
> ....
> ....

REVIEW AND DEVELOPMENT

REVIEW OF UNIT 14

1

Give the learners two minutes to read through the pairs of sentences, then follow the instructions in the Class Book. In the second part of the exercise, monitor carefully so you can decide if differences of opinion are the fault of the listener or the speaker.

Answer key

1. She broke it.
2. When I arrived he'd left.
3. He hadn't been before.
4. I was angry because she lost it.
5. They met a man who'd lived there.
6. She'd injured her ankle; that was the problem.
7. I hope she's gone.
8. We did it because he'd asked us to.

2

Jokes do not always travel well. If you do not think your group will understand or appreciate these short anecdotes, leave this exercise out. If you do decide to do it, see if the learners can contribute any funny stories of their own.

REVIEW OF UNIT 15

1

The learners could read through the list and ask you or their partner about the meaning of any vocabulary they have forgotten. Give them a few minutes to complete the column on the right alone, then put them in pairs to discuss their answers.

2

You could ask the learners to do this alone, in pairs or groups.

Answer key

moved
have lived / have been living
started
arrived
bought
was working
realised
was watching
noticed
had left
hurried
laughed
complained
told
had had
got
brought
have now written
have been thinking

```
QUICK NOTES

This went well:

.................................................................

.................................................................

There was a problem with:

.................................................................

.................................................................

Things to think about:

.................................................................

.................................................................
```

PACKAGING

```
                        CONTENTS

Language focus:    partitives
                   numbers and quantities
                   making associations

   Vocabulary:     holiday arrangements
                   prices and costs
                   abstract nouns

       Skills:  Speaking:  barbecues in different countries
                           discussing advertisements and advertising
                               brand names
                           travel agent / customer role play
                Listening:  a shopping list
                            an advertising expert explaining the
                                rationale behind an advertisement
                Reading:   holiday brochure information
```

SACKS AND BARRELS

Introduction

The language focus of the lesson is types of container, and the context is preparing for a barbecue. The learners listen to and complete a shopping list for the barbecue; they talk about their own barbecues and barbecues in their country; and they speculate on the rubbish that may be left after the barbecue. The lesson begins with the presentation of the various types of container, e.g. *packet, box, bowl*; and there is also a lexical focus later in the lesson on ways of expressing different numbers and quantities, e.g. *a couple, half a dozen, loads of*, etc.

Suggested steps

1

Follow the instructions in the Class Book and then check the answers with the group.

Answer key

1. tube   2. box   3. bucket   4. jar   5. barrel
6. packet   7. bag   8. can/tin   9. tub   10. bottle
11. carton   12. mug   13. bowl   14. sack   15. jug

2

Do one or two examples with the group before putting them in pairs.

Answer key

Possible answers (There will be cultural differences here. These answers would be possible in Britain.)
sack: coal, potatoes
carton: milk, orange juice
barrel: beer, wine
tube: toothpaste, glue
bag: apples, sweets
box: chocolates, matches
bucket: water, coal
can/tin: soup, cola
jar: jam, mustard
packet: crisps, biscuits
bottle: milk, wine
jug: water, milk
bowl: fruit, soup
tub: cream, ice cream
mug: tea, coffee

3 📖

First let the learners read through the shopping list and check that they understand the vocabulary, e.g. *fizzy, peanuts, glue* and *string*. (To explain the last three items, the best thing would be to take in examples to show the group.) Then play the recording, pausing it so that the learners have time to write down their answers. Let them compare with a partner. If they have failed to note down some of the information, play the recording a second time, then check the answers. The tapescript is on page 154.

Answer key

They need to buy:
a dozen cartons of fruit juice
5 or 6 bottles of wine
5 or 6 bottles of mineral water
a few cans of beer
half a dozen loaves of bread
lots of green salad
a few tomatoes
a large box of matches
They need to borrow:
some bowls

4

You may need to do an example with the class so that they understand what they have to do, and you should also make it clear that two items may go on the same place on the line.

Answer key

the least   the most

one or two	half a dozen	a dozen	plenty of★
a couple of	a few★★		loads of
several			hundreds of

★ Plenty of means a large quantity, but has the added meaning of being sufficient or more than enough.
★★ How many constitutes a few will depend on the maximum number that might be involved. For example, a few people in a class might be three or four, but a few people in an audience (at a concert) might be thirty or forty. In other words it is relative.

Option

If you want further practice of the above quantities, you could play this short game. Say a sentence and then ask a learner to paraphrase using a number from above. For example:

TEACHER: *Did you see two people?*
LEARNER: *Yes, a couple.*
TEACHER: *There were lots of people?*
LEARNER: *Yes, hundreds.*
TEACHER: *We've got lots of time.*
LEARNER: *Yes, loads.*
TEACHER: *Did you say six?*
LEARNER: *Yes, half a dozen.*
etc.

When you have demonstrated five or six examples with different learners, put the class into pairs for further practice. Move round and listen.

5

This discussion may be more interesting with learners from a range of countries. With a monolingual group you may wish to introduce a few additional questions to tease out more ideas and information. For example:
How often do you have barbecues? When was the last one?
Do you normally plan them in advance or are they spontaneous?
How many people are there at your barbecues?
What do you normally cook on the barbecue?
What makes a good/bad barbecue?
etc.

6

For the sake of simplicity, tell the group that all the food was eaten, so all the containers are empty. They can then decide what to do with the empty containers. If they decide certain containers can be reused, encourage them to suggest what they might be used for.

Option

You could provide for some slightly different language practice by changing the focus of Exercise 6. Ask the groups what will be left or might be left at the end of the barbecue. For example:
There will probably be some glue left.
There might be some wine left.
I doubt if there will be any crisps left.

As you can see from the examples, this will provide practice in ways of expressing probability and possibility. Following this, groups can decide what they would do with the things that are left. Would they keep them for later use or throw them away?

Personal Study Workbook

1: A packet of biscuits, please: containers
2: How many, how much, how far?: vocabulary
5: Food facts: how could they eat all that?: reading
6: Sorry, I got it wrong: listening
9: Visual dictionary

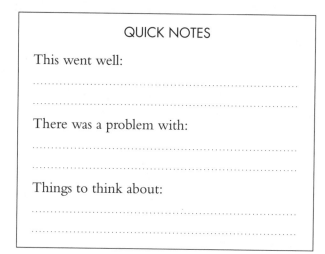

QUICK NOTES

This went well:

....

....

There was a problem with:

....

....

Things to think about:

....

....

PACKAGING PRODUCTS

Introduction

Most learners find advertising an interesting subject to discuss, and this lesson examines the range of associations conjured up by different brand names and their advertising techniques. This is developed through a range of speaking and listening activities, with the language focus on a group of abstract nouns commonly used to describe advertisements, e.g. *glamour, elegance, status* and *power*. There are a number of opportunities for personalised speaking in which the learners give their opinions about adverts and create their own products and brand names.

Suggested steps

1

If you work with a group from a single country, it will probably be more effective to use products that are well known in that country. Begin by writing three or four brand names on the board. Elicit or teach the word *brand name*, then ask the group if the brand name is important, and if so, what associations are evoked by the name. Do this for one of the products and then let them discuss the others in pairs. Conduct a brief feedback. You can then get the learners to read the two examples in the Class Book.

With a multinational group you could follow the same procedure but using well-known international brand names, e.g. Sony, Swatch, Rolls Royce, Martini, McDonald's, Pepsi, etc.

2

If possible, make monolingual and bilingual dictionaries available, and move round to help individual learners where necessary. Clarify any problems at the end.

Option

If some or all of the group find this lexical set quite easy, you could ask them to add any adjectives that can be formed from the nouns, e.g. *elegance – elegant*; *glamour – glamorous*.

3

You could provide initial practice of the phrases on the left by talking about the brand names you discussed at the beginning of the lesson. For example:
Sony makes me think of quality and reliability.
I associate Martini with sunshine, the Riviera, open-air cafés and trendy young people.
With Rolls Royce, I tend to think of money, luxury and power.
Elicit a few associations from the learners, then put them in pairs to complete the task using the phrases and the vocabulary from the previous exercise. Listen to their ideas at the end.

4

The learners are free to recycle the same language to describe the Cognac advertisement, but most of all we want a personal response to the advert. And the group may also be interested to know at this stage that they are going to listen to an advertising expert talking about the same advertisement afterwards.

When the groups seem to have exhausted the discussion, elicit some of their ideas and put them on the board. Feed in new language as appropriate.

5 ▭

Play the recording. At the end, put the learners in pairs or groups to compare notes on *new* information or ideas. If possible, give them photocopies of the tapescript so they can compare their ideas with the recording. The tapescript is on page 154. Then put them back into groups to invent a product and a name for it.

If your group seems particularly interested in the theme of advertising, you could also try Worksheet 17 on page 127.

Personal Study Workbook

3: Building words and shifting stress: pronunciation and vocabulary

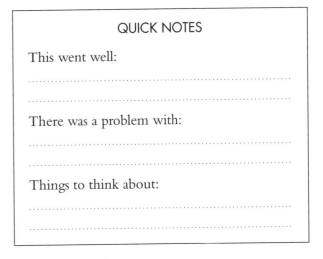

```
QUICK NOTES

This went well:
...............................................................
...............................................................

There was a problem with:
...............................................................
...............................................................

Things to think about:
...............................................................
...............................................................
```

PACKAGE HOLIDAYS

Introduction

A reading text is used to present some of the vocabulary commonly associated with holidays and travel arrangements (much of it connected with money), and this is then consolidated through an extended role play in which the learners take the roles of travellers and travel agents in discussing possible holiday destinations. This is not an original idea, but most learners find the subject useful as they often have to use English when they are on holiday and have to make travel and/or accommodation arrangements.

Suggested steps

1

Your own experience of package holidays is an obvious place to start, then let the learners share their experiences in pairs or small groups. If you hear any particularly interesting anecdotes, get them to tell the whole class.

2

This will be a very brief activity, so you could do it with the whole class and write their ideas on the board. Make sure they don't look at the Holiday Checklist at this stage.

Answer key

Possible answers

The flight
Transport to the hotel from the airport
Some or all meals
Possibly excursions

3

Show the learners the first example, then let them complete the task individually before comparing with a partner. They should also be able to use dictionaries.

Answer key

The first seven questions all refer to costs. Relevant vocabulary is:

covered; pay extra; taxes; charges; pay (for); cost; price reductions; free; surcharges; price increases.

Note: Be included and be provided do not explicitly mention costs, but in this and many other contexts they refer to costs and expenses.

4

This will be most useful if the learners can think up likely contexts for these question forms. For learners studying in an English-speaking country, the obvious context would be their course and accommodation; but others should still find relevant contexts. Move round and monitor while the learners are writing questions, and help where necessary. When they have finished, put them in pairs for the task, and put some of the most relevant examples on the board at the end. In some situations, these sentences will be so common that the learners should learn the whole sentence as a lexical item.

Answer key

Possible answers

1. Is the price of textbooks included in the fees? (e.g. a language school)
2. Is there any reduction for students? (e.g. in cinemas or on trains)
3. Is gas and electricity covered in the total cost? (e.g. renting a flat)
4. Is paper provided? / Are dictionaries provided? (e.g. in an exam)
5. Are there facilities for cooking? (e.g. accommodation)
6. Is the school suitable for teenagers? (e.g. a language school)

5

Obviously it is difficult to recreate a travel agent's in the classroom, but learners usually have no difficulty throwing themselves into this situation, and for many this may be a situation where they will need to speak in English, so it is worth preparing it carefully.

First divide up the group between customers and travel agents (if you have an odd number, one of the customers can be a couple). The travel agents can then be directed to their information at the back of the book. There is

quite a lot of information to digest and the role play will be more effective if they have a good grasp of the facts. Tell them to try to remember as much as possible, and put them in pairs to test each other when they have read through once or twice. While they are working (in different parts of the room or a separate room if at all possible), divide the two situations between the customers and direct each one to their role card. Once again, tell them to prepare their questions carefully and then rehearse them with a partner who is preparing the same situation. While they are doing this, move round and monitor both groups.

When you are satisfied that they can act out the situation without referring to their books too much, put them in pairs for the task. Monitor as carefully as you can and when they have finished, give them feedback on the way they handled the situation and any significant language points that emerge. Then, they can do it again, only this time customers move round to a different travel agent who dealt with the other situation.

Personal Study Workbook

4: That's not what I asked for: vocabulary
7: Letter of complaint: writing
8: Speaking partners

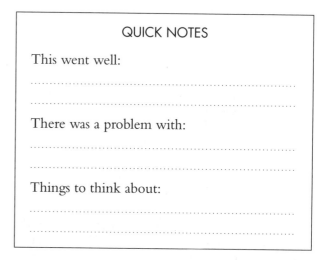

QUICK NOTES

This went well:

....
....

There was a problem with:

....
....

Things to think about:

....
....

REVIEW OF UNIT 15

1

Give the learners enough time to think about the last few days, and if possible, provide one or two examples from your lessons to illustrate some of the verbs, e.g. *I thanked Andrea for opening the window yesterday, and then I made everyone do that exercise on prepositions.* Then put the learners in small groups to compare answers. If the response is poor, you could ask the learners to keep a record of these actions over the next few days so that they can do the exercise again in a later lesson.

2

Go through the example in the Class Book, and then elicit answers from the group for the first question. After that, put them in pairs to complete the task, then listen to some of their answers. If you want further practice, mix up the pairs, let them practise again, and ask them to think up two more short dialogues of their own following the same pattern.

Answer key

Possible answers
1. I've been jogging.
2. I've been working in the garden.
3. I've been working hard.
4. I've been cooking.
5. Yes, I've been sitting in the sun.
6. I've been walking by the river.
7. Yes, I've been studying hard.
8. Yes, I've been trying to do my homework.

REVIEW OF UNIT 16

1

This is based on an old game that was very popular on British television many years ago. It is a game, however, that many nationalities play in some form or other. Play the recording and elicit the rules from the learners. Then play the recording a second time, pausing where necessary, and elicit the contestant's answers. The tapescript is on page 155.

Answer key

A
The rules of the game are that you can't answer *yes* or *no* to any question. (And of course, you can't nod or shake your head.)

B
It is.
It is indeed.
I have two names. Two christian names.
I do.
That's right.
That's right.
Gail.
Correct.
Absolutely.
I did indeed.
It is. Julia Gail.
I was born in Runcorn.
I was, yes. Oh, no!

She loses because she says *yes*.

Finally, set up the game in class. Put the learners in pairs and give them a few minutes to write down some *yes/no* questions. It is important they have a good battery of questions because the success of the game depends on a good pace and it is important that the questioner does not run out of questions and dry up. Then reorganise them into groups of three or four – if there are at least two questioners, this should ensure a rapid pace of

questions – and let them play the game. At the end, let one or two groups demonstrate for the whole class.

2

The most important thing is to go through the examples carefully so that the learners understand what they have to do. Follow the instructions in the Class Book, and monitor the pairs carefully when they ask each other questions. Clarify any problems at the end.

```
┌─────────────────────────────────────────┐
│            QUICK NOTES                   │
│                                          │
│  This went well:                         │
│  ......................................  │
│  ......................................  │
│                                          │
│  There was a problem with:               │
│  ......................................  │
│  ......................................  │
│                                          │
│  Things to think about:                  │
│  ......................................  │
│  ......................................  │
│                                          │
└─────────────────────────────────────────┘
```

18

HONESTLY SPEAKING

CONTENTS

Language focus: reported speech
reported questions

Vocabulary: reporting verbs
politics and economics
triumphs and disasters

Skills: Speaking: discussing honesty in everyday situations
interviewing a famous person
current news stories
discussing if there is too much bad news
in our news

Listening: an extract from a Dorothy Parker short story
a telephone conversation (based on above)
news headlines

Reading: a text about the balance of good and bad
news in our media

Writing: reporting direct statements and questions

DIFFERENT POINTS OF VIEW

Introduction

The learners deduce the rules of reported statements from example sentences and consolidate their understanding with controlled practice. The main part of the lesson, however, is the exploitation of an extract from a Dorothy Parker short story (recorded), which involves the natural use of a number of common reporting verbs as well as a discussion around the theme of honesty and self-deception.

Suggested steps

1

Follow the instructions in the Class Book, pointing out that the significant point is the change that takes place from the first to the second picture for each conversation. You shouldn't have too much difficulty eliciting the correct answers.

Answer key

In the first conversation *I'm tired* becomes *she was tired*, i.e. from present to past. In the second conversation the change is from *will* to *would*. These changes take place when we are *reporting* what someone has said at a later date.

2

This may seem as if you are letting the learners loose on something without any preparation, but in fact most learners soon grasp what should happen and the effect of discovering the rules for themselves can be much more memorable. Check the answers and clarify any problems, e.g. *must* has no past form; simple past and present perfect are both often represented as past perfect in reported speech.

Answer key

He said he was going out.
She told me they worked in Rome.
They told us they didn't know him.
He told her he'd (he had) found the letter.
He said she'd (she had) lost her wallet.
She told him she couldn't remember.
He said I had to pay the fees before Friday.

3

In this exercise it doesn't matter if your learners write two examples or twelve; just make sure they are using the correct tenses and using the correct constructions with *say* (no direct object) and *tell* (must have a direct object). Go through the examples first.

You could get your learners to read the Grammar Reference at this point or ask them to read it at home. If you choose the latter, you may wish to explain the following Language Point on the board, otherwise your learners may think the Grammar Reference contradicts what you have told them.

The rest of the lesson provides some practice of reported speech, but the emphasis switches to a range of reporting verbs. If you feel your group needs more controlled practice in changing tense from direct to reported speech, you could do Worksheet 18 on page 128 at this point. If you do, you will need to clarify certain points contained in the Grammar Reference, e.g. *come* often becomes *go* in reported speech; *yesterday* becomes *the day before*; the change in pronouns; etc.

Answer key for Worksheet 18

1.
Paul said he was going out for half an hour.
Jane replied that he couldn't because Mary was going to phone at seven.
But Paul said that Mary had rung him earlier so it was OK.
Jane said in that case she would go with him.

2.
Jim told Sue that he had finished.
Sue said she would check it in a minute because first she had to finish some filing.
Jim said he could do that for her, but Sue replied that she wanted to do it herself so she would know where everything was.

3.
Sam said he had lost his gloves.
Pam said they were in the cupboard.
Sam said they weren't because he had already looked there.
Pam replied that she had seen them in the cupboard that morning, so Sam said he would have another look.

4 ▭

This is a rather different type of listening – a lonely woman describing to herself the desperation she feels because the man she loves hasn't phoned her. There is a general question on the listening (commenting on the character of the woman), followed by more detailed comprehension, so you will probably have to play the recording twice. For this reason, try to encourage the learners not to focus too much on information in the first listening, but to think about the woman and her emotional state. Get the class sitting back relaxed, then play the whole thing without stopping.

At the end, invite reactions and ask for words to describe the woman. If possible, ask the learners to explain their reasons. The tapescript is on page 155.

Answer key

Possible answers
nervous; agitated; neurotic; desperate; shy; weak; sensitive; insecure

5

For this more detailed understanding of the text, direct the pairs to the questions and give them a few minutes to see what they can answer from memory. They will probably be able to answer some but not all the questions. If that is the case, play the recording again, so they can focus on the information they need to complete the answers. Check at the end.

Answer key

1. She wanted the man to phone her.
2. The man promised to phone her at five o'clock.
3. When she rang, she asked him how he was.
4. When she rang, he told her he would telephone her.
5. She admitted you shouldn't keep telephoning men.
6. She refused to believe he didn't want to speak to her / he wasn't going to phone her.

Option

At this point you could invite more discussion of the story based on some of these questions:
– What do you think is going to happen?
– What do you think the real relationship is between this woman and the man she talks about?
– Do you sympathise with this woman?
– Do you feel sorry for her?
– Do you like the story from what you have heard?
– Do you think this shows women in a negative way?
– Do men generally behave in the same way as the man in the story?

6 ▭

If you have followed the option above, you may have to save the listening for a future lesson. If not, you could begin by telling the group they are about to hear the actual conversation which took place between the man and woman before the time of the earlier recording. Ask them to predict how the conversation began, developed and ended. Then play the recording and put them in groups to discuss their predictions and the question of the woman's honesty. At the end, you may wish to invite class discussion and give some feedback on their use of language. The tapescript is on page 155.

Personal Study Workbook
2: How did they say it?: reporting verbs
5: Does your job make you lie?: reading

```
┌─────────────────────────────────────────┐
│              QUICK NOTES                  │
│                                           │
│   This went well:                         │
│                                           │
│   .....................................   │
│                                           │
│   .....................................   │
│                                           │
│   There was a problem with:               │
│                                           │
│   .....................................   │
│                                           │
│   .....................................   │
│                                           │
│   Things to think about:                  │
│                                           │
│   .....................................   │
│                                           │
│   .....................................   │
└─────────────────────────────────────────┘
```

HONEST ANSWERS

Introduction

Following the lesson on reported statements and reporting verbs, the learners now focus on the rules governing reported questions. This is largely done cognitively, with the learners first transforming reported questions into direct speech. They then reflect on their answers and decide if the rules they are given for reported questions are true or false. This is followed by a freer activity in which the learners, in groups, prepare and conduct interviews with famous people; and finished off by the learners reporting their interviews, i.e. the questions they asked, to a different person in the group.

Suggested steps

1

This first exercise utilises knowledge from the previous lesson in helping the learners to grasp the construction of reported questions. Go through the two examples carefully, but after that see if the learners can deduce the rule correctly to form the other direct questions. The question about speaker and context is a further check on understanding and makes the learners think about meaning as well as form. Move round and help the pairs where necessary, and check the answers carefully with the group at the end.

Answer key

Direct question	Speaker/context
3. Do you have anything to declare?	customs official to passenger going through customs
4. Can you do overtime this evening?	boss to employee
5. Have you done this kind of work before?	interviewer to interviewee
6. Where does it hurt?	doctor to patient
7. Why are you carrying a knife in the street?	policeman to youth
8. When will you be able to pay the rent?	landlord to tenant

2

This activity checks and consolidates the rules the learners will/may have deduced from the first exercise. Monitor any pairs who seem to have a disagreement over any of the statements, and clarify any problems with the class.

Answer key

1. True   2. False   3. True   4. False   5. True

3

This returns to the theme of honesty and provides a break from the grammar analysis. Put the learners in small groups and monitor carefully.

Option

If the above exercise prompts a lot of discussion and you feel your group have had enough grammar for one lesson, you could continue by asking them, in pairs, to write questions of their own which might produce honest and dishonest replies. For example:
– *Why were you late this morning?*
– *Do you like my new dress?*
– *Would you like to come round and have dinner with us?*

When they have written three or four questions, they can try them out on other pairs. At the end, the group could select the question which seems to provoke the greatest number of potentially dishonest replies.

4

This provides further practice of reported question forms but does allow more freedom and creativity. If time is short, you could ask pairs to form alternative questions for the first four or five questions before they work with a new partner.

5

This is quite a complicated rubric so explain it carefully and give one or two examples to clarify the procedure.

Personal Study Workbook

1: Get it right: reported speech and questions
6: Honestly!: listening
7: She said in her letter that …: writing
8: Speaking partners

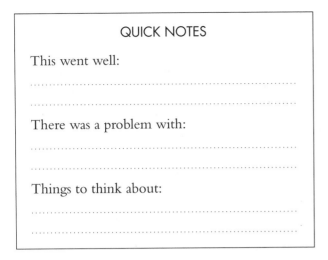

GOOD NEWS, BAD NEWS

Introduction

Listening to the news in English is a relevant and valuable activity for many learners. The lesson provides an opportunity to listen to an example of news headlines; to learn and practise vocabulary that regularly appears in the news (politics, the economy and natural disasters); and also introduces a discussion on the balance of good news and bad news that appears on our televisions and in our newspapers. Is there too much of an obsession with bad news? One British newsreader thinks so, and we include a reading text outlining his thoughts.

Suggested steps

1

You could focus this task more by asking for two current domestic news events and two international news events. Then ask each individual to decide on the most important news story a) from the world's point of view and b) from their own personal point of view.

2

Allow pairs to work on the new vocabulary using dictionaries with no pre-teaching, but do stress that words may go in more than one category (there is a clear overlap between *politics* and *the economy*).

Answer key

The economy	*Politics*	*Natural disasters*
redundancies	redundancies	flood
trade agreement	trade agreement	famine
inflation rate	election defeat	drought
industrial dispute	riots	avalanche
trade union victory	ministerial row	earthquake
	peace talks	epidemic
	foreign policy	
	industrial dispute	
	trade union victory	

When you go through the lists check pronunciation of difficult items such as flood /flʌd/ and drought /draʊt/.

3 📖

The recording has the advantage that it provides reinforcement of many of the lexical items in Exercise 2, so it may be worth doing for that reason alone. However, the learners will probably be more motivated to listen to current new stories, so if possible, record the day's news and use that instead or as well. In an English-speaking country this will be easy, but elsewhere you should still have access to the BBC World Service or Voice of America, etc.

Answer key

See the tapescript on page 174 of the Class Book or page 156 of this Teacher's Book.

4

The discussion points are valid regardless of the news you used in the previous exercise, and they are important in providing a link with the text about 'good news' and 'bad news', so focus your feedback on question 3 about the balance in the news.

5

Get the learners to read the text and respond to a partner with their views. If this prompts a lot of discussion, let it develop; if not, you might try to develop the discussion with the whole group.

Option

You could set the group a small project. Over the next week, ask them to listen to or watch the main news (this is usually broadcast at least three times a day on most TV channels) on four separate days agreed in advance by the group. Ask them to keep a record of the news stories and then organise them into 'good news' stories and 'bad news' stories. They can compare their findings in a week's time and discuss a) whether they agree on what is good or bad news, and b) the balance of good and bad news. If you are not working in an English-speaking country and do not have access to English news, the learners can still do the project using news from their country; the classroom discussion will be just as useful and interesting.

6

This just provides some more intensive work on an understanding of the text. If time is short, give it for homework.

Answer key

good policing
new self-help community policy
significant decrease in crime
achievements and successes
hope for the future
the rescue of people trapped near the front
a moving and uplifting story
accomplishments, successes and triumphs
balanced and fair picture of the world

Personal Study Workbook

3: Compounds and word partnerships: political vocabulary
4: Good news and bad news: opposites

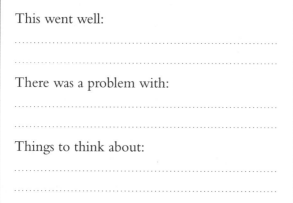

REVIEW AND DEVELOPMENT

REVIEW OF UNIT 16

1

Explain the exercise and do the example with the class. They may be able to think of other possible questions that would uncover whether someone had breakfast or not. While the pairs are forming their questions, move round and monitor and help where necessary. When you are happy the questions are all correct, let people mingle to ask their questions.

2

Follow the instructions in the Class Book.

Answer key

A
Numbers 2, 3 and 5 are real questions.
B
1. isn't it?
2. aren't you?
3. did she?
4. aren't you?
5. have you?
6. didn't he?

3

If you linger upon each word and think about it, you may end up with very mixed reactions. But for this exercise it is really the immediate intuitive response which we are after. So, tell your learners to read through and write down an answer quickly. If necessary, set a time limit, e.g. between one and two minutes before they compare in groups.

REVIEW OF UNIT 17

1

Do the first one together, then let the learners finish in small groups. Go through the answers with the whole class.

Answer key

1. A bag of rice is smaller than a sack.
2. A basket of fruit is bigger than a tin.
3. A loaf of bread is bigger than a slice.
4. A mouthful of honey is smaller than a jar.
5. A ball of string is bigger than a piece.
6. A jug of water is smaller than a bucket.
7. Half a dozen bottles of wine are smaller than a barrel.
8. A tub of ice cream is bigger than a spoonful.
9. A handful of peanuts is bigger than several.
10. A packet of spaghetti is bigger than a portion.

2

Follow the instructions in the Class Book.

Answer key

1. elegance; elegant
2. luxury; luxurious
3. warmth; warm
4. danger; dangerous
5. comfort; comfortable
6. grace; graceful
7. simplicity; simple
8. mystery; mysterious

19

PLAIN ENGLISH

CONTENTS

Language focus: formal and informal English
should, ought to, had better
verb + *-ing* form; preposition + *-ing* form
adjective + infinitive

Vocabulary: bureaucracy
symptoms of fear
a curriculum vitae

Skills: Speaking: paraphrasing formal English
common fears and how to overcome them
giving a short talk on a chosen topic
Listening: a woman talking about 'Plain English'
a recruitment consultant advising on how
to write a good curriculum vitae
Reading: a text about The Plain English Campaign
mistakes in CVs

PLAIN ENGLISH OR GOBBLEDYGOOK?

Introduction

The lesson focuses on The Plain English Campaign: an organisation whose aim is to persuade official bodies to use clear simple English in their literature. It would be interesting to know if the learners have any knowledge of similar organisations in their own country.

The learners find out about this organisation through reading and listening activities, and towards the end of the lesson they have an opportunity to paraphrase rather formal language into more informal spoken English.

Suggested steps

1

If you think that most of your learners will not be very familiar with any of the documents we have listed, substitute anything you think might be more relevant or familiar, e.g. university or college application forms, language school enrolment forms, etc.

You could provide a cursory explanation of the vocabulary items in the box, or let them work out the meanings with the aid of dictionaries, each other and the context (most learners should be able to predict that concepts concerning length, clarity and complexity are the most obvious ones in relation to official written documents). Clarify any problems of meaning when you get feedback at the end of the activity.

2

Introduce the text and ask the group if they know of anything similar in their country. You can also tell them that when they complete the task, they can write down more than three points if they can find more in the text. We have restricted it to three because, arguably, the text includes different ways of saying the same thing.

When they have finished, let them compare with a partner then check with the whole group.

Answer key

1. They should write in everyday English. In other words, they should avoid jargon and difficult words.
2. They should be as brief as possible and use short simple sentences.
3. They should use clear headings and support the text with diagrams.
4. Any technical terms must be explained in simple English.

3 ▭▭ ▨▨

The above text will have introduced the learners to many of the ideas that are mentioned on the recording, so their task is now to sift out the new information. Choose the appropriate version of the recording and play it once. Let the learners compare with a partner, then go through the answers if you think they have extracted most of the new information; if not play the recording again. The tapescript is on page 156.

Answer key

Version 1:

Texts are easier to read if the average sentence length is 15–20 words.

They are easier to read if there are no more than 7–12 words per line.

Good typesize and clear typeface are important.

Texts should use active verbs rather than passive verbs.

Version 2:

As for Version 1 plus the following:

Texts should avoid indirectness by using *we* and *you* rather than terms such as *the applicant* or *the insurer*.

4

We do not want the learners to waste time on 'gobbledygook', but the rest of the lesson does relate to the main theme by asking the learners to simplify examples of formal English and turn them into more informal everyday language. Go through the example carefully clarifying the formal items and the more informal words and phrases that are being put in their place. The introductory phrase *that means* is a very common way of introducing a paraphrase or reformulation, so encourage its use.

Allow pairs to use dictionaries, but stress that you do not want dictionary definitions in their answers; the reformulation must be in language which will sound natural coming from their lips.

Discuss their answers at the end, and remember that there is no single correct answer here, and those given below are just sample answers.

Answer key

Possible answers

1. That means the driver was not thinking about other people. Maybe he was driving dangerously.
2. That means you must give the right money and say where you are going.
3. That means you mustn't take more (medicine) than it says.
4. That means he/she can't give you permission to take time off.
   or
   He/she doesn't have the power to let you take time off.
5. That means they can't give you your money back if you haven't got a receipt.

Personal Study Workbook

5: Word stress, sentence stress: pronunciation
6: Keep it simple!: reading and writing

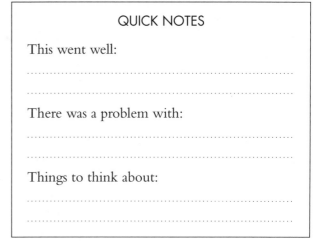

WRITING A CURRICULUM VITAE

Introduction

The learners talk about their own experiences of writing a CV, and also discuss what it should or shouldn't contain. They listen to the views of a recruitment consultant to compare their views with his, and also correct some amusing errors that people have made in their CVs. The linguistic focus is on *should* and *ought to*, which emerge quite naturally out of the topic. These modal verbs are finally compared and contrasted with *had better* and there is a testing exercise to conclude the lesson.

Suggested steps

1

Most nationalities understand what a CV is, and the function it performs. If you are working in a country where this is not a familiar concept, however, your learners may find it hard to tackle some of the tasks in this lesson, and you may be advised to omit it.

With most groups, the warm-up activity will be quite straightforward, although the scope of the activity and the time required will depend much on the age of your group. If many of your group are still studying, you could do this as a class activity. Do not, at this stage, go into the details of the CV, as this is covered in a later activity.

2

Point out that the mistakes they are about to uncover include language errors, cultural errors (including information that is not relevant to the task), and some plain stupidity. Do the first one as a group so they grasp the idea, then put them in pairs to discuss the others.

Answer key

1. Anyone with an excellent memory would not write it twice, as it implies that they forgot they wrote it the first time.

2. It should be *Dear sir or **madam*** and *a quick **learner***.
3. *756 words a minute* is clearly impossible, therefore demonstrating that her typing is probably not very good. *Maturity leave* should be ***maternity*** *leave*.
4. It should be … *hearing from you **shortly***, i.e. *soon*.
5. The information is too long, inappropriate and silly.
6. These hobbies are not only irrelevant to a job application, they are probably the type of hobbies that the applicant should keep quiet about.
7. A shoeshine man is not normally a suitable person to act as referee, and this applicant is either culturally naive or stupid.

In feedback, try to elicit both the answers and explanations from the learners.

Option

If your learners really enjoyed this activity, you could put them in groups to try to make up two or three stupid errors that a CV might contain. They can then give them to other groups to correct.

3

Put the learners in groups for the task, and during the discussion listen to see whether they use *should* or *ought to*, and if they do, if they use them correctly. At the end, conduct a short feedback and put their ideas on the board. Do not confirm or reject any of them at this stage.

4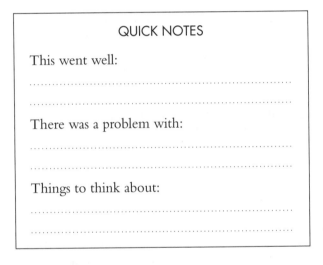

Play the recording and ask the learners to see if the speaker includes all their ideas. Are there any additional ideas? Let the learners compare, then check answers. You could ask the group if they agree with these ideas. The tapescript is on page 174 of the Class Book and page 156 of this Teacher's Book.

Answer key

A good CV should:
- be brief (no more than two pages);
- always be typed;
- only include information relevant to the job you are applying for;
- contain short, businesslike sentences;
- start with name, address, phone number, age, marital status, etc.;
- then continue with professional and educational qualifications;
- and then continue with previous jobs in reverse order (the most recent first);
- accompany a covering letter in which you explain why you are the right person for the job.

Finally, you should make it clear if you are not available for interviews at a particular time.

An important point that the speaker does not mention which your students may have picked up is that a CV should also contain the names of referees who are prepared to speak on your behalf.

5

With a class, it is probably better to go through the explanations on the board, highlighting both the form and conceptual differences. Then direct the learners to the tapescript and the exercise, pointing out that some of the sentences are correct. Check the answers at the end.

Answer key

1. You really ought **to** leave now.
2. correct
3. You **had** better take your umbrella today.
4. I don't think people **ought to / should** use …
5. correct
6. correct
7. correct
8. You'd better go to the bank now. (no **to** after *better*)

Personal Study Workbook

2: Tell them what you think: *should, ought to, had better*
4: Employees and employers: word building
8: Put your life into words: writing
9: Speaking partners

QUICK NOTES

This went well:

....

....

There was a problem with:

....

....

Things to think about:

....

....

....

PUBLIC SPEAKING

Introduction

The learners are introduced to many ways of describing physical and mental symptoms of fear, and talk about them in the context of their own experiences of giving talks, speeches, presentations, etc. Further input comes in the form of different verb and adjective constructions, e.g. adjective + infinitive, verb + preposition, and these are practised in the context of discussing ways to reduce fear and anxiety. Finally, the learners prepare their own presentations which they will give in a future lesson.

Suggested steps

1

Go through the topics to check that they are clearly understood. Put the learners in pairs to talk about their experiences, monitor the discussions, then ask one or two learners to recount their stories to the rest of the group.

2

If any of the group have experienced fear during a speech or presentation, ask them to describe exactly how they felt to see how much they can express in English. Then move on to explain that they are going to focus on ways of expressing fear and anxiety. Put them in pairs, making sure they have access to monolingual and/or bilingual dictionaries, then set them to work on the task. Clarify any problems when you check their answers.

Answer key

Mental symptoms	Physical symptoms
your mind goes blank	you wake up sweating in the night
you feel intimidated	you blush
you lose the thread of your argument	you start to shake
	you bite your nails or your lips
	you feel tension in your neck
	you start to stammer
	your mouth goes dry

Asking the learners to add more symptoms gives them an opportunity to find out how to express other symptoms which may be of interest to them.

3

Give the learners a chance to absorb this new input – one useful technique is to make a connection between the words and what they mean, e.g. rub the back of your neck while you say the expression to yourself – then tell them to shut their books and tell a partner which symptoms they have experienced. If they forget, they can quickly refer to their books to check a word or phrase.

Option

For a further check on the new vocabulary, you could write the beginnings of some phrases on the board, then see how many they can finish and in what different ways they can finish them. For example:

You start to ...   Your mind ...
You feel ...   You bite ...
Your mouth ...

4

The table of suggestions includes ideas for discussion and target constructions for the learners to focus on and practise. In your introduction though, concentrate on the ideas, and you may find during the course of their discussion with a partner that the constructions are incorporated quite naturally and accurately without need of prior explanation. During feedback, highlight errors regarding the correct use of preposition or verb form, and ask members of the group to correct them and explain. If necessary, go over the constructions again and clarify any problems with either form or meaning.

Answer key

Possible answers

Try putting your main ideas on cards that you can refer to quickly and easily.
Avoid telling jokes unless you feel very confident.
Concentrate on being clear.
Start by asking experienced speakers for advice.
Reduce fear by doing relaxation exercises.
Don't be afraid to pause and collect your thoughts.
Be prepared to leave something out if you think it is taking too long.

5

It is a good idea to introduce this activity in class and get the learners in pairs to think about the first two questions. After that, however, you may wish to give them time at home to plan and rehearse their talk. Discourage them from reading out a prepared speech. We feel that rehearsal is a very useful activity and can facilitate learning very effectively, so do explain it to the group if you haven't done so already. Some learners like to prepare mentally, others prefer to utter the words and sentences aloud. We would certainly encourage the learners to record their talks if at all possible; and if you have a small group for whom presentations in English are important, you may be very interested in following up with the option below.

Option

Get the learners to record their presentations. They then make a transcript of it (or part of it) and give it to you. You listen to the recordings, correct their transcripts, and if possible, make your own recordings of the corrected transcripts. The learners can then listen and rehearse the new transcripts and talk to you about any language problems or amendments to the original presentations. This may seem a lengthy and time-consuming process, but much of the work is being done by the learners, and it has the great virtue that all the correction and reformulation is taking place to a piece of work that the learner has produced and desperately wants to improve. Motivation is very high and the learning from this activity tends to be very memorable.

We would like to thank Terry Miles and Tim Shearer for the idea for this activity.

6

Make sure the learners have time for one final rehearsal before they give their talks. If space permits, it is also better if the learners can exercise choice in which talk(s) they listen to. This will help to ensure an interested audience. If you cannot do this, we would certainly advise that you do not continue with one talk after another for much of the lesson; the learners will probably get bored and restless. One or two talks will be enough, so spread them over a number of lessons if necessary. If you do this and you are looking for an activity to fill perhaps half a lesson, you could use Worksheet 19 on page 129, which provides consolidation of some of the lexical input from the unit.

Personal Study Workbook

1: Familiar symptoms: vocabulary
3: Fear of flying: *-ing* form or infinitive
7: My mind went completely blank: listening

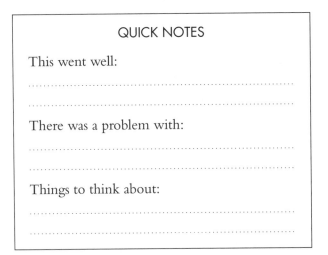

```
QUICK NOTES

This went well:

...............................................................

...............................................................

There was a problem with:

...............................................................

...............................................................

Things to think about:

...............................................................

...............................................................
```

REVIEW AND DEVELOPMENT

REVIEW OF UNIT 17

1

Follow the instructions in the Class Book.

Answer key

1. security   2. insurance   3. price reduction
4. surcharge   5. provided   6. included   7. facilities
8. suitable

Option

When you have been through the answers to the above exercise, put the learners into pairs and give each pair ten minutes to prepare eight to ten definitions of other words or expressions from the unit. Move round and monitor to try to ensure that the definitions are clear and unambiguous. Then let pairs test each other. At the end, you can discuss whether any of their definitions could be improved, and if so, how. This can be an enjoyable and useful class activity.

2

First check that the learners can name the objects in the pictures. When they have done that, let them discuss the items in pairs and groups. At the end, you could ask for any answers that the learners found surprising. You could also extend the activity by asking the learners to add more items for their partner or group to talk about.

REVIEW OF UNIT 18

1

This is quite a complicated rubric as the exercise involves the learners in both writing and answering a questionnaire. Writing the questionnaire involves the correct use of various verb patterns, so go through the example very carefully with the class. Put the learners in pairs and ask one person to write questions for Box A while the other writes questions for Box B. Emphasise that they should not try to answer the questions at this stage. Monitor their questions as carefully as possible, and when they have finished, they can then ask each other their questions and discuss their answers.

Answer key

Sample questions
Box A
1. a.   ask them to make less noise.
   b.   tell them to stop the noise completely.
   c.   say you are going to call the police.
2. a.   ask them not to smoke.
   b.   tell them that they are in a no-smoking compartment.
   c.   say you will call the guard if they light their cigarette.

Box B
1. a.   ask them to return the stolen goods.
   b.   tell them to return the goods or you will call the police.
   c.   say nothing.
2. a.   ask them why they were crying.
   b.   tell them to stop crying.
   c.   say nothing and leave the room.

2 ▭

There are at least two ways of doing this. You could allow your learners to write down the questions during and after the listening activity. If you do this, the learners then have a relatively straightforward task in transforming them into reported questions before you check to see who has the most 'correct' questions, i.e. grammatically correct and factually accurate.

A more challenging variation is not to allow the learners to write down anything while they listen – they simply have to try to remember the questions. Then, they turn their remembered questions into reported questions and write them down. If you use this second option, you could make it a bit easier by putting them in groups of three rather than pairs, and by telling them beforehand that each group should assign one member to listen to certain questions, e.g. the first person listens to question 1 and 4, etc. The tapescript is on page 156.

Answer key

Someone asked her if she really had one of these things.
Someone asked her if it was big.
Someone asked her if it was very long.
Someone asked her if you kept it indoors.
Someone asked her if you could read it.

Someone asked her if you would be surprised to find it
  indoors.
Someone asked her if the colour was important.
Someone asked her if a man would wear it or a woman.
Someone asked her if you would wear it on your feet.
Someone asked her if you could wear it on your head.
Someone asked her if it served a purpose.
Someone asked her if it was to protect your head.

```
┌─────────────────────────────────────────────┐
│              QUICK NOTES                      │
│                                               │
│   This went well:                             │
│   ..................................          │
│   ..................................          │
│                                               │
│   There was a problem with:                   │
│   ..................................          │
│   ..................................          │
│                                               │
│   Things to think about:                      │
│   ..................................          │
│   ..................................          │
│                                               │
└─────────────────────────────────────────────┘
```

20

ART AND SOCIETY

```
                        CONTENTS

Language focus:    passives
                   modal passives
                   revision of link words
                   definite, indefinite and zero article

    Vocabulary:    art and design
                   goods

         Skills:   Speaking:   design quality of everyday objects
                               a discussion about the role of court artists
                                   and the role of art
                               personal choice of a painting, sculpture
                                   or ornament
                   Listening:  about a court artist
                   Reading:    a text about the history of bank notes
                               a text about the commercialisation of art
                                   galleries and museums
                   Writing:    sentence transformation
```

THE VALUE OF MONEY

Introduction

The learners are tested on their knowledge of certain link words, and their ability to choose correctly between active and passive verbs. This should be revision for most learners, and if it doesn't present any problems, more time can be spent on the theme of the lesson – discussing the design qualities of everyday objects we carry around with us. Several short reading texts also introduce the learners to various lexical items which may be useful for them in discussing design features.

Suggested steps

1

Make sure your learners do not have an opportunity to look in their pockets before doing the activity. The different bank notes should not be a problem, but few people can actually remember whose face is on the notes. At the end, the learners can take out their bank notes to check. If you are in an English-speaking country, you could ask your learners in advance to bring to class any bank notes from their own country that they have at home in their suitcases, etc.

2

You could ask these questions to the class as a whole, then move on to the text. At the end, the learners can compare their answers with a partner before you check

with the group. This should be revision, but if the learners are still having problems, elicit more examples from the group to put on the board.

Answer key

although   as a result   however

3

The group should also be familiar with passive constructions, but you could quickly elicit one or two examples of passive forms before setting the task. The learners check with a partner.

Answer key

Active:
was; visited; was; were; are
Passive:
was issued; was used; was produced; can be found; are sought after

The extended use of the passive here is largely because the focus of interest is the history of paper money, and not, in most cases, those responsible for its production, distribution and use.

4

This is a straightforward testing activity on passives, but allow the learners to use dictionaries to help with new vocabulary. Check answers at the end and clarify any problems with the use of the passive or the meaning of new vocabulary. You could also refer the learners to the Grammar Reference on page 164 of the Class Book with further details on the use of the passive.

Answer key

replaced	varied	be printed
were designed	had	be seen
were chosen	were decorated	remained
became	were based	was produced

Option

You could follow up this language testing exercise with a more creative task. Put the learners in groups and get them to design their own bank notes. These could be serious designs or something more amusing.

5

Your learners may have come to class with all sorts of interesting everyday objects. But just in case they haven't, remember to bring along some examples of your own which they could also discuss, e.g. wallet, purse, key ring, paper tissues, pens, pencils, credit cards, cheque books, etc. If possible, clear a space where people can display some of these objects, then let groups examine them in detail and make notes before they sit down and discuss which ones they like and why, and what changes they would suggest. At the end, each group can give their opinions and recommendations.

Option

You could extend the discussion to include other objects as well. Ask the class if they can think of any examples of something that is particularly well-designed and why. You could ask them to volunteer any particularly good examples of original or elegant design.

Personal Study Workbook

3: We've been sold a forgery: passives
5: Dear Vincent ...: reading

```
┌─────────────────────────────────────────┐
│            QUICK NOTES                   │
│                                          │
│  This went well:                         │
│  .......................................  │
│  .......................................  │
│                                          │
│  There was a problem with:               │
│  .......................................  │
│  .......................................  │
│                                          │
│  Things to think about:                  │
│  .......................................  │
│  .......................................  │
└─────────────────────────────────────────┘
```

Introduction

Following vocabulary input revolving around a number of items which are commonly misunderstood or confused, the lesson looks at the work of a court artist. Information about this unusual occupation is introduced through a listening task, and after a brief focus on modal passives, the learners have the opportunity to discuss some of the issues surrounding the work of a court artist, using some of the modal passives they have looked at.

Suggested steps

1

The initial activity involves distinguishing between lexical items which sometimes overlap in meaning and often cause problems for learners from different countries. The learners can compare, and then you can discuss any areas of difficulty when you go through the answers. In particular, see the Language Point below.

Answer key

1. an exhibition; gallery   2. paint
3. an artist; illustrations   4. reproduction   5. statue
6. drew   7. portrait   8. landscapes

> ### Language Point: scenery, landscape and view
>
> The *view* is what you can see when you look at scenery / the landscape. For example:
> *We had a wonderful view of the mountains from the room in our hotel.*
>
> *Scenery* (U) is used to describe the general appearance of an area, particularly in describing how beautiful it is:
> *It's worth taking the train because the scenery along the route is so beautiful.*
>
> *Landscape* can describe the general appearance of a place (like *scenery*), but is often used to describe the more specific qualities of a place which give it its character, i.e. whether it is mountainous, flat, barren, built-up, industrial, etc.:
> *As you move inland the landscape changes and becomes quite hilly.*
>
> *Note:* A painting of a scene from the country is called a *landscape*, not *scenery*.

2 ▭

Direct the learners to the picture and ask them what they think the woman's job is. (It may seem obvious to some people, but we are not sure if every country has court artists.) When you have elicited or explained what she does, introduce the listening and give the learners a minute or two to read through the questions and the explanations of the abbreviations. Play the recording and let the learners make notes. If necessary, play the recording a second time as the learners are required to answer quite detailed questions on the text. Put them in pairs to compare, then check with the group. You could also play the recording again and let the learners see the tapescript while they listen. The tapescript is on page 157.

Answer key

1. She drew people in a nightclub, then she started her own gallery, then she worked for NBC, then she started working for the BBC.
2. In Britain a court artist has to draw from memory because they are not allowed to draw people in court, whereas in the United States they can.
3. 15 minutes is the time the artist has to study the subject before going into a different room to do the drawing.
   One and a half hours is the time she has to do the drawing before the next news broadcast
   15 seconds is the amount of time that viewers usually see these drawings on television.

3

This transformation consolidates work from the previous lesson, only this time the focus is on sentences using modal passives, which the learners have to transform into the active. This is a preparation for the final activity in which they are likely to need modal passives. Talk the learners through the example, i.e. what kind of change is being made, then let them do the rest of the task individually. Check answers at the end.

Answer key

2. The artist cannot make sketches in the courtroom itself.
3. The artist should draw people accurately in court.
4. The artist has to produce the drawings quickly for the television news.

4

Explain any unknown vocabulary in the six statements, then follow the instructions in the Class Book. For the most part we do not believe the learners should be forced into a particular point of view just for the sake of language practice, and that is why we have only asked the learners to respond to one or two statements out of a total of six: given this choice, there seems a fair chance of genuine agreement or disagreement with at least one statement. Then form small groups on the basis of the statements the learners wish to attack or defend, and monitor their discussions. At the end, give positive feedback; suggestions for language items that might have been useful to them (you may already have slotted in one or two items into the discussion of individual groups); and important error correction.

Personal Study Workbook

1: What's a forgery?: vocabulary
4: A self-portrait that's forgery-proof: prefixes and suffixes

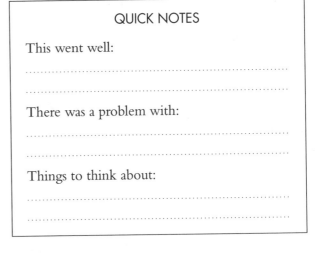

QUICK NOTES

This went well:

....
....

There was a problem with:

....
....

Things to think about:

....
....

ARTICLES AND PRECIOUS ARTICLES

Introduction

There is a warm-up activity in which the learners talk about works of art they would like to own, but the main focus of the lesson is a text about the growth in sales of art-related accessories from museum and art gallery shops. This provides discussion as the learners select the accessories they find attractive, and leads into the exploitation of the text for its use of definite and indefinite articles. The learners have an opportunity to identify and analyse these uses in the text before moving on to controlled practice at the end of the lesson.

Suggested steps

1

If you know what your own answer would be to this question, start the lesson by telling the group your own personal choice. Then open up the discussion to the class, putting them in small groups.

Option

If you are not confident your class have either the knowledge to answer this question or the inclination to do so, ask them about any pictures, sculptures or ornaments they have in their own home. They could describe something they have, something they like, or something they particularly dislike (this may be popular with learners who are still living with their parents).

2

As well as underlining the objects that can be bought, you could also ask the learners to see how many pictures they can identify in the text. Let them compare with a partner before checking answers.

Answer key

reproductions of ancient Egyptian and Roman jewellery
disposable tablecloths decorated with Lautrec's dancing girls
long black gloves

a reproduction of Lautrec's walking stick
a pocket watch
a copy of Cezanne's blue vase
a glass and jug from a Degas painting
garden shears
Egyptian board games
terracotta figurines
reproduction Roman coins
statues of Apollo
postcards and books
educational games
aeroplane kits and other toys

3

Your learners will probably have come across some basic rules governing the use of articles in English, so you could begin by asking them for any rules they know, with examples. Put them on the board without confirming or rejecting them at this stage. Then put the learners in pairs to discuss the four questions and complete the rules below. When they have finished, discuss their answers as a class, make connections with any previously stated rules they may have given you, and reject/clarify anything which is clearly wrong.

Answer key

1. If a person bought *the pocket watch* in Stevens's *Le Bain*, it would mean specifically the one in the painting. This is not the case. People are simply buying one of many that are available for sale; therefore *a watch*.
2. Because the watch is a copy of a very specific watch, i.e. the one in the picture, and not any watch.
3. Because the writer of the text does not specify which picture the glass and jug come from, it is therefore *a painting*.
4. Because it refers to any garden shop and not a special garden shop.

Rules:
1. b   2. a

Option

If you feel your particular group of learners do not need this fairly detailed work on articles – it may be the case if they have few difficulties with articles at this level of analysis, or they are on a short intensive course which attaches greater importance to speaking, listening and lexical input – you could follow up with Worksheet 20 on page 129, which is based loosely on a task in the Review of Unit 20 at the end of Unit 21. You could use this worksheet after doing the review activity if you wished.

You need to warn your learners in advance that they will need to bring in a postcard or picture of a painting/drawing that they like. These can be well-known pictures or something that they have done themselves. Follow the instructions in the worksheet. You could either mount a wall display of the results, or if you have generous photocopying facilities, make them into a booklet for each of the learners in the class.

4

With any language analysis there is the danger that a learner may have understood the point but lack the language to articulate that knowledge or understanding. This exercise is an opportunity for the learners to demonstrate/test their understanding of the concepts that have been discussed. When they have finished, they can discuss their answers first with a partner and then with the group as a whole.

Answer key

1. a; a
2. the; the; the
3. a; the; a
4. the; the; the; a; the; a/the★; the

★ Both answers are possible here because we don't know how many trees are next to the statue. If there is only one, it must be *the* tree; if there are several, it could be 'a' tree, assuming they are all equidistant from the statue.

5

Put the learners back into pairs to discuss the question and fill in the rule. Check their answers.

Answer key

When we want to talk about something in general, we don't use *the* with a plural or uncountable noun.

When we want to talk about something particular or specific, we use *the* with a plural or uncountable noun.

6

Give the learners a few minutes to complete their answers. If you are short of time, give the exercise for homework but do one in class as an example.

Answer key

Possible answers
1. Museums are wonderful places.
2. The museums I went to when I was a child were free.
3. Jewellery is expensive to insure.
4. The jewellery in my case was all stolen in the burglary.
5. Money doesn't buy happiness.
6. The money they raised is going to a charity for the deaf.
7. Works of art give huge amounts of pleasure to millions of people.
8. The works of art they lost in the fire were some of the most valuable in the collection.

Personal Study Workbook

2: *A(n), the* or nothing at all: articles
6: I know what I like: listening
7: Describing a painting: writing
8: Speaking partners
9: Visual dictionary

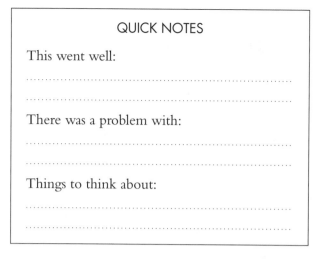

QUICK NOTES

This went well:

....

....

There was a problem with:

....

....

Things to think about:

....

....

REVIEW AND DEVELOPMENT

REVIEW OF UNIT 18

1

Follow the instructions in the Class Book and make sure the learners write down reported questions and not direct questions.

Answer key

Possible answers

1. Someone asked her where the ladies' toilet was.
2. Someone asked her if (some) flights to India were delayed this/that morning.
3. Someone asked her why the flights were delayed.
4. Someone asked her if there was a chemist's in the airport.
5. Someone asked her how far the city centre was and how to get there.
6. Someone asked her how often the buses ran.
7. Someone asked her if the shops were open.

2 ▭

Do the first one or two with the class, then let them complete the task on their own. They can compare with a partner when they have finished.

Play the recording so they can check their answers, then let them practise saying the words with a partner. Once again, do several examples with the class first.

Answer key

famine	balance
third	hurt
industrial	justice
triumph	priority
police	achievement
dispute	refuse
rate	inflation
fair	area
threaten	success

3

If you are working with a group from the same country, you could do the activity in class, then ask them to find the answers to any questions they cannot answer for the next lesson.

If your group has no interest in politics, omit this particular revision activity.

REVIEW OF UNIT 19

1

You could ask the learners to choose a topic, then match them accordingly, either in pairs or small groups. If one topic is not chosen by anyone, use this as your example. Give them one or two ideas of your own using the sentence beginnings, then elicit more from the class. When they have clearly got the idea, let them complete the task in their pairs or groups. When they have finished they can try out their suggestions on a different pair/group.

2

Follow the instructions in the Class Book.

Answer key

Possible answers

Situation	Speaker/hearer
2. someone has just cut themselves	friend to injured person
3. in part of a building with restricted access	e.g. a school teacher to student
4. domestic problem between husband and wife	friend to wife
5. in an office at work	secretary to secretary
6. child jumping on furniture	parent to child

Check answers with the group and discuss any problems, then put them back in pairs to think of suitable replies. When they have finished, you can mix the pairs so that they can practise the dialogues and decide if each other's replies are appropriate. Move round and listen to some of the dialogues and adjudicate at the end in the event of any disagreements. Finish with part C in which the learners decide on contexts and write their own sentences using the target verbs in brackets.

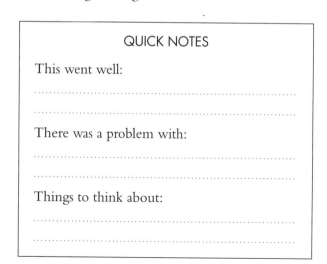

QUICK NOTES

This went well:

....

....

There was a problem with:

....

....

Things to think about:

....

....

21

DARE YOURSELF TO SUCCEED

CONTENTS

Language focus: *should have* + past participle
past conditional

Vocabulary: applying for jobs
outdoor activities
verb or adjective + preposition

Skills: Speaking: role play: admitting to a lie
discussing job applications / interviews
anecdotes about personal successes
and failures
managing on an outdoor executive
training course

Listening: people talking about their experience of
an outdoor executive training course

Reading: a text about telling white lies in job
applications

A WHITE LIE?

Introduction

The lesson opens with a brief explicit presentation of *should have* + past participle, but for the rest of the lesson, practice of the structure is woven into a variety of skills activities: first through a response to a reading text about the unfortunate consequences of lying in a job application and interview; then in a role play arising from the reading text; and finally in discussion involving various cross-cultural issues connected with applying for jobs.

Suggested steps

1

You could begin by asking the learners to imagine that two of them (one male, one female) were going for an interview for an office job. Ask the others to list some of the things these two people should do, e.g. the man should wear a tie; the woman shouldn't wear jeans. When they have compiled a short list – individually, in pairs or as a class – refer them to the pictures in the book and explain that these two people went for interviews like this and didn't get the jobs. What do the class think they should(n't) have done? Go through the examples, then let them work individually to add others before comparing in groups.

Answer key

Possible answers
The man:
– should have trimmed his beard.
– should have worn a tie.
– should have had his hair cut.
– should have worn a suit.
– should have sat up straight during the interview.
The woman:
– shouldn't have worn so much jewellery.
– shouldn't have smoked during the interview.
– shouldn't have brought shopping bags into the
interview room.
– should have worn more conservative clothes.

2

Eventually the text will be exploited for freer practice of *should(n't) have* + past participle, but first of all the class need a good grasp of the text; this is the purpose of the comprehension task. Let the learners complete it individually (using dictionaries if necessary, although the vocabulary is not very difficult), then they can check with a partner.

Answer key

1. At school Melanie studied German but she wasn't good at it and her teacher told her to give it up.
2. The job advertisement stated that applicants should be able to speak good German.
3. At the interview Melanie said she could speak German.
4. When she started the job she didn't need to speak German.

5. In the evenings she tried to learn German but she was still terrible at it.
6. When her boss told her she was going to Germany she realised she would have to be able to speak German.

3

The learners may need help to put some of their ideas into English, so be prepared to move round and help. When they have a few examples, elicit answers from the class and see if there is agreement on all of them.

Answer key

Possible answers

She should have noticed German was necessary in the advertisement.

She should have told the truth in the interview. (She shouldn't have lied in the interview.)

She shouldn't have accepted the job.

She should have accepted the job but then told her boss that her German was not as good as she thought.

He should have tested her on her knowledge of German.

He should have realised that something was wrong when she didn't volunteer to go to Germany.

4

This type of role play often works better if the learners have had a chance to prepare a strategy. You could, therefore, ask each pair to find another pair who have chosen the same role play (if it is easier you may just assign role plays to each pair, but in principle it is better if the learners can choose), then let the learners playing the same role get together and discuss what their strategy is going to be, and what they are going to say. This not only gives the opportunity for mental rehearsal, but also assists weaker learners. When they feel they are well-prepared, put them together to role play their situations. At the end, discuss the situations and how they were approached and give feedback on language use.

5

Ask the learners if they know what a *white lie* is, and explain if you do not get a satisfactory answer. Ask them if they think Melanie told a white lie, then put them in groups to discuss the other questions. With the first question, you could ask the learners to try to think up white lies that may be acceptable in a job application. For example, someone might say they have worked in a particular job for a year, when in fact they only did the job for ten months. Conduct feedback at the end.

Option

You should obviously tread carefully here, but you could ask the group if any of them are prepared to confess to telling white lies in a job application they have made.

Personal Study Workbook

7: A letter of application: writing
8: Speaking partners

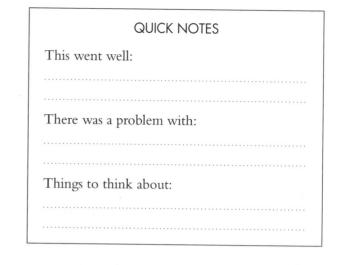

QUICK NOTES

This went well:

....

....

....

There was a problem with:

....

....

Things to think about:

....

....

....

NOTHING SUCCEEDS LIKE SUCCESS

Introduction

The learners will be familiar with the form of the past perfect (Unit 14), and the form of modal perfects, e.g. *should have* + past participle from the previous lesson; this lesson takes one step further and puts them together in the form of the past conditional, which the learners practise in controlled activities and then in more creative and personalised activities at the end. The topic throughout the lesson is reflecting on past success and failure.

Suggested steps

1

While some learners grasp the concept of the past conditional immediately, others find it difficult to disentangle the complex forms that are involved. If you wish, you could start with this option before doing Exercise 1.

Option

Write this sentence on the board:
If I'd known about the film on TV, I would've watched it.

First check that the learners know what the contractions represent (you could write them in a different colour above each contraction), then ask them this question: *Did I watch the film on TV last night?* If you elicit the answer *no*, follow up by asking: *How do you know?* If you wish, give more examples until you feel confident the whole class (or most of them) have got the idea. Another example could be:
If he'd told me it was a secret, I wouldn't have told Barbara.

Questions:
Did I tell Barbara?
Why did I tell her?

Then direct the learners to Exercise 1 in the Class Book. Check that they understand the vocabulary in the sentences, e.g. *to get a contract, evidence, a case.* Let them complete the exercise individually and compare with a partner. Then you can check with the whole class.

Answer key

1. No 2. Yes 3. Yes 4. No 5. No

2

Although the form is in the Class Book, try to elicit it from the group and put it on the board. Add *could* and *might* and clarify the difference between them, and the difference between these forms and *would*. Explain why this structure is used – it may help to point out that we often use it to express anger or regret about past actions – and then move on to the examples. They are in the Class Book but it is still probably more effective if you write them on the board so that there is a single focal point for the whole group. Give them the first clause of the transformation, i.e. *If he hadn't driven so fast*, and see if the group can finish it for you. With the second example, i.e. *If he had driven slower*, see if they can provide the whole sentence. Give them the task in the book and allow them to work with a partner if they wish.

Answer key

1. If she'd done well in the interview, she would've got the job.
2. She wouldn't have come first if she hadn't worked harder than everyone else.
3. He wouldn't have won the card game if he hadn't cheated.
   (He would've lost the card game if he hadn't cheated.)
4. The meeting would've been a success if she had planned it carefully.
5. The patient wouldn't have lived if the operation hadn't been successful.

Note: Might and/or *could* are also possible in a number of these sentences, e.g. *might've got the job* in 1 and *couldn't have won the card game* in 3.

3

Divide the class in half and direct one half to the text on page 173, while the other half look at the text in the unit. Ask them to read their respective texts, complete the last line, and then compare their answer with someone who read the same text. While they are doing this, move round and monitor and help where necessary.

4

When they have finished Exercise 3, put each learner with a partner who read the other text. They can then tell each other their stories and see if their partner can finish their story in a suitable way.

Answer key

Possible answers
1. If he hadn't made that speech, sales wouldn't have fallen.
2. If she hadn't been so dedicated, she wouldn't have won a medal.

5

Tell the class the two examples in the book as if they were your own experiences or those of a friend. This not only provides listening practice and a model for their own anecdotes, but is more interesting and motivating as well. Then give them one or two minutes to think about their own experiences before putting them with a partner or in small groups to share their experiences. This may then provoke a great deal of genuinely interesting discussion, or it may produce almost total silence. If it is the latter and you find you cannot prompt any discussion and still have fifteen or twenty minutes left in the lesson, you could do Worksheet 21 on page 130 instead.

Personal Study Workbook

1: Letter of explanation: job vocabulary, past conditional, *should have* + past participle
3: I wouldn't have done that: past conditional
5: A chance meeting: reading
6: Different lives: listening

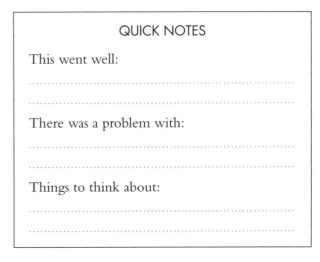

```
QUICK NOTES

This went well:

..........................................................
..........................................................

There was a problem with:

..........................................................
..........................................................

Things to think about:

..........................................................
..........................................................
```

EXECUTIVE TRAINING

Introduction

Although the context of the lesson is executive training courses, the topic should be relevant to everyone as it asks the learners to assess how well they might cope in different physical conditions which are potentially stressful. There is extensive and intensive listening (the latter recycles the past conditional from the previous lesson); a wide range of vocabulary items related to various outdoor activities; and throughout the lesson a number of personalised speaking activities with opportunities for discussion and creative thinking.

Suggested steps

1

You could begin by talking about the picture at the top of the lesson. Can the learners identify this activity? Does anyone have any experience of it? From this, you could then tell the learners that this is an activity that executives are sometimes called upon to perform in outdoor executive training courses. Tell the class about Andy Booth (in the Class Book). Elicit a few reactions to draw the learners into the topic (or put them in groups to discuss reactions), then introduce the listening.

2 ▭

Play the recording, pausing after each speaker to allow time for the learners to complete the table. At the end, let the learners compare, and play the recording again if they appear to have missed some of the information or have different answers. Check with the whole group at the end. The tapescript is on page 157.

Answer key

	Opinion	Why?
1. Michael	hated it	he was humiliated in front of colleagues
2. Caroline	good and bad	good because it is fun; bad because women are at a disadvantage in some of the physical activities
3. James	good	it gave him confidence and taught him to work in a team
4. Sonia	a waste of time	not relevant to her life and job, and she also found the conditions unpleasant

3 ▭

Follow the instructions in the Class Book. The tapescript is on page 157.

Answer key

Michael suffers from vertigo, so he was unable to do the abseiling even when he was ordered to do it. As he was in front of colleagues, he felt humiliated by this experience and he started crying.

4

Keep the class arranged in their groups, and direct them to the vocabulary in the exercise. You can then get them to retrieve the meaning themselves using dictionaries and each other; or you can explain certain items yourself if you wish to allow more time for the speaking activities to follow. When you are satisfied that the group have a good initial understanding of the items, let them discuss their own reactions to these activities. This will, of course, provide the practice and consolidation of the new items. At the end you could conduct a brief feedback on their ideas and use of language.

Option

If you would like to provide more controlled practice of the vocabulary, you could ask them to complete a table like this:

	Easy	Quite Difficult	Very Difficult
sleeping in a tent			
having no hot water			
sleeping in a cave			
on your own			
etc.			

Then put the learners in pairs to go through the list and get their reactions to each one. Doing it this way ensures that each item on the list is mentioned.

5

This final activity gives the learners a chance to contribute their own ideas on executive training, and if any in the group have experience of different types of course, this is the time to draw on that knowledge. As the learners are given a number of choices, encourage them to rank the courses in order of effectiveness if they wish to choose more than one example. You should also encourage them to think up their own courses which may be useful.

Personal Study Workbook

2: What follows what?: prepositions and adverbs
4: Weak forms and linking: pronunciation
9: Visual dictionary

QUICK NOTES

This went well:

....

....

There was a problem with:

....

....

Things to think about:

....

....

REVIEW AND DEVELOPMENT

REVIEW OF UNIT 19

1 ▭

This may be of particular interest in those parts of the world where the learners are often exposed to American and British English, e.g. Japan and South America. In our experience, however, most learners are quite intrigued by the differences. Follow the instructions in the Class Book. At the end, you could put the learners in groups to see if they can add more examples of

---

differences in pronunciation, spelling and grammar. Alternatively, ask them to discuss their preferences. Which pronunciation sounds more attractive? Which spelling is more logical to them?

Answer key

B

American English	British English
color	colour
labor	labour
center	centre
theater	theatre
jewelry	jewellery
traveled	travelled
license (noun)	licence
(bank) check	cheque

C
1. I'm visiting with her tomorrow.
2. Could I speak with Albert, please?
3. I just had some coffee.
4. I'll go get the car.
5. a half hour
6. I can't remember if it starts at twenty of four or five after five.

2

This exercise revises vocabulary from the unit, but also illustrates the important skill of reformulation. The learners often need to do this themselves when they are talking to someone with less command of English than them, so it is worth practising in class on a regular basis. The expression *in other words* is also very useful receptively, as it is an important discourse marker in introducing a reformulation. Once the learners can identify this phrase, they know that a previous item or concept is being redefined, and this may be of considerable help to them in understanding a piece of discourse.

Follow the instructions in the Class Book.

REVIEW OF UNIT 20

1

See if the learners can grasp the basic gist of the comments without using dictionaries. And for a more precise assessment of the comments, you could ask the learners to put their reactions on a scale of liking and disliking, like this:

---

like a lot   quite like   mixed feelings   don't like much   can't stand

Let them compare answers, then ask them to write their own reactions. Move round and be prepared to help learners who are searching for a particular word or expression they might need to express their feelings. At the end, they can compare in groups.

Option

If there is real interest in this kind of activity, you could bring in some pictures of your own for the learners to discuss and write about, or ask them to bring in their favourite pictures. One way of doing this is to bring three or four pictures which all have something in common, e.g. they are all portraits, or landscapes, or abstract paintings; then ask the learners to write comments about one or two of the pictures without naming them. The learners can then walk round the class, read each other's comments and try to identify which picture is being described.

2

Follow the instructions in the Class Book.

Answer key

Possible answers
1. It's been stolen.
2. They're being knocked down.
3. They are sent back to the theatre.
4. They'll be thrown away.
5. They are seen by a nurse.
6. They are sent back to the post office.
7. They've been cleaned.
8. It's been attacked by another dog.

QUICK NOTES

This went well:

....

....

There was a problem with:

....

....

Things to think about:

....

....

FORCES OF NATURE

CONTENTS

Language focus: *used to* + verb
be *used to* + noun or *-ing*
get *used to* + noun or *-ing*

Vocabulary: health problems and natural remedies
abstract nouns
word building

Skills: Speaking: describing things you are used to and
things which would be difficult to get
used to
inventing remedies for illnesses
beliefs and superstition
Listening: people talking about features of Britain
which foreigners may find strange
advice on unusual remedies for illnesses
a description of *feng shui*
Reading: a text about an earthquake

ONE MINUTE CHANGED OUR LIVES

Introduction

The lesson contrasts *used to* + verb and *be/get used to* + noun or *-ing*. These structures are lifted out of a text which forms the basis for the first half of the lesson, and then consolidated through further practice. The learners start by working on vocabulary which appears in the text, and then use their reading skills to put the jumbled text in the right order.

Suggested steps

1

This exercise gives the learners their first look at a number of lexical items which appear in the text they read later. You could start by putting them on the board or OHP, and you could also ask the learners if they have any idea what two of the four categories might be. With this start, the learners can then complete the rest of the task with a partner and the help of a dictionary.

Answer key

Possible answers

Animals	Time	Verbs	Objects
snake	eventually	grab hold (of something)	a gravestone
lizard	a fortnight	crawl	tiles
squirrel	dawn	to last	concrete
	a while		pavement
	to last		

2

Try to elicit the meaning of the headline and explain, if necessary, the word *earthquake*. Then let the learners piece the text together and compare answers. When you go through the answers with the group, try to get them to justify the order of their paragraphs.

Answer key

1. It was midnight …
2. I came in but I couldn't relax.
3. My first thoughts were for my daughter.
4. It suddenly occurred to me …
5. When we crawled out …
6. The rescue operations moved quite quickly …
7. My daughter and I …

3

The learners should be able to answer the question without a full understanding of the structures. Don't explain anything yet, just elicit the answers.

Answer key

Mary was used to picking oranges and going to San Francisco for the weekend. She can't get used to a small house and garden in rural England.

4

You could put the three structures on the board and see if any learners can explain the differences. If possible, get them to put the structures into sentences and write the sentences on the board. Don't confirm or reject any suggestions at this stage.

When you have a number of suggestions, correct or otherwise, direct the learners to the sentences and definitions in the book and get them to complete the task. At the end, you can check the answers and ask them which of their suggestions were right or wrong.

For speakers of romance languages, *be accustomed to* is a useful and helpful paraphrase of *be used to*, and you can explain that we also use this structure in English but it is less common and natural than *be used to*.

Answer key

1. *used to (do)*
2. *be used to (doing)*
3. *get used to (doing)*

Some learners find it helpful if you explain that *be* represents the state, while *get* describes a process (which leads to a state).

5

This is an opportunity to practise and consolidate the structures in a freer personalised activity. The learners are obviously free to talk about anything they like, but you could encourage them to be quite specific, e.g. it is more interesting if a learner says they are used to *extremes of hot and cold*, than if they just say they are used to *the weather*. When they have finished, let them compare in groups, and encourage the learners to ask each other why they might find certain things difficult in Britain.

6 ▭

Before listening, ask the learners to predict the things the speakers might talk about. Then follow the instructions in the Class Book. The tapescript is on page 158.

Answer key

1. queuing
2. driving on the left
3. the English sense of humour

Personal Study Workbook

1: Things you're familiar with: *used to* + *-ing* form
4: Text reading: pronunciation
6: I couldn't get used to that: listening
7: Fill in the details: writing
8: Speaking partners

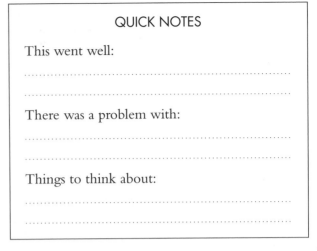

QUICK NOTES

This went well:

....

....

There was a problem with:

....

....

Things to think about:

....

....

NATURE'S REMEDIES

Introduction

The learners do encounter some rather unusual vocabulary items in the course of this lesson, but the subject is one that many groups find fascinating, i.e. the debate concerning the use of natural remedies for illness rather than conventional medicine; and in a multinational group, a number of interesting cross-cultural differences should emerge.

The lesson develops through a series of speaking and listening activities, which are punctuated with vocabulary input and consolidation.

Suggested steps

1

This may appear a slightly unusual lexical set, but the inclusion of several items, e.g. *warts* and *cold sores* is simply because they appear later in the listening passage and are likely to cause significant problems if they are not understood.

Give the learners five or ten minutes to work on the vocabulary and move round to help where necessary. For the practice activity, you could get them to stand up and mingle with others in the class.

2

Ask the class if they know of any natural remedies for particular illnesses; start with an example of your own if possible. Help them with words they do not know in English and write the examples on the board. Then they can label the items in the pictures. As some of these items may not be common in some cultures, we would suggest that if you work with a monolingual group, you try to find out translation equivalents before the lesson.

Option

There is an opportunity for some discussion later in the lesson, but this is the type of subject where you may find members of the group with a very real interest or commitment. If so, they may be quite keen to talk about their beliefs and opinions; and if the rest of the group are clearly interested by this, be prepared to depart from the scheduled lesson plan.

Answer key

1. bicarbonate of soda   2. cayenne pepper
3. cloves of garlic   4. teabags   5. ice cubes
6. a bar of chocolate   7. sellotape   8. ginger root

3

When you have checked their answers and clarified any problems, the learners can try to match the items on the left with the problems on the right. Listen to their suggested answers but don't give the correct answers.

Answer key

Ginger root relieves nausea.
Sellotape gets rid of warts.
Cayenne pepper warms cold feet.
Ice relieves insect bites and blocked sinuses.
Bicarbonate of soda relieves itching.
Garlic fights colds and flu.
A tea bag soothes cold sores.

4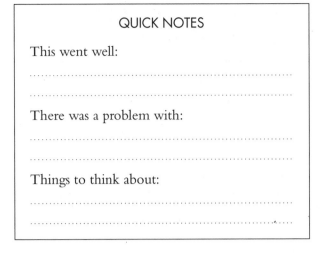

Play the recording so that the learners can check their answers, and then play it a second time for the learners to note down further information. At the end, elicit information from the group and then make the tapescript available to them. The tapescript is on page 158.

Answer key

See the tapescript on page 158.

5

The questions are really just prompts for a more general debate about the use of natural (homeopathic) medicine rather than conventional medicine which makes extensive use of drugs. Let groups find their own points of interest for discussion, but make notes on their ideas and language use for later feedback.

6

The two examples demonstrate that the learners are being encouraged to enjoy themselves with this exercise, but you can encourage them to try to think up remedies which sound far-fetched but might just be possible. The final exchange may be more fun if you work with the whole group rather than pairs.

Personal Study Workbook

5: Fight disease through food: reading
9: Visual dictionary

SEND FOR THE *FENG SHUI* MAN

Introduction

We hope the title alone will be sufficiently intriguing to generate interest, and in our experience the topic is often the trigger for some very interesting stories and experiences from members of the group. The cross-cultural interest in multinational classes is obviously a bonus, but even among monolingual groups it can stimulate very interesting discussion.

In the second part of the lesson there is a focus on some of the vocabulary from the recording, which is then extended through a word building exercise before final consolidation in an activity that also compares and practises *if* and *unless*.

Suggested steps

1

It will be more interesting if you tell the class about the examples in Exercise 1, direct them to the pictures in the Class Book, and then ask for possible explanations of *feng shui*. Write their ideas on the board.

2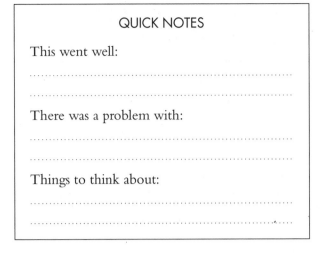

Play the recording so that the learners can compare their ideas on the board with the facts. Play the recording again for the learners to extract more detailed information (most of question 1 may already have been answered). The tapescript is on page 159.

Answer key

1. Human beings must live in harmony with their natural surroundings and the position of your home or workplace in relation to the environment is very important.
2. A *feng shui* priest advises people how to change their environment and be healthier and wealthier.
3. It exists in China where it is not officially recognised. It is widely practised in Hong Kong, and it has begun to spread to the USA.

4. A woman moved out of the apartment where she had lived for ten years on the advice of a *feng shui* priest. Another man was burgled six times, so he consulted a *feng shui* priest. He installed a red clock and a tank of fish, and since then he hasn't been burgled.

3

The discussion generated here will depend partly on the culture of your learners and partly on their own individual interests. If they have a lot to say, the second question can be ignored; but if they don't have a lot to say, the second question may be very useful as it does direct the conversation along completely different lines and may be very generative. See the option below.

Option

If you sense that some learners are very interested in the topic but others less so, you could ask the group to look at the two questions in Exercise 3 and choose which one they want to discuss. Then organise the groups accordingly (maximum four or five per group) and let them discuss their chosen question.

4

Elicit the meaning of the nouns in the table – this is an excellent place to make use of translation if you work with a monolingual group and you are also a native speaker or proficient in the language – then let them work individually or in pairs on the adjectives. Conduct a brief feedback at the end and make sure the learners can pronounce the words correctly.

Answer key

successful; powerful
healthy; wealthy; lucky
philosophical; environmental
wise; poor

5

Write the second sentence on the board: *Unless she moved, she wouldn't survive*, and then explain that we can rewrite this sentence with *if*. Put the first clause on the board:
If she didn't move, ...

See if you can elicit the rest of the sentence. If not, write it yourself, then do the same with the second paraphrase, i.e. put the first clause on the board:
If she stayed in her house, ...

and then elicit the second part. Ask the learners what *unless* means, and if you wish, follow up with more examples for them to transform. For example:
Don't touch it unless it breaks.
Unless the weather improves, we'll have to stay here.
You'll never know unless you ask.

6

This is designed to provide controlled practice of the structure, but you should also encourage the learners to complete the sentences in ways that accurately reflect their feelings and opinions. Move round and monitor while they are writing, helping where necessary, and when they have finished, put them in groups to read out and discuss their answers. At the end, you might also invite other groups to comment on two or three examples of completed sentences.

If the group has enjoyed the topic of *feng shui*, you could follow this lesson with Worksheet 22 on page 131, which is a reading text on the subject and develops some of the ideas a bit further.

Personal Study Workbook

2: Transformations: *if* and *unless*
3: Parts of speech: word building

QUICK NOTES

This went well:

....

....

There was a problem with:

....

....

Things to think about:

....

....

REVIEW AND DEVELOPMENT

REVIEW OF UNIT 20

1

Follow the instructions in the Class Book.

Answer key

Possible answers

Money and banking	Art and design	Both
currency	an engraving	to print
a transaction	to decorate	to be worth
coins	a portrait	
financier	a reproduction	
an amount	a sculpture	
to be in debt	to illustrate	
	landscape	
	a drawing	

2 ▭

The importance of this exercise will obviously depend on the nationality of your learners. If they are not accustomed to consonant clusters in their first language, you may wish to repeat this kind of activity for clusters that cause particular problems. Follow the instructions in the Class Book.

3

The learners can work with a partner (as instructed in the Class Book), or they could work individually and then check their answers with a partner.

Answer key

an experienced housewife
the label
the washing powder
the curtains
a kind of
the paste
a bowl
a slice
bread
the kitchen table
indigestion

REVIEW OF UNIT 21

1

There are many ways of demonstrating that you understand a lexical item: through synonyms, antonyms, definitions, example situations, etc. Explain this to your learners (with examples if necessary), and encourage them to make use of these different techniques if required.

Go through the example with the group, then let them work on the rest of the task on their own. When they have finished, they can read out and compare their answers in small groups, and decide if each of their explanations is clear and accurate. Check with the whole class at the end.

Answer key

Possible answers
1. … they are funny.
2. … they don't like strong coffee. They don't like a lot of 'coffee' in their coffee.
3. … you were very happy with it.
4. … the service is OK but not fantastic.
5. … you enjoyed it.
6. … you are very tired.
7. … you enjoy them and find them very interesting.
8. … you didn't get the job.
9. … you found it difficult but in a positive sense. It was interesting.

2

Divide the class into two groups, then get each group to complete their sentences individually. When they have finished, pairs from each group can compare their answers to see if they are correct and also to see how similar they are. After this, put pairs from each group together so they can explore a wider range of possible answers. Have any individuals reproduced the same sentence as any of their partners?

QUICK NOTES

This went well:

....

....

There was a problem with:

....

....

Things to think about:

....

....

WORKSHEETS

WORKSHEET 1A

Your partner's country: what do you know?

Your partner's name ....

Your partner's country ....

Capital city ....

Name of President / Prime Minister ....

Size of population ....

Language(s) spoken ....

Famous food/drink ....

Famous places ....

Famous people ....

What is this country most famous for? ....

What would you like to know about it? ....

TRUE TO LIFE INTERMEDIATE   © Cambridge University Press 1996

WORKSHEET 1B

Your partner

Ask about your partner:

Name ....

Job ....

Family ....

Where they live exactly ....

Why they are doing this course ....

Interests/hobbies ....

Any more questions? ....

TRUE TO LIFE INTERMEDIATE   © Cambridge University Press 1996

1. Which sounds and/or spelling combinations do you find most difficult in English? Look at the examples in the table. Do you have these problems? Think about them, then add some more of your own.

PROBLEM	EXAMPLE
1. I don't know how to say the letter 'v' in English.	I say *werb* and not *verb*.
2. I make mistakes with 'ous' at the end of words.	I say *famous* /feɪmʊs/ or /feɪmaʊs/ not /feɪməs/.
3. I have problems with 'th'.	I say 'ze' and not 'the'.
4. I often have problems with the letter 'o' in words.	I often say /ɒ/ and not /ʌ/, e.g. I say *love* /lɒv/ and not /lʌv/.
5.	....
6.	....
7.	....
8.	....

2. Try to find someone who speaks the same language as you. Do they have the same problems? Is there a solution to any of these problems?

3. Are there learners with a different first language to you in your class? If so, look at their problems. Can you help them with any?

4. Use the table to keep a record of your special problems. Focus on a different problem each week, practise the correct pronunciation as much as you can, and ask others in the group to tell you if you are getting it right more often.

TRUE TO LIFE INTERMEDIATE   © Cambridge University Press 1996

WORKSHEET 3

1. The verbs before each set of dots in the following sentences are followed by an infinitive or -*ing* form. Write infinitive or -*ing* above each verb. (Both verbs in the sentence may take an infinitive or -*ing* form.) Look at the example first.

    infinitive   *-ing*
Example: *I want* .... *but I can't stand* ....

1. I never enjoy .... but someone persuaded me ....

....

2. I decided .... because I couldn't risk ....

....

3. I managed .... but I couldn't avoid ....

....

4. I can't imagine .... because you have to spend so much time

....

5. I offered .... but he refused ....

....

6. I don't mind .... if the others want ....

....

7. I spent four months .... but you really need ....

....

8. I wanted .... so I decided to give up ....

....

2. Now go back and complete each sentence in a way which is logical and grammatically correct. Work with a partner and then compare your answers with another pair.

Example: *I want* ..*to go to the wedding*.. *but I can't stand* ..*wearing a suit*........ .

TRUE TO LIFE INTERMEDIATE © Cambridge University Press 1996

WORKSHEET 4

How much do you know about newspapers in your country?
See how many of these questions you can answer. Work with a partner from the same country if possible.

1. How many national daily newspapers are there?

....

2. Do you have regional daily newspapers in the morning, and if so, how many are available in your region?

....

3. How many daily (and regional papers in your area) are tabloid size, and how many are broadsheet size?

....

4. Do you know which paper has the largest circulation? If so, do you know what it is?

....

5. Can you identify any of these papers as being aimed at a particular sex or age group?

....

6. How would you describe the political position of these papers? Complete the table if you can.

extreme left	moderate left	centre	moderate right	extreme right
....	....	....	....	....
....	....	....	....	....
....	....	....	....	....
....	....	....	....	....

7. Which paper do you read, if any, and why?

8. What is the general opinion of the press in your country? Would you say people have a high opinion of papers or a low opinion? Do you think this opinion has changed in the last ten years?

TRUE TO LIFE INTERMEDIATE   © Cambridge University Press 1996

WORKSHEET 5

Complete the sentences using names of people in your class. Your sentences can be true, possibly true or not true.

.... has got two older sisters.

.... likes fast cars and motorbikes.

.... is going to get married this year.

.... has spent several months abroad.

.... paints in his/her spare time.

.... can speak more than two languages.

.... is a fine singer.

.... can't cook.

.... hates getting up in the morning.

.... is the youngest in his/her family.

Tell some of your completed sentences to the class. They will tell you if each sentence:
is definitely true/not true;
is likely/unlikely to be true;
is probably/definitely (not) true;
may/might be true.

Tell them the answer, if you can! If not, ask the person whose name you wrote.

TRUE TO LIFE INTERMEDIATE © Cambridge University Press 1996

WORKSHEET 6

Get + past participle

This structure can have passive meaning (something is done to you), but it is sometimes also used for things we do to ourselves.

Look at these sentence beginnings. Do they describe something passive (done to us) or something reflexive (we do ourselves)? Write your answer at the end of the line and compare with a partner.

Examples: *He got mugged* .... *(passive)*
            He got dressed .... *(reflexive)*

1. He got bitten ....

2. He got lost ....

3. He got knocked down ....

4. He got arrested ....

5. He got changed ....

6. He got stopped ....

7. He got fined ....

8. He got stabbed ....

9. He got undressed ....

10. He got delayed ....

Now go back and finish each sentence in a logical way, and in a way that would be unlikely in any other sentence. Work with a partner and look at the examples first.

Examples: *He got mugged* *by two men who took his wallet and watch as he left the station.*
           He got dressed *and went downstairs for breakfast.*

TRUE TO LIFE INTERMEDIATE © Cambridge University Press 1996

WORKSHEET 7

Be a television critic

1. Write down the names of four or five popular TV programmes, then form groups with others who have some of the same programmes on their list. In your groups, discuss these questions for each programme:

1. Is the programme generally well-written?
2. Is it well-acted? (i.e. better than average). If not, why not?
3. Name one actor who is usually very good in this programme, and one who is below average.
4. Think about the different acting skills you discussed in the lesson in the Class Book. Which of these skills are often needed in this programme?
5. What do you feel about the general quality of acting on television in your country?

2. Report back to the rest of the class on your discussion and the main points of agreement and disagreement.

3. Agree on one programme the whole class can watch before the next lesson. Make notes on the programme, with particular reference to the first four questions in Exercise 1. You can compare your notes in the next lesson.

TRUE TO LIFE INTERMEDIATE © Cambridge University Press 1996

WORKSHEET 8

1. Read through the four situations and make sure you understand them.

A. You have just bought a brand-new board for windsurfing and you are looking forward to trying it out for the first time next month. A friend of yours has just decided to take up windsurfing, so when he learns that you have a new board, he asks you if he can borrow it next weekend. What do you say?

B. Some friends have asked you to go on holiday with them in August. You would love to go but you know that your parents have already rented a cottage in the country for the same period and they are expecting you to go with them. What do you say to your parents?

C. Last week you had a big argument with a friend because he arranged a small party at another friend's house and you invited lots of people to go. The party was not a success because neighbours complained about the noise and some things were stolen from the house.
You are now planning to go to a different party tomorrow evening, but the only way you can get there is if your friend gives you a lift in his car (you think he is going but you are not sure). What would you say to him?

D. You are planning to buy a particular second-hand car and if you don't buy it tomorrow (Saturday), it may be too late. However, you would really like your friend to accompany you as he knows much more about cars than you. He normally spends Saturdays at the local sports centre. What do you say to him?

2. Work with a partner. Decide which role you are going to play in each of the four situations, then spend time preparing what you are going to say in each one.

3. When you are ready, act out the first two situations. If you are satisfied, move on to the final situations. If you are not satisfied, practise the first two situations again before doing situations C and D.

WORKSHEET 9

Interview five people of different ages about what concerns them at this point in their lives.

I spoke to five people about the things that concerned them and their generation at this moment in their lives. Here are their responses.

NAME	AGE	CONCERNS
1.	....	....
....	....	....
2.	....	....
....	....	....
3.	....	....
....	....	....
4.	....	....
....	....	....
5.	....	....
....	....	....

Compare your results in groups. Can you summarise the responses of people at the same (or similar) age? Are their responses similar to those you listened to on the recording?

WORKSHEET 10A

ROLE CARDS

A You are going to telephone your bank (Barclays) because you want to find out if some money has been transferred to your account from your country.

The department you need is the Foreign Desk.

D You are the receptionist at a dental surgery. You are very busy, and have only one emergency appointment this afternoon at 3.30. (You have another appointment at 5.00, but only for patients who have been with the dentist for a long time.) Otherwise, you have an appointment at 5.00 tomorrow.

B You are the telephonist at Barclays Bank. The Foreign Desk is closed for lunch. They have asked you to take any messages so that they can return any calls.

Be sure to write down all the necessary information.

E You are in New York. You want two tickets for any musical on at the moment because a friend is coming to visit you from your country. You need to ring an agency to ask what tickets are available for Saturday. You don't want to spend more than $25 per ticket.

C You have toothache and your landlady has given you the phone number of her dentist. It's three o'clock and you want an appointment as soon as possible. Be sure to allow plenty of time to get there – at least 40 minutes from the end of the lesson.

F You work in a ticket agency in New York selling theatre tickets. Saturday is a really busy time, but you have got a few tickets left for *Blue Moon* ($50 per ticket) and two standing room seats for *Starlight Express* ($12 each).

WORKSHEET 10B

1. In these sentences, the verbs are mixed up. Can you make ten logical sentences by moving the verbs?

1. Do you **wear** chess?
2. Do you ever **leave** crosswords?
3. Do you usually **jump** a message on an answerphone?
4. Do you often **do** the wrong number?
5. Do you ever **use** reversed charge calls?
6. Do you often **sack** a favour of an old friend?
7. Do you sometimes **dial** employees?
8. Do you ever **play** the phone late at night?
9. Do you ever **ask** make-up?
10. Do you ever **make** out of bed in the morning?

1. ....
2. ....
3. ....
4. ....
5. ....
6. ....
7. ....
8. ....
9. ....
10. ....

2. Work in small groups. Find out how many people do the things in the corrected sentences.

WORKSHEET 11

Work alone. Think of something you own which:

is lockable	*my suitcase*	is completely silent	....
needs a licence	....	is both hard and soft	....
is complicated to use	....	gets dirty easily	....
is valuable	....	is portable	....
is unbreakable	....	is interesting to look at	....
is safe and reliable	....	can go fast	....
makes a lot of noise	....	is inflatable	....

Compare your answers in small groups. What is the most common answer in each case?

TRUE TO LIFE INTERMEDIATE © Cambridge University Press 1996

WORKSHEET 12

Look at this mind map. Try to complete it with the words from the box. (You can put words in more than one season if you wish.) Compare your answers with a partner.

> gloves   skis   shorts   mosquito spray   candles
> suntan lotion   barbecue   turn on central heating
> torch   hay fever tablets   short-sleeved shirts

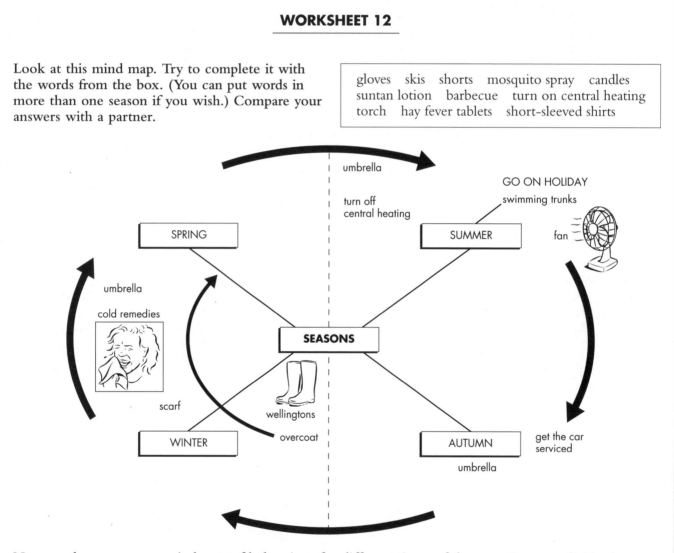

Now produce your own mind map of belongings for different times of the year. You can divide the year into two seasons, four seasons, or as many as you wish.

TRUE TO LIFE INTERMEDIATE © Cambridge University Press 1996

WORKSHEET 13

Work in groups of four. Your teacher will explain what you have to do.

1. A policeman sees a youth (about fifteen years old) running at top speed along a busy shopping street. He appears to have some kind of bag in one hand. The policeman gives chase and shouts to the boy, who takes no notice. Finally the policeman catches up with the boy and knocks him to the ground. The boy's arm is broken and his face is badly cut.

2. A policeman sees a young man in his twenties trying to open the window of a ground floor flat. The policeman approaches the man quietly and is about to speak when the young man finally gets the window open. As he disappears inside, the policeman grabs his foot; the man falls and breaks his ankle.

3. A police car, with its siren on, is driving down the wrong side of the road. A motorist coming in the opposite direction tries to avoid the police car and crashes into the back of a parked car. His car is badly damaged and he has to go to hospital suffering from concussion.

4. A plain clothes policeman (i.e. not wearing a uniform) sees a pair of vases being sold in a street market. The policeman is suspicious, quickly shows the trader his identification, then picks up the vases and asks the trader to accompany him to the police station. The trader puts his hand out to stop the policeman walking off with the vases. In the struggle, one vase falls to the ground and breaks. It is worth £400.

WORKSHEET 14

Discuss these questions in small groups.

1. Are you ever late for …
   - class?
   - meetings?
   - social events?
   - work?
   - meals?

2. In your country, how late is it acceptable to be in the situations in 1 above? For example, can you arrive one minute late for class? or five? or ten? or more?

3. In the situations below, do people often arrive late? If so, how late is acceptable?
   - You arrange to meet a close friend in a bar at 7.00 pm.
   - Someone you know well invites you for dinner at their house at 8.00 pm.
   - You book a hotel room in the capital of your country and they ask you to check in by 9.00 pm.
   - You have an informal meeting with your boss (just the two of you) at 10.00 am.
   - You arrange to go round to your brother's / sister's / close relative's for a chat at lunchtime.
   - You have a dental appointment at 4.30 pm.

4. How important is punctuality to you personally? How do you feel when other people arrange to meet you and are late?

WORKSHEET 15

1. Match the groups on the left with the people or places on the right.

a team — of spectators
a congregation — of representatives
the crew — of hooligans
a choir — of soldiers
a gang — of directors
a committee — of singers
an audience — at a church service
the staff — of a ship
a crowd — of rugby players
a regiment — of a school
a board — at a play

2. Have you ever been a member of any of these groups? Tell a partner.

3. Choose two or three of the groups and then turn back to the sentences in Exercise 2 on page 104 of your Class Book. Are these sentences *true, not true,* or *not important* for the groups you have chosen?

TRUE TO LIFE INTERMEDIATE © Cambridge University Press 1996

WORKSHEET 16

1. Read through these questions. Make sure you understand them.

1. Did you wear the same shoes yesterday?
2. Did you go to bed quite late (e.g. after midnight) last night?
3. Did you have something to eat for breakfast this morning?
4. Did you come to school by bus?
5. Did you buy a newspaper this morning?
6. Have you used the phone today?
7. Have you got angry with anyone this week?
8. Have you had your hair cut this month?
9. Do you watch much television?
10. Are you planning to go out this evening?
11. Are you usually punctual?
12. Do you enjoy learning English?
13. Does it annoy you when you get things wrong?
14. Are you normally an optimistic person?
15. Are you in a good mood today?

2. You are going to ask a partner these questions. What do you think their answers will be? Write down *yes* or *no* to each one, but do not let your partner see.

3. Now ask each other your questions. Who predicted the most answers correctly? Did anyone in the group predict all their partner's answers correctly?

4. Write five more questions of your own, then predict your partner's answers. Ask and find out if you were right.

TRUE TO LIFE INTERMEDIATE © Cambridge University Press 1996

WORKSHEET 17

You are going to design and write an advertisement for one of the following:

- the language class you are in
- the school you are studying in
- the company you work for

1. Organise yourselves into small groups of about three or four and decide what you are going to advertise.

2. Discuss and agree on the following:

- who your advertisement is to be aimed at (new learners? learners from other groups? customers?)
- where you will advertise
- what you think will attract the learners/customers
- what the text of the advertisement should say (It might include some superlative forms!)
- what kind of artwork you need (photographs? drawings? a cartoon? a sketch? a diagram?)

3. When you have decided, make a rough copy of the advertisement on a large sheet of paper. Display it to the rest of your class and see what your classmates think of it.

TRUE TO LIFE INTERMEDIATE   © Cambridge University Press 1996

WORKSHEET 18

Read the dialogues then complete the statements below in reported speech.

1.
PAUL: I'm just going out for half an hour.
JANE: You can't. Mary is going to phone at seven.
PAUL: No. She rang me earlier. It's OK.
JANE: Well, in that case, I'll come with you.

Paul said he ....

Jane replied that he .... because ....

But Paul said that Mary .... , so it .... OK.

Jane said in that case she .... ,.... .

2.
JIM: I've finished.
SUE: Good. I'll check it in a minute. I have to finish some filing first.
JIM: I can do that for you.
SUE: No, I want to do it myself actually so I'll know where everything is.

Jim told Sue that he ....

Sue said she .... because first she ....

....

Jim said he .... , but

Sue replied that she .... so she

....

3.
SAM: I've lost my gloves.
PAM: They're in the cupboard.
SAM: No, they aren't. I've already looked there.
PAM: I saw them in the cupboard this morning.
SAM: OK. I'll have another look.

Sam said he ....

Pam said they ....

Sam said they .... because he ....

Pam replied that she .... , so

Sam said he ....

TRUE TO LIFE INTERMEDIATE © Cambridge University Press 1996

WORKSHEET 19

Work in small groups. Take turns to find pairs of words that are connected in some way. Cross out each word as you make a connection.

Example: *You can **fill in** an **application form**.*

fill in	concise	leaflet	blush
confusing	clear	referee	document
should	reduce	refund	increase
certificate	application form	straightforward	applicant
curriculum vitae	long-winded	employer	ought to
embarrassed	qualification	complicated	be entitled

Continue until you have found connections for all the words.

TRUE TO LIFE INTERMEDIATE   © Cambridge University Press 1996

WORKSHEET 20

Class art gallery

Instructions

1. Find a postcard or copy of a drawing or painting that you like very much. It can be a painting by a famous artist or someone you know, or even your own painting/drawing. Bring it to class.

2. Put your picture at the top of a large sheet of paper, and write a short paragraph about the picture. Include any of the following information:
   - the name of the artist
   - the title of the painting
   - the date it was painted
   - the context of the painting, and what you feel it represents/illustrates

Don't write your own opinion of the painting yet.

3. Now circulate your painting. Let other people write their opinions of it underneath your paragraph. These opinions should be short – a sentence, or a phrase. When your teacher tells you that 6–8 people have written comments on your picture, take it back and read them. If you like, talk to the people about their comments.

4. Put your picture and the comments on the wall and then look at other people's pictures and comments.

TRUE TO LIFE INTERMEDIATE   © Cambridge University Press 1996

WORKSHEET 21

1. In conversation it is quite common for the speaker to provide the first part of a conditional sentence, then the listener, predicting the second part, finishes the sentence. Look at these examples:

A: *It was a pity because if I'd won that point in the fifth game …*
B: *You might've won the match.*
A: *Yes, maybe.*

C: *If I'd known about the party …*
D: *You would've gone.*
C: *Yes, definitely.*

Now complete these short dialogues in a similar way:

1. A: If I'd got to the station five minutes earlier …

    B: ....

    A: ....

2. A: If I'd worked a bit harder …

    B: ....

    A: ....

3. A: If I'd known they were coming this evening …

    B: ....

    A: ....

4. A: If I'd phoned the restaurant last week …

    B: ....

    A: ....

5. A: If I'd taken a map with me …

    B: ....

    A: ....

6. A: If I hadn't gone to the bank yesterday …

    B: ....

    A: ....

2. Practise the dialogues with a partner. Read the first line, then listen to your partner's answer, then be prepared to respond to their answer. Repeat with your partner reading the first line, so you can give your replies. Are the two dialogues similar? Are they both logical?

TRUE TO LIFE INTERMEDIATE © Cambridge University Press 1996

1. Do you notice anything strange or unusual about the room in the picture? If so, what explanation could there be for it? Discuss with a partner.

2. Now read about the woman in the picture, and discuss the questions below in groups.

'I'm currently concentrating on my relationships corner,' says Gina Lazenby. 'I've hung two small mirrors upstairs and I'm trying to bring more "paired energy" into the house.' She believes that arranging ornaments in a certain way will lead to the arrival of a new man in her life.

Gina is not stupid – she has created her own successful marketing consultancy – but is a devotee of *feng shui*, an ancient Chinese philosophy which has been practised for over 3,000 years. According to *feng shui*, the organisation of one's home, office and possessions along certain sacred principles can produce health, wealth and domestic harmony. 'It's like acupuncture for the home,' says Gina. But rather than needles, a *feng shui* master uses mirrors, plants, wind-chimes and pictures – objects which have an energising effect on the area around you. And Gina's own home is a model of good *feng shui*. The open plan living room has a wall of mirror (in her 'inner knowledge area'), and reverberates with music ranging from Mozart to bird song.

Feng shui also advocates a harmonious blend of shapes and colours, and so Gina softened the sharp angles in her room by introducing the natural curves of bananas (in the painting), and natural objects such as stones and driftwood. The harsh scheme of black and white was also softened with the introduction of a yellow wall.

1. You learned various things about *feng shui* in the lesson in your Class Book. Does this text introduce any new information If so, what?
2. Do you think Gina's comparison of acupuncture with *feng shui* is reasonable? If not, why not?
3. Based on the information in the text, would you say your own living room is an example of good or bad *feng shui*?

TRUE TO LIFE INTERMEDIATE © Cambridge University Press 1996

TESTS

1 Grammar: tense review   15 marks

Underline the correct verb form in brackets.

1. I think it (*is raining/will rain*) this evening.
2. I can't come today because I (*will meet/am meeting*) Paul for lunch.
3. They (*build/are building*) a new motorway outside town.
4. I don't think people (*will play/are playing*) records in ten years' time.
5. A: Can I see you after work?
   B: OK. I (*meet/will meet*) you at six o'clock.
6. What (did you do/have you done) at the weekend?
7. I (*didn't see /haven't seen*) him for two weeks.
8. I (*wrote/have written*) to my sister a few days ago.
9. A: How long (*did you work/have you worked*) there?
   B: It's almost three years now.
10. I (*visited/have visited*) my relatives in India three times, and I'm planning to go again next year.
11. I (*cut/was cutting*) my finger when I was slicing the oranges.
12. When I (*arrived/was arriving*) Paul and Jean (*played/were playing*) cards.
13. When I (*saw/have seen*) Tim yesterday, he (*prepared/was preparing*) his speech for this evening.

2 Verb/adjective + preposition   10 marks

Fill the gaps with the correct preposition.

1. She's not very keen .... it.
2. I'm afraid .... spiders.
3. The magazine is aimed .... teenagers.
4. You can't rely .... the buses.
5. They're not interested .... sightseeing.
6. I feel I can talk .... her and trust her.
7. She never confides .... me.
8. We can cope .... it, I'm sure.
9. He gets on very well .... his brother.
10. I suffer .... hay fever in the summer.

3 Grammar: uncountable nouns   5 marks

Tick (✓) the uncountable nouns in this list.

bomb	luggage	machine	toy
weather	advice	cough	traffic
hammer	equipment		

4 Vocabulary: verb + noun collocations   10 marks

Write down a noun that can follow these verbs.

1. turn on ....
2. fasten ....
3. lock ....
4. do up ....
5. plug in ....
6. pack ....
7. wrap up ....
8. commit ....
9. load ....
10. light ....

5 Pronunciation: word stress   10 marks

Put the words into the correct column on the right according to the main stress.

		1st syllable	2nd syllable
Japan	Arabic	....	....
advantage	necessary	....	....
reliable	industry	....	....
decide	policeman	....	....
interesting	comfortable	....	....

6 Vocabulary and paraphrase   10 marks

Fill the gaps in the definitions or answers with a suitable word or expression.

1. It means the same as *awful*.
   Answer: ....
2. It's the opposite of ....
   Answer: improve
3. It's a .... of .... game.
   Answer: chess
4. It's the place where you borrow books.
   Answer: ....
5. It's the .... you use for .... a door.
   Answer: key
6. It's the .... you use to wash your face.
   Answer: soap
7. It's someone who .... buildings.
   Answer: architect
8. It's the opposite of *whisper*.
   Answer: ....

7 Grammar: –ing form or infinitive?   10 marks

Put *doing* or *to do* after each verb.

can't stand ....

manage ....

avoid ....

refuse ....

enjoy ....

want ....

promise ....

imagine ....

spend time ....

persuade someone ....

8 Vocabulary: topic groups   10 marks

Organise the words in the box into four groups and give each group a title.

| headline niece stage drugs actress play |
| only child cancer treatment cousin editor |
| performance relative tabloid suffer article |

1. ....   3. ....

....

....

....

2. ....   4. ....

....

....

9 Pronunciation: sounds   5 marks

Tick (✔) the odd one out in each group based on the pronunciation of the underlined letters.

1. shock<u>ed</u>   delight<u>ed</u>   embarrass<u>ed</u>   watch<u>ed</u>
2. n<u>ow</u>adays   d<u>ou</u>bt   c<u>ou</u>ntable   c<u>ou</u>gh
3. c<u>a</u>reer   m<u>a</u>chine   Br<u>a</u>zil   m<u>a</u>gazine
4. scr<u>ea</u>m   h<u>ea</u>lth   w<u>ea</u>ther   d<u>ea</u>th
5. c<u>o</u>mplain   c<u>o</u>mplicated   c<u>o</u>mpare   c<u>o</u>mpetitive

10 Vocabulary: synonyms and opposites   10 marks

Match words from the two boxes to form five pairs of synonyms and five pairs of opposites.

| simple loud |
| great give up |
| anxious temporary |
| delighted love |
| terrified reveal |

| terrific can't stand |
| worried show stop |
| disappointed |
| permanent quiet |
| scared stiff |
| complicated |

11 Probability and possibility   5 marks

Complete these sentences with a suitable word.

1. It is .... true because I looked it up in the dictionary.
2. I'm not 100% sure but I think he's .... to be there.
3. It's possible but I .... if it's true.
4. I really don't know, but it .... be true.
5. I don't know for certain that it's false but I think it's very .... to be true.

Total = 100 marks

TEST 2 UNITS 7–11

1 Grammar: obligation and prohibition   10 marks

Fill the gaps with one of these: *have to, had to, don't have to, didn't have to, are(n't) allowed to, were(n't) allowed to.*

1. In my English class we .... speak our first language. If we do, the teacher gets quite angry.
2. When I was in the army we .... get up at 6.30.
3. When I was at school the girls .... wear make-up until they were 16.
4. In many jobs you .... wear a tie, but it is necessary in my job.
5. When I was at school we .... wear a uniform, so I could wear what I liked.
6. The teacher gives us homework most days but we .... do it if we are very busy doing other things.
7. My boss is very strict but we .... take off our jackets and ties on hot days.
8. If you want to smoke, you .... go outside. I'm afraid you .... smoke in any part of this building.
9. In my first job I .... work seven days a week when we were very busy, but I still enjoyed it.

2 Grammar/vocabulary: correct the mistakes   10 marks

Correct the mistake in each of the sentences.

1. I have studied economic.
2. A: Where have you been?
   B: I went to see my hairdresser to cut my hair.
3. She made a course in word processing.
4. The last shop what I visited was closed.
5. She did very bad in her exam.
6. I explained him we were busy.
7. Lorry drivers haven't to be creative.
8. He told him go away.
9. The money is not very good. On the other side, the holidays are very good and you get a company car.
10. I must wake up him now.

3 Vocabulary: synonyms   10 marks

Find words in the box on the right that can be synonyms for the words on the left.

| install   apologise |
| dismiss   get worse |
| chat   wait |
| hostile   call |
| child   expected to |

| aggressive   sack |
| conversation   ring |
| deteriorate   fit |
| supposed to   kid |
| say sorry   hang on |

4 Vocabulary: verb + noun collocation   10 marks

Which noun on the right often follows the verb on the left?

solve	an agreement
reach	a hobby
go	a problem
fail	the drinks
take up	in an election
vote	a course
pour	on holiday
apologise	a colleague
do	for a mistake
consult	an exam

5 Pronunciation: word stress   10 marks

Put the words in the correct column according to the main stress.

	1st syllable	2nd syllable	3rd syllable
economist			
organise			
agriculture			
manager			
financial			
obligation			
electronics			
computer			
politician			
politics			

6 Functional language   5 marks

Underline the correct words in the brackets.

1. I'm afraid (*that she's busy*/*but she's busy*).
2. Would it be possible (*that you*/*for you to*) help him?
3. I'd be (*grateful*/*pleased*) if you could send it to me.
4. I'm afraid that's out of the (*question*/*discussion*).
5. (*Do you mind*/*Is OK*) if I open the window?

7 Vocabulary: word building   10 marks

Complete each sentence with the correct form of the word on the right.

1. We'll find a ....   solve
2. The company has become very
   ....   profit
3. He wants to become a
   ....   psychology
4. Why did he ....
   for the job?   application
5. The tablets are ...., so
   you can take quite a few.   harm
6. That toy is safe because it is
   ....   break
7. The strap on this bag is
   ....   adjust
8. I lived in France during part of my
   ....   child
9. What plans does he have for his
   ....?   retire
10. I got .... from my
    boss.   permit

8 Vocabulary: topic groups   10 marks

Organise the words into four groups and give each one a title

| adolescent   exam   colleague   bride |
| early twenties   headquarters   subject   adult |
| degree   budget   ceremony   appointment |
| retirement   reception   certificate   honeymoon |

1. ....   3. ....

2. ....   4. ....

9 Grammar: would *and/or* used to   5 marks

Can you use *would* **and** *used to* in these sentences, or just *used to*? Underline the correct answer.

1. When I was a boy in Canada we (*would/used to*) build snowmen in the garden and then paint them.
2. I (*would/used to*) be much fatter when I was younger.
3. My father (*would/used to*) bring us back presents from his business trips, and we had to guess where he had been.
4. In my teens, I (*would/used to*) have long hair and I had lots of arguments with my parents about it.
5. This place (*would/used to*) be very quiet until it was discovered by tourists.

10 Vocabulary: verbs and nouns   20 marks

Write ten logical sentences using suitable nouns and verbs from the two boxes. (Remember to put the verbs into the correct form.) You cannot use each word more than once.

| hair eyes film |
| present phone |
| portrait car suit |
| shopping skirt |

| install service |
| cut make paint |
| gift-wrap test deliver |
| develop shorten |

1. I want to have a/my ....
2. I want to have a/my ....
3. I want to have a/my ....
4. I want to have a/my ....
5. I want to have a/my ....
6. I want to have a/my ....
7. I want to have a/my ....
8. I want to have a/my ....
9. I want to have a/my ....
10. I want to have a/my ....

Total = 100 marks

TEST 3 UNITS 12–17

1 Vocabulary: compound nouns   10 marks

Match words from the two columns to create ten compound nouns.

electric	pool
sleeping	alarm
classical	holiday
package	juice
burglar	bag
leisure	site
swimming	centre
baby	music
fruit	sitter
camp	fan

2 Grammar: tense review   11 marks

Underline the correct word or words in brackets.

1. I (*have known/have been knowing*) him for five years.
2. A: You look hot.
   B: Yes, I (*have run/have been running*).
3. She (*has lived/has been living*) there for about six months.
4. I (*have read/have been reading*) your new book. It's fascinating, and I can't wait to find out what happens at the end.
5. A: There's about 10 centimetres of snow on the ground.
   B: Yes, I know. It (*has snowed/has been snowing*) for over an hour.
6. I (*haven't been/hadn't been*) there before last year.
7. We (*sat down/had sat down*) and had a drink.
8. When we got there I realised I (*left/had left*) my books on the bus.
9. I (*enjoyed/had enjoyed*) the film last night but Mary (*saw/had seen*) it before.
10. I wish I (*have/had*) enough money for a new car.

3 Vocabulary: containers and contents   5 marks

Choose the most likely container on the right for the contents on the left.

a .... of cola
a .... of water
a .... of toothpaste
a .... of marmalade
a .... of juice

| carton jar |
| tube can |
| bucket |

4 Functional language: excuses and reassurance

12 marks

Complete each gap with a suitable word or phrase.

1. A: I'm sorry .... late.
   B: That's OK. .... mind.
2. A: The bus .... down on my way to work.
   B: That's OK. Don't ....
3. A: I got .... up in the traffic.
   B: That's OK. It doesn't ....
4. My alarm clock didn't .... , so I .... As a result, I was half an hour late for work.
5. I'm really sorry but I got off the bus at the wrong .... , and then I had to ask someone the ....
6. I can't help just at the moment because I'm .... a phone call.
7. I wish I .... help, but I'm afraid it's impossible at the moment.

5 Grammar: verb patterns   10 marks

Complete each sentence with *go*, *to go*, or preposition + *going*. (If the answer is preposition + *going*, write the correct preposition.)

1. He promised ....
2. He made us ....
3. He thanked me ....
4. He prevented me ....
5. He agreed ....
6. He refused ....
7. He let me ....
8. He blamed me ....
9. He offered ....
10. He threatened ....

6 Vocabulary: topic groups   10 marks

Organise the words in the box into four groups and give each group a title.

```
drizzle  jury  balcony  lake  lightning
mountain  cave  judge  basement  cellar  sleet
hurricane  sentence  witness  attic  rockface
```

1. ....   3. ....
   ....
   ....
   ....
   ....

2. ....   4. ....
   ....
   ....
   ....
   ....

7 Grammar: conditionals   5 marks

Underline the correct answer or answers.

1. If we had more time, it .... a difference.
   a) will make   b) would make   c) might make
2. If we ...., we'll get there.
   a) hurry   b) will hurry   c) would hurry
3. I would spend the money if I ....
   a) win   b) will win   c) won
4. If I work hard, I ....
   a) will pass   b) would pass   c) may pass
5. I'm sure that she .... if you explain it in French.
   a) doesn't understand   b) won't understand
   c) wouldn't understand

8 Pronunciation: sounds   5 marks

Circle the odd one out based on the pronunciation of the underlined letters.

1. c<u>o</u>ver   d<u>o</u>zen   c<u>o</u>mb   c<u>o</u>mpany
2. fl<u>oo</u>d   typh<u>oo</u>n   f<u>oo</u>d   p<u>oo</u>l
3. fr<u>ui</u>t   j<u>ui</u>ce   gl<u>ue</u>   m<u>u</u>stard
4. dr<u>u</u>g   t<u>u</u>be   p<u>u</u>nish   j<u>u</u>dge
5. thr<u>ough</u>   c<u>ou</u>ple   r<u>ough</u>ly   t<u>ough</u>

9 Vocabulary: opposites   10 marks

Write the opposite of these words. In some cases you need a prefix and in others a different word.

Examples: good   opposite = bad
           friendly   opposite = unfriendly

```
honest  innocent  chilly  boil  similar to
satisfied  obedient  reduce  almost always
roughly
```

10 Vocabulary: very and absolutely   4 marks

Can you use *very* or *absolutely* before each of these adjectives?

.... tired   .... unbelievable
.... enormous   .... dreadful
.... useful   .... angry
.... exhausted   .... useless

11 Vocabulary   8 marks

Complete each sentence with the correct word.

1. Why don't we get .... of these records? We never play them.
2. The two boys look very similar, ... that Paul has slightly darker hair than Michael.
3. There is a bus .... tomorrow, so there will be no buses.
4. I .... the room and it is 3 meters by 5 meters.
5. I was parked illegally and I had to pay a £50 ....
6. She couldn't swim, so he had to .... off the cliff and into the lake and rescue her
7. It really annoys me when people drop .... in the street. Why can't they put it in the bins where it belongs?
8. I like Joe but unfortunately we have nothing in ....

12 Pronunciation: word stress 10 marks

Put the words in the correct column based on the main stress.

	1st syllable	2nd syllable	3rd syllable
advertisement	....	....	....
facilities	....	....	....
mystery	....	....	....
unbelievable	....	....	....
criminal	....	....	....
entertainment	....	....	....
reduction	....	....	....
insurance	....	....	....
education	....	....	....
compromise	....	....	....

Total = 100 marks

TEST 4 UNITS 18–22

1 Grammar: reported speech 8 marks

Report these statements and questions.

1. 'I'm going to the dentist.'
   She said she ....
2. 'I'll help you.'
   She said she ....
3. 'I've seen him.'
   She said she ....
4. 'I lost it.'
   She said she ....
5. 'Did you win?'
   She asked me ....
6. 'When are you leaving?'
   She asked me ....
7. 'Do you often stay there?'
   She asked me ....
8. 'Why did you stop?'
   She asked me ....

2 Vocabulary: adjectives 5 marks

Complete the sentences with adjectives from the box.

serious   sore   strict   strong   steep

1. I think I'm getting a .... throat.
2. She had a .... accident in her car.
3. We had to climb a .... rockface.
4. My parents were very .... with me when I was a child.
5. I couldn't swim far because the current was too ....

3 Grammar and vocabulary: reporting verbs 8 marks

Using the verbs in the box, report the sentences below.

tell   promise   refuse   admit

1. 'I will not do it.'
   He ....
2. 'Leave a message on the answerphone.'
   He ....
3. 'I broke the vase.'
   He ....
4. 'I'll bring it back this evening.'
   He ....

4 Vocabulary: opposites 6 marks

Find six pairs of opposites from the two boxes.

boring thrilled poor straightforward concise clear	stimulating wealthy disappointed long–winded confusing complicated

5 Grammar: conditionals 10 marks

Put the verbs in brackets into the correct form.

1. If I (get) home by 6 pm, I (give) you a ring.
2. If I (have) more free time, I (learn) another language. Unfortunately, I'm too busy.
3. If we (stay) at the party a bit longer yesterday, we (see) Tom.
4. Come on, Julia. If we (not go) now, we (be) late.
5. She failed most of her exams, but if she (work) harder, she (pass).

6 Grammar: passives and tense revision 15 marks

Put the verbs in brackets into the correct tense and in the correct active or passive form.

1. The accident (report) at 10.20 pm and the ambulance (arrive) within six minutes. The driver of the car (be) in a bad way, so he (take) to hospital where he (have) an emergency operation. Later, a spokesman for the hospital (say) the man (do) well but was still in a serious condition.
2. A: Where are the new books?
   B: They (not arrive) yet.
   A: What! I (order) them weeks ago.
   B: Yes, I know. Unfortunately the books (delay) because of staff shortages at the warehouse, and then they (send) to the wrong address. I (speak) to the bookshop and they (be) very sorry. Anyway, a new lot of books (send) tomorrow and should arrive by Thursday. If not, I (telephone) them again and complain to the manager.

7 Vocabulary: collocation   6 marks

Match the verbs on the left with the nouns on the right.

bite   the truth
climb   an operation
relieve   your nails
have   the pain
make   some rocks
tell   a speech

8 Pronunciation: sounds and spelling   10 marks

Look carefully at the underlined letters in these words. Find a word on the left with the same sound as a word on the right and form ten pairs.

r<u>io</u>t s<u>u</u>ccess
<u>ough</u>t to g<u>oo</u>d
r<u>ow</u> (= argument)
v<u>a</u>se b<u>o</u>ss s<u>a</u>vings
fl<u>oo</u>d f<u>a</u>mine

dr<u>ough</u>t j<u>u</u>stice
tr<u>iu</u>mph w<u>a</u>tch
infl<u>a</u>tion dis<u>a</u>ster
c<u>a</u>mpaign c<u>o</u>rrect
c<u>augh</u>t underst<u>oo</u>d

9 Vocabulary: verb forms   6 marks

Complete the table on the right for these verbs

	past tense	past participle
bite	....	....
sting	....	....
wear	....	....
draw	....	....
feel	....	....
shake	....	....

10 Vocabulary: topic groups   10 marks

Organise these words into four groups and give each one a title.

lizard   exhibition   sweat   trade union   dispute painter   shake   stammer   snake   gallery sculpture   squirrel   mosquito   election   blush redundancy

1. ....   3. ....
   ....
   ....
   ....
   ....
2. ....   4. ....
   ....
   ....
   ....
   ....

11 Grammar and vocabulary: mistakes   8 marks

Correct the mistakes in each of these sentences.
1. We had better to go.
2. We'll be late unless we don't go now.
3. I'm not used to get up early.
4. I can't concentrate in my work at the moment.
5. We should have went earlier.
6. I wanted to avoid to go there.
7. He said me he was busy.
8. It was a beautiful scenery.

12 Vocabulary: word building   8 marks

Complete each sentence with the correct form of the word on the right.

1. It's a very .... area.   industry
2. Pronunciation is my main

   ....   weak
3. I like her ....   draw
4. He didn't have the ....

   to lift it.   strong
5. I think .... is a major

   cause of crime.   poor
6. Are they going to ....

   the match?   television
7. The two brothers worked hard all their

   lives, but unfortunately they were both

   ....   success
8. .... doesn't always

   increase with age.   wise

Total = 100 marks

TEST ANSWER KEYS

1 Grammar: tense review

1. will rain   2. am meeting   3. are building   4. will play
5. will meet   6. did you do   7. haven't seen   8. wrote
9. have you worked   10. have visited   11. cut
12. arrived; were playing   13. saw; was preparing

2 Verb/adjective + preposition

1. on   2. of   3. at   4. on   5. in   6. to   7. in   8. with
9. with   10. from

3 Grammar: uncountable nouns

luggage; weather; advice; traffic; equipment

4 Vocabulary: verb + noun collocations

Possible answers
1. a TV, a radio, a light, a video
2. a seatbelt
3. a door, a suitcase
4. a shirt, a jacket, a coat
5. the TV, the washing machine, the food mixer
6. a suitcase
7. a present
8. a crime, murder
9. a car, a lorry, a van
10. a fire, a cigarette

5 Pronunciation: word stress

1st syllable: interesting, Arabic, necessary, industry. comfortable
2nd syllable: Japan, advantage, reliable, decide, policeman

6 Vocabulary and paraphrase

1. terrible   2. get worse   3. kind/type/sort; board
4. library   5. thing; locking   6. stuff   7. designs
8. shout/yell

7 Grammar: -ing form or infinitive?

-ing form: can't stand, enjoy, avoid, imagine, spend time
infinitive: manage, refuse, want, promise, persuade someone

8 Vocabulary: topic groups

NEWSPAPERS	FAMILIES	THEATRE	ILLNESS
headline	niece	stage	drugs
editor	only child	actress	cancer
tabloid	cousin	performance	suffer
article	relative	play	treatment

9 Pronunciation: sounds

1. delighted   2. cough   3. magazine   4. scream
5. complicated

10 Vocabulary: synonyms and opposites

SYNONYMS	OPPOSITES
great – terrific	simple – complicated
give up – stop	loud – quiet
anxious – worried	temporary – permanent
terrified – scared stiff	delighted – disappointed
reveal – show	love – can't stand

11 Probability and possibility

1. definitely   2. likely   3. doubt   4. may/might/could
5. unlikely

1 Grammar: obligation and prohibition

1. aren't allowed to   6. don't have to
2. had to   7. are allowed to
3. weren't allowed to   8. have to; aren't allowed to
4. don't have to   9. had to
5. didn't have to

2 Grammar/vocabulary: correct the mistakes

1. I have studied economics.
2. A: Where have you been?
   B: I went to see my hairdresser to have my hair cut.
3. She did a course in word processing.
4. The last shop I visited was closed.
5. She did very badly in her exam.
6. I explained (to him) we were busy.
7. Lorry drivers don't have to be creative.
8. He told him to go away.
9. The money is not very good. On the other hand, the holidays are very good and you get a company car.
10. I must wake him up now.

3 Vocabulary: synonyms

install – fit
apologise – say sorry
dismiss – sack
get worse – deteriorate
chat – conversation
wait – hang on
hostile – aggressive
call – ring
child – kid
expected to – supposed to

4 Vocabulary: verb + noun collocation

solve a problem   vote in an election
reach an agreement   pour the drinks
go on holiday   apologise for a mistake
fail an exam   do a course
take up a hobby   consult a colleague

5 Pronunciation: word stress

1st syllable	2nd syllable	3rd syllable
organise	economist	obligation
agriculture	financial	electronics
manager	computer	politician
politics		

6 Functional language

1. I'm afraid that she's busy.
2. Would it be possible for you to help him?
3. I'd be grateful if you could send it to me.
4. I'm afraid that's out of the question.
5. Do you mind if I open the window?

7 Vocabulary: word building

1. solution   2. profitable   3. psychologist   4. apply
5. harmless   6. unbreakable   7. adjustable   8. childhood
9. retirement   10. permission

8 Vocabulary: topic groups

STAGES IN LIFE	WEDDINGS	WORK	EDUCATION
adolescent	bride	budget	certificate
early twenties	honeymoon	colleague	degree
retirement	reception	appointment	subject
adult	ceremony	headquarters	exams

9 Grammar: would and/or used to

1. would/used to   2. used to   3. would/used to
4. used to   5. used to

10 Vocabulary: verbs and nouns

1. I want to have my hair cut.
2. I want to have my eyes tested.
3. I want to have a/my film developed.
4. I want to have a/my present gift-wrapped.
5. I want to have a phone installed.
6. I want to have my portrait painted.
7. I want to have my car serviced.
8. I want to have a suit made.
9. I want to have my shopping delivered.
10. I want to have my skirt shortened.

TEST 3

1 Vocabulary: compound nouns

electric fan   leisure centre
sleeping bag   swimming pool
classical music   babysitter
package holiday   fruit juice
burglar alarm   campsite

2 Grammar: tense review

1. have known
2. have been running
3. has lived/has been living (both answers are possible here)
4. have been reading
5. has been snowing
6. hadn't been
7. sat down
8. had left
9. enjoyed; had seen
10. had

3 Vocabulary: containers and contents

a can of cola   a bucket of water   a tube of toothpaste
a jar of marmalade   a carton of juice

4 Functional language: excuses and reassurance

1. A: I'm sorry **I'm** late.
   B: That's OK. **Never** mind.
2. A: The bus **broke** down on my way to work.
   B: That's OK. Don't **worry**.
3. A: I got **held** up in the traffic.
   B: That's OK. It doesn't **matter**.
4. My alarm didn't **go off**, so I **overslept**.
5. I got off the bus at the wrong **stop**, and then I had to ask someone the **way**.
6. I'm **expecting** / **waiting for** a phone call.
7. I wish I **could** help.

5 Grammar: verb patterns

1. He promised to go.
2. He made us go.
3. He thanked me for going.
4. He prevented me from going.
5. He agreed to go.
6. He refused to go.
7. He let me go.
8. He blamed me for going.
9. He offered to go.
10. He threatened to go.

6 Vocabulary: topic groups

WEATHER	COURT	PARTS OF A HOUSE	GEOGRAPHY
drizzle	jury	balcony	lake
lightning	judge	basement	mountain
sleet	sentence	cellar	cave
hurricane	witness	attic	rockface

7 Grammar: conditionals

1. b and c   2. a   3. c   4. a and c   5. b

8 Pronunciation: sounds

1. comb   2. flood   3. mustard   4. tube   5. through

9 Vocabulary: opposites

honest – dishonest
innocent – guilty
chilly – warm or hot
boil – freeze
similar to – different from
satisfied – dissatisfied
obedient – disobedient
reduce – increase
almost always – hardly ever or rarely
roughly – exactly (or gently/smoothly)

10 Vocabulary: **very** and **absolutely**

very: tired, useful, angry
absolutely: enormous, exhausted, unbelievable, dreadful, useless

11 Vocabulary

1. get rid of   2. except that   3. strike   4. measured
5. fine   6. dive or jump   7. litter   8. common

12 Pronunciation: word stress

1st syllable	2nd syllable	3rd syllable
mystery	advertisement	unbelievable
criminal	facilities	entertainment
compromise	reduction	education
	insurance	

TEST 4

1 Grammar: reported speech

1. She said she was going to the dentist.
2. She said she would help him.
3. She said she had seen him.
4. She said she had lost it.
5. She asked me if I had won.
6. She asked me when I was leaving.
7. She asked me if I often stayed there.
8. She asked me why I had stopped.

2 Vocabulary: adjectives

1. sore throat   2. serious accident   3. steep rockface
4. strict 5. strong

3 Grammar and vocabulary: reporting verbs

1. He refused to do it.
2. He told me to leave a message on the answerphone.
3. He admitted breaking the vase.
4. He promised to bring it back this evening.

4 Vocabulary: opposites

boring – stimulating
thrilled – disappointed
poor – wealthy
straightforward – complicated
concise – long-winded
clear – confusing

5 Grammar: conditionals

1. If I get home by 6 pm, I'll give you a ring.
2. If I had more free time, I would learn another language. Unfortunately, I'm too busy.
3. If we had stayed at the party a bit longer yesterday, we would've seen Tom.
4. Come on, Julia. If we don't go now, we'll be late.
5. She failed most of her exams, but if she had worked harder, she would've passed.

6 Grammar: passives and tense revision

1. was reported; arrived; was; was taken; had; said; was doing
2. haven't arrived; ordered; were delayed; were sent; spoke; were; will be sent/is being sent; will telephone

7 Vocabulary: collocation

bite your nails   climb some rocks   relieve the pain
have an operation   make a speech   tell the truth

8 Pronunciation: sounds and spelling

r<u>io</u>t – tr<u>iu</u>mph   v<u>a</u>se – dis<u>a</u>ster
s<u>u</u>ccess – c<u>o</u>rrect   b<u>o</u>ss – w<u>a</u>tch
<u>ough</u>t to – c<u>augh</u>t   s<u>a</u>vings – infl<u>a</u>tion
g<u>oo</u>d – underst<u>oo</u>d   fl<u>oo</u>d – j<u>u</u>stice
r<u>ow</u> (= argument) – dr<u>ough</u>t   f<u>a</u>mine – c<u>a</u>mpaign

9 Vocabulary: verb forms

bite: bit, bitten
sting: stung, stung
wear: wore, worn
draw: drew, drawn
feel: felt, felt
shake: shook, shaken

10 Vocabulary: topic groups

LIVING THINGS (animals, insects, reptiles): lizard, snake, squirrel, mosquito
ART: exhibition, painter, gallery, sculpture
INDUSTRIAL RELATIONS/POLITICS: trade union, dispute, election, redundancy,
PHYSICAL RESPONSES: sweat, shake, stammer, blush

11 Grammar and vocabulary: mistakes

1. We had better go.
2. We'll be late unless we go now. (or: We'll be late if we don't go now.)
3. I'm not used to getting up early.
4. I can't concentrate on my work at the moment.
5. We should have gone earlier.
6. I wanted to avoid going there.
7. He said he was busy. (or: He told me he was busy.)
8. It was beautiful scenery.

12 Vocabulary: word building

1. industrial   2. weakness   3. drawings   4. strength
5. poverty   6. televise   7. unsuccessful   8. wisdom

TAPESCRIPTS

UNIT 1 LOOKING BACK AND LOOKING FORWARD

I CAN VAGUELY REMEMBER ...

Exercise 3

Version 1

1.

LYNDHAM: When I first started to drive a car, I didn't have any idea how difficult it was going to be to keep the car on the road, so, er, we started moving off. My instructor was sitting beside me. Er, I had to use my hands to turn the steering wheel; then I had to use another hand to change gear. I also had to use both my feet, er, to change gear and tó accelerate the car forward. Um, I suddenly realised that I could perhaps control my feet at once, but not also move my hands at the same time, and look, er, in front of me to see where the car was going. We moved about three feet before I stalled the car and we stopped.

2.

JULIET: My first kiss happened when I was eight. I was at a party, and there was one particular boy who I was very fond of, and he of me. His name was Lee Portnoy. And, er, he, um, he'd been sort of making advances towards me in the way that 7 year olds do, and, er, finally I succumbed. And he pressed his mouth up against mine very hard, um, and he kissed me very, very hard, and I didn't really enjoy it at all. I thought, 'Is this all it is?'

Version 2

1.

WILLIE: The first room I ever lived in after I left school was in London, and I remember moving in, and my room was on the second floor. And the landlord lived downstairs. And on the first day, I brought in all my stuff, including a great big barrel of homemade beer, which I put in the middle of the floor.

And about a week later, the landlord started complaining that there were stains appearing in his ceiling. And was I aware that something was leaking? I said I wasn't, forgetting entirely about the beer. And it was only a few weeks later, when I went to pour the first pint of beer, after it had brewed for a month or so, that I picked it up and realised that the barrel was entirely empty and that 40 pints of beer had drained out into the landlord's ceiling.

2.

JULIA: Well, I can remember the night before my first day at primary school being really, really excited, and I had my little bag with my pumps in all ready to go; and my mum had sewn little name tapes into all my clothes, and my best friend Sarah Williams and I just could hardly wait.

And I remember in the morning, we got on the bus and got to school, and it just seemed massive, the whole school seemed huge. And we had little pegs to put our coats on, and our little pump bags and we had our little bottles of milk; and it was all really fantastically exciting.

But the best thing that Sarah and I thought, was that on the way back, we were going to go on the top of the double decker bus, which we were never usually allowed to do. And so we just scurried up the stairs, got on the top deck, and as soon as the bus pulled into the bus stop, I fell down all the stairs, like a little ball, rolling down to the bottom deck, and then cried and refused to go to school the next day.

Exercise 4

1.

Erm, I suppose the main way I revise the German I learn at night school is, is by going through the work I do each evening and just having another look at it; for example, er, I might go through the grammar exercises, um, where I've filled in all the answers and I might rub them out, and then try doing them all again on my own without any help, um, and then other times, just when I'm walking around, for example, I'll just say things, um, out loud to myself but in German, um, and imagine that I'm actually in Germany. So if I go into a shop and buy, I don't know, a loaf of bread, I'll do it in English, and then I'll do that again in my head afterwards in German. Erm, sometimes I actually get a book out and, and read from the book out loud, er, in German. Er, I, one thing I do sometimes late, late at night, if I'm trying to go to sleep, is to go through my vocabulary – any new words that I've learnt and I just, um, I just say fifty of them, for example, and that helps me remember the German and helps me to get to sleep. Erm, the only other thing I do is sometimes I tape the lessons. I use a little tape recorder and I play back the cassette and just go, go through everything once again, only stopping the tape recorder every now and then so I can just listen to something a bit more carefully than I had done before.

2.

Well, I'm quite busy, I work every day, and I travel from home to work on the train, so I do a bit of work on my Japanese.

On the way to my class, I usually look at the last lesson we did in the coursebook. And, er, I have a Walkman, so I often listen to this on the train, which is very useful.

But at home, I also do things like, um, I, I use a tape recorder, and I tape sentences from the book, and then listen to them and see what my pronunciation's like.

And, er, oh, I've thought of all kinds of other little ways as well, like I have little cards that I write down new words on, to help me learn new vocabulary. Usually about five or ten words a day, pop them on little cards, and then as soon as I feel confident about them, I just put them in a box, so that I've learnt them.

Er, also my coursebook has got a very good grammar section at the back of it, and quite often at the end of my class, I look at this on the train as well, just to go over what I've done in the lesson.

UNIT 2 HOW DOES THAT SOUND?

HOW DO YOU SOUND IN ENGLISH?

Exercise 2

Version 1

People think that pronunciation is about speaking, but it's also about listening. We usually listen for meaning, naturally, but it's also useful sometimes to listen to how people are saying things. So, listen outside class to radio or tapes or videos and for five minutes each day, choose one thing to listen to. It can be a sound that you find difficult; or listen to the regular rhythm and stress of English; or listen to how high and low the voice goes, and when it goes high and low. Now, for many students the thing that can improve their pronunciation most quickly is work on stress, so notice the stress on new words and when you speak English, make regular stress in phrases and sentences. A useful technique is 'shadowing': listen to a recording or the radio, and as soon as you understand, repeat it just after the person speaks and say it exactly like they said it. Finally, look at speakers of English when they are talking. Do they look different from speakers of your language? Look at the face, the way the mouth moves, the way they hold their head, their body – try imitating that when you speak English.

Version 2

DAVID: I'm interested in pronunciation at the moment as I'm learning a language – Spanish. Um, what advice would you give to someone in this position?

CLAIRE: Well, people think that pronunciation is about speaking, um, and of course it is, but actually it's also about listening. Now, usually when you listen to somebody, you listen to the meaning, you listen to what they're trying to say. But for pronunciation it's very useful sometimes to listen to how they're saying it. Um, so if you listen, you know, to radio or tapes or videos or to people speaking English if you can – uh, or your language.

DAVID: Right.

CLAIRE: Um, and say for five minutes each day you choose one thing to listen to. Now, it could be a sound that's difficult, that you don't have in your own language. Um, or you could listen to the regular rhythm and stress of English, which is different from some languages like Spanish, for example. Um, or listen to how high and low the voice goes, and, and where it goes up and down … OK. And for a lot of people five, five minutes a day intensive listening really can help the pronunciation.

DAVID: Right. Uh, what would you think would be a way to improve your pronunciation most quickly, more than anything else?

CLAIRE: Well, for a lot of students of English, I think the thing that can improve the pronunciation most quickly is work on stress.

DAVID: Right.

CLAIRE: Um, so that if people learn new words with more than one syllable, um, and notice which syllable is stressed and make sure they say it that way. And then when they're speaking English continuously, um, to make regular stress in phrases and sentences.

DAVID: Right.

CLAIRE: That can make a lot of difference to the overall sound of, of English.

DAVID: And would there be any, for example, any technique that could help a student of the language?

CLAIRE: One useful technique is, is what's sometimes called 'shadowing': um, this means that you listen to a recording or the radio, and for each phrase that you hear, you repeat it just after the speaker has said it, and you try and say it in exactly the same way that they've said it. Very useful technique.

DAVID: And is there any more advice?

CLAIRE: Well, I think it's useful to look at speakers of a language when they're talking. Um, do they look different from speakers of your own language? Er, look at the face, look at the way the mouth moves, the way they hold their head, their body. If people try imitating that, then see what happens to their pronunciation.

DAVID: Thank you.

Exercise 4

1. Come and look at this shirt.
2. I've lost my glasses.
3. Could you lend me £5 till tomorrow?
4. Excuse me, could I get through, please?

5. Do you come here often?
6. Excuse me, is there a toilet near here?

DOES IT MAKE A NOISE?

Exercise 2

1. Does a hammer make a noise if you use it?
2. If you tear up paper, does it make a noise?
3. Does traffic make more noise than air conditioning?
4. What's this noise?
5. Which is noisier: opening luggage or using an electric drill?
6. What's this noise?
7. Can you think of three kinds of weather that make a noise?
8. Do people make a noise when they're doing research?
9. What's this noise?
10. Does scenery make any noise at all?
11. Does machinery make a pleasant noise?
12. Can you think of three toys that make a noise?
13. Can you hear time?
14. What's this noise?
15. Would you want accommodation if it was noisy?

REVIEW AND DEVELOPMENT

REVIEW OF UNIT 1

Exercise 1

1. I heard a noise.
2. The children hid behind the door.
3. She told me she felt sick.
4. He wore the same suit every day.
5. I burnt my finger on the iron.
6. I chose the wrong answer.
7. The plant grew very quickly.
8. She kept it in a small box.
9. He shook his fists at me.
10. I won it in a competition.
11. I dreamt in English last night.
12. The holiday cost a fortune.
13. He stood next to me.
14. I fell over on my way to school.
15. That dog bit me.
16. My finger bled for ages.
17. We flew over the Sahara.
18. I lent him £50.
19. I meant what I said.
20. That boy stole my pen.
21. She spent the money last week.
22. He threw it over the wall.
23. He rode his bike for the first time.
24. She sang the song beautifully.
25. I caught a fish yesterday.
26. I brought that recipe for you.
27. They let me stay a bit longer.
28. The fish smelt horrible.
29. They both hurt themselves.
30. She became very angry.

Exercise 3

embarrassed excited scared surprised delighted relaxed interested shocked frightened disappointed confused astonished

UNIT 3 GAMES PEOPLE PLAY

I NEVER LIKED GAMES AT SCHOOL

Exercise 2

MAX: I tried to avoid playing games when I was at school, and I absolutely refused to play physical games such as rugby or football. I could never understand why other boys wanted to kick a ball around on a cold, wet windy afternoon in the middle of winter. But my two sons adore football, and I quite enjoy watching them play for their school teams.

JEAN: I decided to take up golf because friends of mine played. At first it was just for fun and I wasn't interested in winning at all. Gradually though, as I improved, I became more and more competitive. Now I can't stand losing.

PATRICK: I used to be afraid of going up ladders, then I met a couple of people who spent every weekend rock climbing, and they persuaded me to go with them. At first I was terrified, but gradually I overcame my fear, and now I can't imagine being afraid of heights.

SALLY: Not long ago I decided it was time I learnt to swim properly. I've always felt embarrassed that I couldn't, and I was worried about taking my grandchildren to the beach. I did quite well, and after a few lessons, I managed to swim 100 metres. It made me feel really great!

GAME SHOWS

Exercise 4

A: Er, it's a machine ... it's the thing you use for, um, copying, paper things, things on paper ...
B: Oh, a photocopier.
A: Yes. Ah, right. Next one. Um, it's ... it's a thing you put money in, you keep one, everyone has one ... well, not everyone, but most people have one, they keep money in it.
B: A purse?
A: ... and their cards. A *man* keeps ...
B: Oh, a wallet.
A: Yes. Erm, it's the stuff you use to clean your clothes ... in a machine.
B: Washing powder.
A: Yes! Er, it's the, it's the opposite of slow.
B: Fast.
A: Like fast, another word for fast.
B: Quick?
A: Yes. Um, oh, another one. Er, this is the opposite of beautiful.
B: Ugly.
A: Oh, yes, got that first time. Erm, right, it's, er, someone who writes music, erm, yes, writes music.
B: Musician?
A: Er, no, actually *writes* music.
B: Oh, composer.
A: Yes. Um, oh, it's a type of fruit. Er, it's a citrus fruit. Um, it's in the song: 'Oranges and ....'
B: Oh, lemon.
A: Yes.

Exercise 5

1. It's the opposite of 'go to sleep'.
2. It's the stuff you use to make you smell nice.
3. It's someone who writes newspaper articles for a living.
4. It's where you buy stamps.
5. It's a kind of animal and it has a very long neck.
6. It's the thing you use for drying yourself after you've had a shower.
7. It means the same as 'frequently'.

REVIEW AND DEVELOPMENT

REVIEW OF UNIT 1

Exercise 1

1. She didn't knew any students at all.
2. I want meet a few people.
3. I don't looking forward to next week.
4. We listen music every day.
5. I might to see him this evening.
6. He's worried for his exam results.
7. They going to meet him at five o'clock.
8. I like to find a new job.

UNIT 4 NEWSPAPERS AND MAGAZINES

¡HOLA! AND *HELLO!*

Exercise 2

Version 1

The Spanish magazine *¡Hola!* started as long ago as 1944, and since then it has been owned and run by the same family, Sánchez Junco. The current boss is Eduardo Sánchez Junco. He's been in charge now since 1984, and he continues to run the magazine, like his father before him, as a small family business from his apartment in Madrid. Which is incredible, because the magazine sells about 675,000 copies a week, and makes a profit of about £10m a year.

In most respects, Eduardo has not changed the philosophy of *¡Hola!* very much. The secret of the magazine's success is that it has never had serious views or opinions, never attacked or criticised the famous people it writes about, and so famous people trust *¡Hola!* and will give them exclusive interviews.

In May 1988, Eduardo introduced a British version called *Hello!* The format was the same: pictures of the royal family, and pictures and articles about the aristocracy and famous film stars and celebrities. And always the same treatment, never rude or critical of the people it features. At first, the British version wasn't so successful, but by the end of 1990, *Hello!* was profitable. Since then, sales have continued to go up, even though it costs twice as much as most weekly magazines. Unusually, *Hello!* only gets 25% of its revenue from advertising: most magazines get about 50%.

Version 2

The Spanish magazine *¡Hola!* started as long ago as 1944, and since then it has been owned and run by the same family, Sánchez Junco. The current boss is Eduardo Sánchez Junco. He has been in charge now since 1984, and he continues to run the magazine – like his father before him – as a small family business from his apartment in Madrid – which is fairly unusual when you consider that the magazine sells about 675,000 copies a week and makes about £10m profit a year.

But in most respects Eduardo has done little to change the philosophy of the magazine. It was created by Eduardo's father who called *¡Hola!* the 'froth of life', by which he meant something without weight or density. And that really has been the secret of its success. *¡Hola!* has never held serious views or opinions, it has never attacked or criticised the famous people it writes about ... and as a result, famous people trust *¡Hola!* and will give them exclusive interviews that other magazines can't get. An example of this was Elizabeth Taylor's wedding to Larry Fortensky – *¡Hola!* was the only magazine allowed to attend the ceremony and take pictures.

One change Eduardo has made though, is to expand. In May 1988 he introduced a British version of the magazine called *Hello!* The format was the same: lots of pictures of the British royal family – the Spanish version has a similar pre-occupation with the Spanish royal family – plus pictures and articles about the aristocracy and famous film stars and celebrities. And always the same kind of treatment: never rude or critical of the people it features.

At first the British version struggled a bit, but exclusive pictures of Prince Andrew and the Duchess of York gave the magazine a big lift in 1990, and by the end of that year, *Hello!* was profitable. Since then sales have continued to rise despite the fact that the magazine is almost twice as much as most weekly magazines.

But the magazine in Britain does have one other unusual feature which is also its greatest problem … only 25% of the total revenue comes from advertising (that's very low … the norm is for a magazine to get about 50% of its revenue from advertising). The reason for this is that few readers of *Hello!* can afford to buy the products of the fashionable companies such as Givenchy, who advertises in the magazine. In the longer term this could be a big problem because these companies may decide to stop advertising and *Hello!* would find it difficult to continue if they lost more of their advertising revenue.

UNIT 5 RELATIONSHIPS

WHO WAS OONA MARRIED TO?

Exercise 2

Version 1

Charlie Chaplin was a famous actor from a theatrical family: his parents, Hannah and Charles, were both music-hall performers. He went on stage with his stepbrother, Sydney. (His mother had been married before to a man called Sydney Hawkes, and their son was also called Sydney.)

Charlie became rich and famous, but his first three marriages were unhappy. With his second wife, Lita, he had two sons, Charles Junior and Sydney. At last, in his fifties, he met and married the young Oona O'Neill, and they had eight children. Oona was herself from a theatrical family. She and her brother, Shane, were the children of the famous American playwright, Eugene O'Neill and his second wife, who was called Agnes. Their Irish grandfather, James O'Neill, had also been a successful actor.

The family tradition continued into the next generation: Charlie and Oona's first child, Geraldine, became an actress like her father. She lived for a while with the Spanish film director, Carlos Saura. Another daughter, Victoria, entered the world of the circus with her husband Jean-Baptiste Thierree. A remarkable group of people!

Version 2

Charlie Chaplin was a famous actor who came from a theatrical family: his parents, Hannah and Charles, were both music-hall performers. He followed his parents onto the stage together with Sydney, who was his stepbrother from his mother's first marriage to a man called Sydney Hawkes. But soon he turned to films, and almost immediately achieved enormous fame. On the screen he played a poor, unlucky little man with a sad face and a funny walk. In his life he was rich and famous, but his first three marriages were unhappy ones. With his second wife, Lita, he had two sons, Charles Junior and Sydney. At last, in his fifties, he married a girl in her teens, Oona O'Neill, and they had eight children. Oona was herself from a theatrical family. She and her brother, Shane, were the children of the famous American playwright, Eugene O'Neill, and his second wife Agnes. Their Irish grandfather, James O'Neill, had also been a successful actor. Eugene O'Neill was extremely angry when Oona married Charlie Chaplin, because Chaplin was about the same age as him! But the marriage was a happy one and lasted until Charlie's death. The family tradition continued into the next generation: Charlie and Oona's first child, Geraldine, became an actress like her father. She lived for a while with the Spanish film director, Carlos Saura. Another daughter, Victoria, entered the world of the circus with her husband Jean-Baptiste Thierree. A remarkable group of people!

WHO ARE YOU CLOSEST TO?

Exercise 2

Who could you talk to?
Who could you confide in?
Who could you spend a week with?
Who would you call on for help?
Who would you turn to for advice?
Who could you borrow money from?
Who could you rely on to keep a secret?
Who would you be prepared to lie for?

Exercise 4

1.

ALAN: Isabelle, tell me about your star diagram.

ISABELLE: Well, I've also picked five people. Erm, the one closest to me in the centre is my brother, although he's, er, the furthest away. He lives in Berlin, but, um, we were very, we grew up very close together, so he's, he I would consider is the closest, er, person to me. And then there are two people who are at the same distance to myself, and one of them is my best and oldest girlfriend, Frederike, and, um, another friend of mine who is a very, very old friend, Michael, who is also my flatmate.

ALAN: Right.

ISABELLE: And then we have … two people at a longer distance. One of them is an old man, an old puppeteer, actually, who's been a friend for a few years, and, um, who is like an uncle, I consider him like an uncle in England, and the other one is a family friend, who lives in England and who, sort of substitutes my family here, so whenever I have a problem he, he would sort of, um, sort that out, and so these two are the furthest away.

ALAN: Right.

2.

ISABELLE: How about you, Dev?

DEV: Well, I have five people as well, so I'll go through them one at a time. The first person who is closest to me is my wife, mainly because she is my, my best friend as well. Next, the second person, who is a little bit further away from me is my grandfather. Er, he's a lovely man, and I can talk to him about all kinds of things and he listens to everything that I have to say to him, and occasionally he is very helpful to me if I have got a problem, which I think he would understand about. Then come my parents; er, they are very close to me but well, I, I, I think a little bit further away from me than my grandfather perhaps, because I find it not as easy to talk to my parents about certain things.

Then I have a professional relationship with my agent, and he comes a little bit, quite a bit further away from me, but it's a, it's a relationship that I, I need for my work and for my, er, existence really, I suppose in many ways.

The, well, it's not really a person who comes next that is furthest away from me, it's actually a pet. I have a pet falcon, a peregrine falcon, and I have just started falconry, and I find when the two of us are together alone, oh, it is a wonderful experience, and I think he too listens to me.

UNIT 6 LIFE'S LITTLE CHORES

TURNING ON AND TURNING OFF

Exercise 5

Version 1

1.

I learnt to do this when I was about four, and I can remember finding it very hard at first, I suppose because my fingers weren't very skilled at that age. My mother used to get quite angry with me if I didn't do it. She said I'd fall over and hurt myself.

2.

I quite enjoy doing this, though I wouldn't say I was very skilled at it. Some people make a beautiful job of it and it can really look special. I usually have the most trouble if it's a strange shape, and I often get in quite a mess with the sellotape; it nearly always gets stuck together.

Version 2
1.

It sounds like a really simple task but you would be surprised how many people do it badly. My brother-in-law has perfected it and now does it for the whole family. He usually starts by laying everything out carefully and arranging similar things together, wrapping certain things in tissue paper and folding everything beautifully. I tend to throw everything in and then iron it at the other end.

2.

I remember the first time I did this, it was a complete disaster. Basically, I was too impatient, I think, and I started putting the coal on too quickly, and I just choked it and it went out. In the end we all went indoors and I had to use the oven. But that was a long time ago and now I'm quite good at it. The important thing is to start it long before you actually need to use it.

DO YOU QUEUE?

Exercise 4

1.
A: Excuse me, could I get through?
B: It's OK, I'm getting off here too.
A: Oh, fine.

2.
A: Excuse me, is this the front or the back of the queue?
B: It's the front. The back's down there.
A: Oh, right.

3.
A: Oh, no! I've forgotten the milk. Look, would you mind if I just went and got some?
B: Oh, OK.
A: I'll be very quick. Thanks.

4.
A: Excuse me, I think I was here before you.
B: Oh, sorry, I thought this was the *end* of the queue.
A: No, this is the front.
B: Sorry.

5.
A: Er, excuse me, my train leaves in a couple of minutes. Do you think I could possibly jump in?
B: Oh. All right then.

REVIEW AND DEVELOPMENT

REVIEW OF UNIT 4

Exercise 2

Words with the /ʌ/ sound, like *some*:
company courage other son

Words with the /əʊ/ sound, like *home*:
hello cope social radio

Words with the /ə/ sound, like *complain*:
editor famous compare section

Words with the /uː/ sound, like *who*:
lose through too scoop

UNIT 7 COURSES

TURNING POINTS

Exercise 4

Um, I suppose I was about 12 or 13, and, uh, talking to my parents the subject came up of what the curriculum should be – what I should be studying at school. And the first thing they said it was very important that I should learn Latin, and I had absolutely no interest in that – I couldn't see the sense of it. And there were terrific arguments about it, and I refused and I said I'd learn German instead, which I did, without a great deal of success, I must confess, but because I'd refused to learn Latin, I never could go to university. So, it's a turning point but rather a negative one.

NOT EASY TO BE A BUTLER

Exercise 5

A: I'm fascinated by what you said about quietly removing a drunken guest. How exactly is the butler supposed to do that?
B: Well, first you tell your employer very discreetly that a drunken guest is annoying the people beside him. The employer will probably tell *you* to deal with the situation yourself, so you instruct another servant to return to the dining room in five minutes to announce a phone call. You then ask the guest to take the call in another room. If the guest doesn't want to go, tell him you will have another drink brought to him at the phone.

Once he is outside the room, apologise and say there is no call, but the host is worried that he is embarrassing himself, and so you ask him to leave.

You can then ask him to give you his car keys and order a taxi for him. You tell him that you will have his car delivered the following day.

AN ACTOR'S LIFE FOR ME

Exercise 4

Version 1
JUDY: When I was at drama school, um, we had to learn all kinds of things. I remember we had to learn to fall – we spent a lot of time just standing in the middle of the room and then, um, falling as though we'd been shot or something like that. Also, I remember, we had to learn how to laugh and how to cry, and again we would stand in the room and the teacher would say 'breathe in and breathe out laughing' or 'breathe in and breathe out sobbing'. Um, we didn't have to learn to dance. We did dancing as a form of exercise but we didn't have to learn to dance because we might need to do it professionally on stage. I think that's all quite different nowadays.

WALTER: When I was at drama school, a lot, there was a lot of concentration on the voice, and we had to learn to do a thing called 'rib reserve breathing'. And this was quite difficult to do, and, er, we tried hard to learn it and I learnt it, and I've since discovered that it's totally false – it doesn't work. So we had to learn to do something that, um, was absolutely useless. What we didn't have to learn to do was sing, and I find that I'm being asked to sing all the time.

Version 2
FRANCES: When I was at drama school we had to learn to fence. We had to learn how to do stage fights. Um, I was pretty hopeless at this 'cause I was left-handed so nobody could fence with me. We didn't have to be a professional level, but we had

to be able to look after ourselves in a fight on stage. It was horrible.

STUART: When I went to drama school, er, we had to learn a lot of things. We had to learn to, um, develop characters: to explore the emotions of a character in a scene; to be able to use our own experiences and to be able to relate them to a scene. And we had to learn how to, to be able to take all that information and put it into a scene in front of our other students for 'scene studies', this was called. But we didn't have to learn how to speak verse, that was never taught. And we didn't have to learn how to sing, or dance.

UNIT 8 ALL IN A DAY'S WORK

HOW DO YOU COPE?

Exercise 3

Dialogue 1

A: I wanted to ask you about the, the one week course in, in Stockholm, erm, because I'd, I'd like to go if that was possible. Um, I know there've, there've been a lot of cutbacks but I wondered if there was still enough in the budget for, for training schemes like that.

B: Well, as you know, we are already sending three or four representatives over. I'm not really sure there's scope for you as well.

A: Yes, I know; I had heard that, that the other three were going. It's just that if I don't go on this course, there isn't a similar one here, um, and I'll get left behind.

B: Well, it's really a course, you know, for senior management.

A: But they said in the, um, in the details they sent that it was, it was for the, for other levels as well. I mean, I'd, I'd just be grateful if you'd think about it because I think it … I would get a lot out of it.

B: Well, I'll have another look at the budgets but, er, I suspect that it's, it's going to be out of the question.

A: Right. But if you, if you could just give it a thought.

B: Surely. Yes.

A: Thank you, thank you.

Dialogue 2

C: Good morning.

D: Good morning.

C: I just came in to see if you knew about the management course in Stockholm.

D: Yes.

C: Yes, well I wonder if I could put myself forward for the course. I'd really like to do it and I'd be grateful if you could spare the time to discuss it with me.

D: Well, as you know, the training budget for this department has been cut quite drastically recently, so I do have to be careful. And other people have applied.

C: Yes, I know that.

D: So, why you?

C: Well, I think I have a lot to contribute and I need to improve my skills in this particular area. It would give me more confidence. Would it be all right if I came back tomorrow and we can discuss it further? I can make an appointment with your secretary …

D: I'm afraid that's out of the question. I'll be out all day tomorrow.

C: OK, how about Friday?

D: Well, if you let me come back to you on this. I need more time to think about it.

C: Well, I'd very much like to go.

D: I understand.

C: Thank you very much.

D: OK.

REVIEW OF UNIT 7

Exercise 2

mathematics mathematician   politics politician   athletics athlete
economics economist   engineering engineer   chemistry chemist
philosophy philosopher   history historian   physics physicist
interpreting interpreter

UNIT 9 FROM THE CRADLE TO THE GRAVE

AGES AND STAGES

Exercise 4

DAVID: Well, I'm 20 and, um, I suppose me and my mates, what we really want most is a really nice girlfriend, um, if I'm honest. Uh, it's really difficult our age, because you find generally that most of the girls kind of want older boyfriends and you know all the girls of our age have got boyfriends of 25, so it's a bit difficult. Um, also I'd like, like a car 'cause I think that'd help maybe get a nice girlfriend. Um, and obviously I need a job before I can buy a car. Some of my friends have got cars and we generally help each other and give me lifts here, there and everywhere. We go to the football together – we really like that, that's a good day out – and, um, then we go to the pub in the evening. Um, I guess we're really most worried about the wars in the world. There's always wars somewhere it seems to be. It would just really be great if it could be peace everywhere in the world, but I suppose that's not realistic.

JUDY: I'm in my forties now and I think, um, the thing that occupies my mind mostly, um, is my children's education, and I think this probably goes for most of my friends. Um, our children are at secondary school age now, so it's quite important what happens to them now. Um, I also worry for them, looking ahead, I find that I'm advising them to take exams, to think of going to college or university, and then I read in the paper that more people from university are unemployed than people who haven't been to university. And, er, so I end up really not knowing if I'm giving them good advice or not.

Um, I think another thing that is starting to, um, to be on my mind now is death – my own father died about two years ago, and that's quite a turning point in your life. You start to realise that, um, that your parents are going to cease to be the senior members of your family, and you are going to take' that position.

WALTER: I'm over 60 and I imagine a lot of people who are round about my age are either thinking about their retirement or actually retiring or maybe they've retired early and thinking how they're going to spend the rest of their life. So I'm sure that that's a big preoccupation of people of my age. Another preoccupation I think is the way the world has changed and the way things are different, er, for young people – lots of unemployment and that sort of thing. How they're going to make their way in the world. And also the way people behave differently, the way they seem to be to older people, to be very unmannerly, push you off the pavement and so on. And also the way they look through you as if you're invisible. I suppose the main thing is that one says 'uh, in my day' or 'of course you won't remember this, but …' I think that's a bit of a preoccupation of people of my age.

UNIT 10 PHONAHOLICS

MAKE THAT CALL!

Exercise 2

1.
A: Good morning. Doctor's Surgery. Can I help you?
B: Oh, yes, er, good morning. Er, I'd like to make an appointment. Um … as soon as possible, please.
A: Right. And is there a particular doctor you wish to see?
B: Er, yes, er, Dr Jackson, please.
A: Right. I'll just have a look. Uh … Well, I'm afraid Dr Jackson is very busy … the earliest appointment I can give you with her is the day after tomorrow. Well, if that's no good …

2.
A: Good morning. Cambridge Chemicals.
B: Oh, good morning. Could I speak to Mr Roberts, please? In the marketing department.
A: Right. And who shall I say is calling, please?
B: My name is Carol Barnes. He doesn't actually know me.
A: OK. One moment please … Er, I'm afraid Mr Roberts isn't at his desk at the moment. I believe he's just popped out.
B: Oh. Do you know when he'll be back?
A: No, I'm afraid I don't. But I can give him a message … or shall I get him to ring you or something like that?

3.
A: Hello.
B: Is that Joanne?
A: Yeah.
B: Hi. It's Nigel. How are you?
A: Oh, busy … you know … but otherwise fine. How about you?
B: Well, I wish I could say the same. But unfortunately I haven't had a particularly good week … I had a slight accident with the car at the weekend.
A: Oh, no. Was anyone hurt?
B: No, no, nothing like that. But there's a bit of damage to the car and it's going to be off the road for a week or so. Actually that's part of the reason why I'm ringing. I was wondering if I could ask you a big favour?
A: Oh, yeah.
B: Yeah … uh, I've got to … to go to Wales at the weekend and without the car I'm a bit stuck. I was wondering if I could possibly borrow your Golf for a couple of days?
A: What next week?

Exercise 4

1.
B: Oh …
A: Well, if that's no good, there are two doctors with appointments this afternoon.
B: I would rather have Dr Jackson, but I don't think I can wait for another day.
A: Well, I'm very sorry but I could give you an appointment with Dr Morton at 3.45 this afternoon. He's very nice.
B: I've never met Dr Morton, but would that mean I would have to explain everything all over again?
A: Well, not really, he will have your notes. Would that be all right? 3.45?
B: Well, I should take it. I suppose it's …
A: Right. Could I have your name, please?
B: Yes, it's, er, it's Mr Jones.
A: Mr Jones …

2.
B: No, it's just that I'm in meetings all morning and I'm not going to have a lot of time, you see. I think, I think I'd like to speak to somebody else if I can. Isn't there anybody else I can speak to?
A: Er, well, I could see if Mr Roberts' secretary is there.
B: Yes, well, I think I have to speak to someone. If you could put me through, I'd be very grateful …

A: Right, right, I'll put you through to Denise, then.
B: Thanks very much.
C: Hello, Marketing Department. How can I help you?
B: Ah, yeah, good morning …

3.
A: … What, next weekend?
B: Yeah, if it's, if it's possible.
A: Oh, look, Nigel, I'm really sorry, but, well, I'm afraid I need it. I've got to go up to Manchester.
B: Oh, Joanne, don't worry. Look, I just hope you didn't mind me asking.
A: No, any time, I'm really sorry.
B: It's … it's really left me in a bit of a hole as far as transport goes …

REVIEW AND DEVELOPMENT

REVIEW OF UNIT 8

Exercise 2

1. company organise difficult positive manager flexible
2. appointment solution effective advantage agreement financial
3. orders sickness colleague training cutbacks budget
4. collect involve consult employed discuss accept

UNIT 11 GOODS AND SERVICES

CAN YOU SELL IT?

Exercise 5

Version 1
ANDY: Joe, can I interest you in buying something really unusual? Something that none of your friends will have?
JOE: Well, it depends. I mean, is it expensive?
ANDY: No, that's what is so fantastic – actually, it's incredibly cheap.
JOE: OK, go on, then, tell me.
ANDY: Well, how much do you spend on dry cleaning bills for your suits?
JOE: I don't know … really, I've no idea.
ANDY: Well, I can sell you twelve suits for only £25.
JOE: So what's wrong with them?
ANDY: Nothing! They are really attractive, smart suits, very fashionable … *and* they are throwaway.
JOE: What do you mean, throwaway?
ANDY: Exactly that – they are disposable.
JOE: So you think my friends would be impressed by that, do you?
ANDY: Well, yes, of course … people will think you've got an enormous number of suits and that you are really rich …
JOE: Hmm … I think they'd probably look a bit cheap.
ANDY: No, look, I'm wearing one right now.
JOE: Yes. Exactly. That's what I mean.
ANDY: I think it looks pretty good. Come on, what do you say?
JOE: No, thanks all the same. I think I'll leave it.
ANDY: Well, it's your loss …

Version 2
LORELEI: Juliet, I have a product you are going to love.
JULIET: Really?
LORELEI: Do you want to know what it is?
JULIET: Oh, please, I'd love to know about it, yeah.
LORELEI: Everything you wanted to know about socks.
JULIET: Socks?
LORELEI: Odourless socks.

JULIET: You're joking.

LORELEI: No, I'm not. You know when you do your aerobics class, your feet get a little bit sweaty, the socks are less than fresh, let's face it – solves that problem. What do you think? Are they beautiful, look? Are they gorgeous? They come in all colours, they go with everything. This pair will go fabulous with your shoes.

JULIET: I know, but the thing is, are they natural fibres?

LORELEI: Absolutely. 100% natural.

JULIET: Really? So how do they work?

LORELEI: Well, I'm afraid that's a secret, but it's a completely natural, patented product.

JULIET: So does that mean I don't have to wash them?

LORELEI: I'm afraid you do have to wash them – yeah, of course you do, but only after a while; but they won't smell at any point.

JULIET: Wow!

LORELEI: How many pairs can I put you down for?

JULIET: So how much are they?

LORELEI: £2.50 a pair. How many can I put you down for?

REVIEW AND DEVELOPMENT

REVIEW OF UNIT 9

Exercise 2

In the first pair of sentences, *triplets* means that the children were born to the same mother at the same time. *Children* could be different ages.

In 2, *kids* means the same as *children*, but it's a more informal word, and it is very common indeed.

In number 3, *a young person* could be either male or female, but *a youth* always refers to a male teenager in English, and it's a word with a negative or pejorative meaning: we talk about *a gang of youths* who are perhaps violent or not under control.

In number 4, *adults* and *grown-ups* mean the same thing, but *grown-up* is a more informal word which children often use.

In 5, if a child is *growing up*, we mean they are becoming more adult, or more mature. But a child who is *growing* is just getting bigger physically.

Finally in number 6, *adolescent* is a bit more formal than *teenager* – so you will probably hear it less often in conversation.

UNIT 12 BARE NECESSITIES

I COULD MANAGE WITHOUT IT

Exercise 3

Version 1

1.

A: Stuart, where do you keep things that you don't use very often?

B: Uh, well, in our house, um, at the top of the stairs there's a huge cupboard.

A: Right. What sort of things do you keep there?

B: Oh, well we have lots of children's toys – we have three kids – so lots of children – we could open up a toy store we've got so many toys. And, um, oh, there's a box of Christmas decorations, of course.

A: Yeah.

B: And, uh, well, it's I guess things we use on holiday like, er, buckets, spades, er, beach umbrella, stuff like that.

A: And are there things there that you need or could you really manage without?

B: Well, um, I don't need the toys, I suppose – Barbie dolls, no I don't need those, but the kids use some of them, but we could give away some of them, I guess. Er, Christmas decorations we need, of course. And, uh, well, we like every year we go away we always go to the beach, so we'd need all the beach stuff I suppose.

A: Are there any things that you'd really like to get rid of?

B: Oh, nothing. They like to hang on to things, my family.

2.

A: So Nick, where do you keep the things you don't use very often?

B: Um, well, I live in a, a studio flat, so I haven't got much room; in fact there's only one big room really, um, so I keep everything under the bed, I'm afraid.

A: I see. Well, what sort of things?

B: Well, there's a, there's a case with some old clothes in it, and a, a tennis racket and balls under there as well; but mainly it's where I keep my collection of football magazines. Um, I'm a great football fan you see, and I keep them for nostalgia really.

A: Well are these things that you really need or could you manage without them?

B: Um, well I couldn't do without the magazines and, um, anyway they're, they're really valuable now. Um, I wouldn't get rid of the tennis racket because I'm sure one day I'll, I'll go back and start playing again.

A: Yeah.

B: Well, I suppose I could get rid of the clothes – I don't think I'll ever wear, wear them again. I mean most of them are really unfashionable now, so I don't need them …

Version 2

1.

A: Frances, where do you keep things you don't use very often?

B: I live in a block of flats without a great deal of space, so I've got a store cupboard in the basement.

A: Right. What sort of things do you keep in there?

B: Uh, hi-fi, a couple of speakers, picture frames, some cases of wine, an old bike, oh, and there's an enormous pile of newspapers and old cans, I'm afraid.

A: And are these things you need or could you actually manage without them?

B: Well, um, I don't really need the picture frames, but I do need the bike specially in the summer, I enjoy cycling in the summer. And I certainly need the cases of wine.

A: Yes. Um, and are there any things that you really would like to get rid of?

B: Er, well I want to sell the hi-fi and the speakers, and actually I, I do get rid of the newspapers and things at, um, the recycling places every so often.

2.

A: David, where do you keep things you don't use very often?

B: Oh, in the attic.

A: Oh.

B: Definitely in the attic. That's where everything goes.

A: And what sort of things do you keep in the attic?

B: Oh, there's all sorts. There's a trunk full of things that we've … family heirlooms that have been handed down through the generations; photographs, photograph albums, that sort of thing. Um, there are old lampshades and old curtains – we could, uh, we've got lots of those. Er, sports equipment up there we keep. Things for unexpected guests – there's an old foldaway bed. There's a sleeping bag, um, and, uh, that sort of thing … old furniture.

A: But are they all these things that you … you do need them all or could you manage without?

B: Well, I think, I think the family heirlooms we need – the trunk full of photographs we would need those. We could manage without the old lampshades and curtains. Um, the sports equipment I use, so I would definitely need to keep those. And we'd like to keep, er, the foldaway bed and the sleeping bag for unexpected guests. We don't use them that often but they are useful.

A: Yes, sure. Um, and are there any things you'd really like to get rid of?

B: I think there's a lot of old college notes and books that could be thrown away, I think, yes.

A: Yes.

Exercise 5

... and in fact you now find that airlines provide all sorts of things to improve the comfort for their passengers on long haul flights. We've been investigating these 'creature comforts' and here are a few of the more unusual ones.

Firstly, you would expect to get toiletries such as soap and toothpaste, but it doesn't stop there. Some companies will give you dental floss, toothpicks and even make-up remover.

Then, there are zone oils – these are specially prepared oils for passengers who travel across different time zones, and they are supposed to put the moisture back into your tired, dry skin.

Another thing we found were osmotherapy wipes – I bet there aren't too many people out there who know what they are. Well, these are tissues which have a special aroma on them, and they are meant to relax people, and they are designed particularly to help people who are afraid of flying.

But you know, it's not just the contents that are important these days, but the case they come in too. One airline now provides a special bag which opens out to become a small case with a handle for carrying documents.

And finally of course there are items which may have a special value in certain parts of the world – the most obvious example of this is sunblock, which is for passengers who are going from cold climates to hot places. Probably essential for most British people who ...

REVIEW OF UNIT 10

Exercise 1

1. (Line engaged)

2.

A: Hello.

B: Hello. Is that Paul?

A: No, sorry, no Paul here. I think you must have the wrong number.

B: That isn't 994 8057?

A: No, it's 882 3286, actually.

B: Blimey. I don't know what happened there. Anyway, I'm sorry to bother you.

A: That's OK.

3.

C: Hello.

D: Could I speak to Margaret please? It's Tom.

C: Yes, I know who it is, and the answer is no. She's fed up with you ringing her day and night. Leave her alone, will you?

4.

E: Pronto.

F: Hi, Carla, it's Michael.

E: Michael! Fantastic. How are you?

F: I'm fine. And you?

E: I'm ... wonderful.

F: Great. And what are you doing?

E: I'm just ...

5.

G: Hello.

H: Hi. Is that Tony?

G: No, I'm afraid Tony's out, and he won't be back for at least two hours.

H: Oh, well in that case, could I leave a message?

G: Sure.

H: Could you ask him to ring me this evening at home. My name is Clare ... he knows my number.

G: OK, will do.

H: Thanks a lot. Bye.

G: Bye.

6.

I: Hope and Macgregor. Good morning. Can I help you?

J: I hope so. I'd like to make an appointment to see Mr Macgregor, please.

I: One moment. I'll just put you through to Mr Macgregor's secretary.

J: Right, thanks ...

K: Mr Macgregor's secretary.

J: Good morning. My name is John Cartwright, I'm a client of Mr Macgregor's. Could I make an appointment to see him some time next week ... preferably in the afternoon?

K: Right, Mr Cartwright. How about Wednesday ... he's free from two o'clock onwards.

J: Yeah, two o'clock would be great.

K: Right, I'll put you down, then.

J: Great. Thanks very much. Bye bye.

K: Goodbye.

Exercise 2

Words with the /ɪ/ sound:
business   addict   aggressive   message   promise   anticipate   minute

Words with the /aɪ/ sound:
hostile   dial   tried   mobile   dialogue   exercise   supervisor

UNIT 13 WHO IS REALLY ON TRIAL?

Exercise 2

INTERVIEWER: And what exactly were you doing for 25 years?

JOHN: For twenty-five years, I'm rather ashamed to admit that my whole life was involved in crime, from the age of 16 to the age of 41, when I came out of prison after my last sentence. So my whole lifetime, really, has been spent involved in crime.

INTERVIEWER: And that was mostly burglary, was it?

JOHN: It was nearly all burglary, yes.

INTERVIEWER: And how long exactly did you spend in prison altogether?

JOHN: About fifteen years of my life.

INTERVIEWER: It's a long time.

JOHN: It's a long time.

INTERVIEWER: And what's it like, the daily routine?

JOHN: Very mundane, very boring, very eroding mentally as well as physically. You get up to the same food, you meet the same people, you go to your place of employment, you come in and the first thing you do is look for the letters, in case somebody's written to you; you have the same meals at dinnertime; you are usually locked away then in most prisons for an hour whilst the officers have their meal, you then return to work again, you then come in and have your meal, there is another short break. If you're lucky in an institution that has evening facilities, recreation facilities, you're allowed to watch television for an hour or so, and then you go to bed. And you can ditto that routine times 365.

INTERVIEWER: There's no variety at all?

JOHN: The variety I suppose comes occasionally if you're allowed out on the sports field, or you go out for exercise, weather permitting. If you have a visit, erm …

INTERVIEWER: How many visits can you have?

JOHN: Most institutions now it's two per month.

INTERVIEWER: Oh, is that all? Two a month?

JOHN: Yeah.

INTERVIEWER: For what, about an hour or something or …?

JOHN: Usually about an hour and a half to two hours. That's a pretty standard length of time, I would say, about two hours in most prisons.

Exercise 4

INTERVIEWER: And with your experience now, what, what can people do to protect themselves from burglars? Is there anything they can do?

JOHN: I talk quite a bit to Neighbourhood Watch co-ordinators, and to policemen about this whole business of protecting homes against burglary. I take it on a scale of nought to ten, with ten being the most vulnerable. If you have no lights on when you go out in winter, if you have no alarm, if you leave doors unlocked, you take no security precautions whatsoever, then you are ten, you are very vulnerable.

INTERVIEWER: Yeah.

JOHN: You can go down the scale, shall we say about four notches, down to six, simply by leaving lights on in winter. This is one of the biggest deterrents of all – leave your lights on, leave them on all over your home.

INTERVIEWER: Really?

JOHN: It's visual.

INTERVIEWER: Yeah.

JOHN: The burglar is basically a very lazy person. He wants easy access, he wants easy pickings. Switch lights on, you reduce your chances of being burgled.

INTERVIEWER: Is that more effective than burglar alarms?

JOHN: It's not more effective, but everything has to be, shall we say, um, a progression. If you leave lights on and have an alarm as well, then you're doubly protected.

If you stand outside your home and have a good look when you go out and think to yourself, 'Yes, we're still in,' then you can imagine how the burglar must feel. It's very much visual.

INTERVIEWER: What about dogs?

JOHN: Dogs are a deterrent, yes, but dogs are still dogs, they're not human beings. They may respond well when the owner is actually present, but when the burglar lurks, a dog still doesn't really know who this is.

INTERVIEWER: Right.

JOHN: … and I would suggest as I do to a lot of people that a very good deterrent is to simply have a picture of a dog on your back gate. It's all visual; the burglar can be frightened away in a variety of different ways.

REVIEW AND DEVELOPMENT

REVIEW OF UNIT 11

Exercise 2

1. Do people wear caps on their heads?
2. Are boots normally made of cotton?
3. Do people wear gloves on their feet?
4. Is a jumper the same as a pullover?
5. Do you wear socks over your shoes?
6. Can you keep money in a purse?
7. Are tights made of leather?
8. Is a skirt another name for a dress?
9. Can you try on clothes in a boutique?
10. If something fits you, is it the right size?

11. Are trainers edible?
12. Are jumpers usually reversible?
13. Can you have a dress shortened?
14. Do people wear suits when they play tennis?
15. Do seat belts hold up your trousers?

UNIT 14 TALL STORIES, SHORT STORIES

THE FACE ON THE WALL

Exercise 2

A: We had been talking of strange events when the little man with the white face began …

B: It all started just over a year ago. I was staying in an old house in Great Ormond Street which had large patches of damp on the walls. And you know, one of those patches looked exactly like a human face. I used to sit and watch it and became so fascinated with it that I began to believe there must be a real person with a face like it. My search quickly became an obsession. I watched crowds of people all day long … some must have thought I was mad, and even the police began to look at me suspiciously. Then, one day I saw the face on a man in a taxi. I followed the taxi to a railway station where the man got out and met two ladies and a little girl. They were all going to France. I quickly bought a ticket and got on the same train to Folkestone. From there we boarded the boat and set off for Boulogne. Half-way across the Channel, I finally met the man face to face and asked him for his card. He was clearly shocked but did as I asked and then hurried away. I looked down. It said Mr Ormond Wall, with an address in Pittsburgh, America. I was astonished.

When I returned to Great Ormond Street some time later, I tried to find out more about this man. I discovered that he was a millionaire with English parents who had lived in London. But where? I got no answer … until yesterday morning. I had gone to bed very late and very tired, and consequently, I overslept. When I woke up, I noticed at once that the face on the wall was hardly visible. I got up, went out and bought a paper. On the back page there was a small headline 'American millionaire in motor accident'. Mr Ormond Wall's car had overturned and he was in hospital in a critical condition. I rushed home and stared at the face on the wall. Suddenly it disappeared completely. Later I discovered that Mr Ormond Wall had died at exactly the same moment.

Exercise 4

A: We were all silent in disbelief. The little man went on …

B: Now there are three extraordinary things about my story. The first is that it is possible for damp patches to look like a man, and that the patch should disappear with the man's death. And the second extraordinary fact is that the man's name should be the same as the place where the face appeared. Don't you think so?

A: We all agreed and began an excited discussion about the facts of this fantastic story. At this point the little man got up to leave. Just as he reached the door, someone shouted, 'What about the third extraordinary thing?' The little man looked back.

B: Oh, yes, I almost forgot. Well, the third extraordinary thing is that I invented the whole story only half an hour ago. Goodnight.

EXCUSES, EXCUSES

Exercise 1

Version 1

1.

CHRIS: The football match was supposed to start at 10.30 on Sunday morning. Now, I don't normally like getting up on Sundays that early, but I thought, 'It's no problem; I'll go to sleep nice and early, and set my alarm clock for 9.00; it'll be fine.'

Unfortunately, my alarm clock didn't go off, and I woke up at 11.00. I was in such a panic. I got dressed very quickly, didn't do my teeth or anything – just rushed out, forgot my kit, had to go back and get my kit, my boots and everything, grabbed them in a bag, and ran, ran as fast as I could, and got to the game, just as it was finishing. Everyone was very angry with me, but they had won 4–1. I didn't get picked again after that.

2.

JOUMANA: Well, I was on my way to meet this young man who had asked me out for a date, and I was very excited (he was rather nice), and erm, I thought, 'Well, you have to be a bit late, you can't seem too keen,' so, um, I took my time, had a very long bath and all that; and walked very slowly to the underground station. I've got an underground pass, and so I just walked right through the barrier, and waited for the train, and waited for around five minutes, which is very unusual because the Jubilee line is usually very quick. And then waited another five minutes, and then another five minutes, all in all, I waited around half an hour. Finally, the train arrived. I don't know what the delay was. The train arrived, and, um, I got on, and got off a few stops later, got out of the station, and, um, opened my handbag and realised I'd left all my money at home, and I just didn't know this chap well enough to tell him, and to say that I couldn't even see myself back home in a taxi. So, um, I had to go all the way back home, and I was in fact 45 minutes late, which was rather embarrassing.

Version 2

1.

GARETH: It was during my last year at university, and I still hadn't got a job to go to, and I had news of an interview for a German company. And the German director was coming over to London, and was seeing people on a particular afternoon. So I took the train from Yorkshire, down to London, and unfortunately, er, it was late, er, there was a problem on the line, and I was about three quarters of an hour late getting to London, so I dashed to where the meeting was being held, and unfortunately, I'd just missed the director of the company, er, who was planning to go back to Germany that very afternoon. I was so eager and desperate to get the job that I asked where he'd gone to. I was told that he was taking the shuttle bus to the airport. So I ran over to where the shuttle bus left, got on it just in time, er, asked all the passengers if they were German, and directors of this particular German company, identified this man, and had the interview with him on the way to the airport. Unfortunately, I didn't get the job.

2.

IAN: So there I was, waiting for a bus. First day of a new job. Before the bus arrives, this car pulls up, two guys leap out, flash a warrant card in my face, demand my name, take me down to the local police station, and question me for half an hour on the possibility I've been involved in some sort of ... in a murder!

Ah, I eventually convinced them it was nothing to do with me, but I had to get them to come with me to my new place of work so that I could explain this to my new boss!

CHRIS: My story about the football match and my alarm clock – yeah, that was absolutely true.

JOUMANA: The story about being late for a date and not having my purse with me was completely false.

GARETH: The story about a job interview on a bus to the airport was absolutely true.

IAN: The story about the first day at work was true.

REVIEW OF UNIT 12

Exercise 1

The book I'm reading is absolutely dreadful.
The weather in Sicily is absolutely wonderful.
This room is absolutely boiling.
I thought his story was absolutely incredible.
The bill was absolutely enormous.
His boss will be absolutely furious.

UNIT 15 LOVE THY NEIGHBOUR

NEIGHBOURS

Exercise 2

If you look at the table in Exercise 1, the sentences on the left are in the present perfect, and the ones on the right are in the present perfect continuous.

You've probably realised that sometimes you can use both forms, and they mean the same thing, as in the first pair of sentences, *I've lived here for about two years* and *I've been living here for about two years*. Both of these describe a situation which started in the past and has continued right up to the present moment.

However, there are some verbs that aren't normally used in the continuous form. So, for instance, in the second pair of sentences, you don't usually use the verb *to know* in the continuous form. Other verbs like this are *understand, believe* and *realise*.

Both of the sentences in the third pair are correct, but there is a difference in meaning. *I've read your book* means that the book is finished, but we don't know when the person finished reading it.

I've been reading your book means that the person has stopped the activity of *reading* but hasn't finished the book.

Finally, in the last pair of sentences, the present perfect continuous is used and not the present perfect. This is because the continuous form expresses the idea that it's the *activity* which is tiring, and it isn't important in this context whether it's finished or not. So if you want to emphasise the *result* of the activity, you'll probably use the continuous form.

You'll find some diagrams to explain these tenses in the Grammar Reference section for this unit.

GETTING ON IN GROUPS

Exercise 4

Version 1

1.

STUART: About, er, two years ago I agreed to become the chairman of our local residents' association, which is a group of people living on our estate. And it was one of the dumbest things I've ever decided to do because the whole idea of these organisations is for people to get on well with each other and, and to compromise. And the fact is, we had rows all the time, people would get on each other's nerves, nobody would trust anybody, and the very difficult thing is that very often on these committees you have people who, who really work hard to create conflict.

2.

FRANCES: I went on holiday to Turkey last year on a small boat which was going to sail round the coastline. And there were five other people who I didn't know at all, so it was a bit of a gamble, but we really did all get on very well together. Um, there was just one thing which did get on my nerves. We'd be moored in these beautiful bays, just wonderful with the moonlight and the sound of the water – and they would play very very very loud pop music. I expect I drove them mad too. But we learnt to compromise, and the main thing was that we were all there because we wanted to be there – there was a really good atmosphere because we had a great deal in common: we wanted to see the place; we wanted to be in the country.

Version 2
1.
NICK: I play with a brass band and I've been with them for about four years now so I think I'd have to say it's, er, been a good experience. Um, this is a good bunch of people and we all get on very well with each other, although occasionally there've been sort of moments where, uh, people have, uh, there's been a clash of personality. We had a euphonium player who never really liked the conductor and, and it all came to a head when we had a contest one day and he didn't turn up and they had an emergency committee meeting and decided to sack him – well, I mean not sack him but just tell him not to come anymore.

Um, I suppose we do as a group compromise in a sense that, um, although we, we play together mostly for the enjoyment, if we worked a lot harder, I'm sure we'd do better at contests, but I don't think we're prepared to do that, so we just do the, the bare minimum and, and we scrape by at contests. Um, it's very nice when new people come because they're welcome there and, uh, at the end of the break in the middle of the practice session, the conductor will say 'It's nice to have, er, Graham come to visit us,' and we all clap. And it's very nice. I like that very much when new people come. And, um, I guess the, the atmosphere, er, in the band is very supportive towards one another and if anybody's got a solo or anything and they play it badly in a concert or a contest, then we all laugh about it.

2.
JUDY: A few years ago I started taking riding lessons. I'd never ridden before in my life. And, um, there was a group of, um, mainly women who used to ride at the same time. And, um, it was really good because we really all got on very well together, and, um, they became, um, very supportive as a group. Very often I would get, um, get frightened, you know I had a fall once, and I would get quite frightened and they would, um, encourage me and help me to, uh, to carry on, which was, um, was really nice. But the more we were together, I think the more difficult it became if a new person, um, came to join the lesson. Um, it was quite difficult for them to, uh, to fit in, I think. And, um, I remember one day a woman came along and, um, she was dressed out in all the most expensive gear – you know wonderful hat and jacket and crop and so on. And, and as soon as she appeared there was a tremendous amount of hostility towards her from the rest of us. I mean it was really quite disgraceful. We behaved like, like small children and we, we laughed at her and we giggled at her and we made her ride the worst horse. It was really appalling.

REVIEW AND DEVELOPMENT

REVIEW OF UNIT 13

Exercise 1

A: Oh, look there's this, um, thing in the paper about a new punishment for, uh, for young offenders in the States.
B: Oh, yeah, yeah. What's it say?
A: Well, apparently they've, they've taken all these young kids who've committed all these crimes like theft and burglary and everything, and, and they're teaching them ballet.
B: What?
A: Yes, honestly, yeah – and, and acting as well. And, and they've

persuaded a few film stars to help teach them. You know, do you know Ted Danson?
B: Oh, yeah.
A: Yeah, well, he's doing it.
B: I mean, what's the point of it?
A: Well, I mean, I think the idea behind it is that dancing is hard work and it, and it helps them, you know, because they're so frustrated they can sort of get it out in dancing.
B: Oh, really.
A: Oh, well, I mean, a lot of these kids have got a very low opinion of themselves, and, and the programme it sort of gives them a, a positive image – that's what it said, a positive image.
B: So, so what it's saying is that instead of going to jail, they, they go to dancing lessons. Is that it?
A: Well, no, I mean, they've got to do community service jobs as well, like cleaning up the streets, and picking up rubbish and, and cleaning all the graffiti and everything.
B: Yeah, but isn't a programme like that gonna be expensive?
A: No, no, it says here it costs about the same as keeping them in jail for a year.
B: Well, I mean, you can say what you like, but that just seems crazy to me. I mean, if you commit a crime, you've got to face the consequences – even if they aren't very nice.
A: Well, I dunno. I mean I think it depends if it works or not. Anyway, it's going to be interesting to see.

Exercise 2

1. Can you walk on a path?
2. Is there grass on a lawn?
3. Can you swim on a cliff?
4. Do sparrows have wings?
5. Is a goat a type of animal?
6. Is an eagle a type of fish?
7. Can you hop on two legs?
8. Can you creep through bushes?
9. Can a fence gallop?
10. Do helicopters land?
11. If you bump into someone, do you meet them?
12. Can motorbikes skid?
13. Can you cancel a lake?
14. Do alarm clocks go off?
15. Is grammar fun?

UNIT 16 YES AND NO

SAYING *NO* POLITELY

Exercise 2

Version 1
1.
INTERVIEWER: Lyndham, in your country, um, of origin, where … if, if you were invited out for a meal, let's say for dinner, um, and you were given food that you didn't like or that you really had objections to eating, what would you do?
LYNDHAM: Well, er, something like this did happen to me once. Er, I, I went to a family for dinner and … the meal was presented and I looked at it, and I looked at the meat, and I asked what it was, and it was pork. And I'm a Mohammedan from India; I'm not allowed to eat pork.
INTERVIEWER: So how did you deal with that?
LYNDHAM: Well, as they were people that I … it was to do with work, and I didn't want to upset them, I, I asked if it was

possible for me to have some salad, and that was the way I went round it. And they, they were very understanding. In fact they were quite … they were quite upset that they had presented me with a dish which obviously I wasn't able to eat.

INTERVIEWER: Lucky for you.

LYNDHAM: Yes.

2.

INTERVIEWER: And Gertrude, tell me, what would happen to you in Germany if you sat down for dinner and the food that you were given was something you really didn't like or objected to.

GERTRUDE: Hmm. Well, it depends. If it's something general like being a vegetarian, it is perfectly acceptable to say so, and people will immediately try and provide alternatives, but if it's say you are invited to someone at home for dinner and they made a speciality, something like liver or kidney, and you don't like that specific thing, it would be difficult to, to get out of that one.

INTERVIEWER: Would it depend on how well you knew the people, perhaps?

GERTRUDE: Yes, definitely. It would be, it could be very rude. It could be very impolite to say you don't like this specific thing.

Version 2

1.

INTERVIEWER: And Aisha, how about you?

AISHA: Well, um, I'm British, and, um, and I think I'm probably quite British in my attitude in that I'm rather over polite, so that if somebody served me something that I didn't like I … it's certainly in the past I have tended to eat it … um, as little as possible, um, but to eat it and not really say very much. But now I'm a vegetarian or almost vegetarian, if somebody offered me beef, I think I would have to say something because I simply couldn't eat it.

2.

INTERVIEWER: Lorelei, how about you?

LORELEI: Willie, I'm from Los Angeles, and everyone there has a food fad of some sort or other, so I can assure you that hosts and hostesses of parties are used to people refusing things … 'Oh, I'm on this diet this week, that diet that week …' So it's very common, and no offence is taken. Having said that, I personally would find it rude. So when presented with something I don't like, there is always something on the plate you can eat, so what I tend to do is chop it up, push it around, eat the bits I like and leave what I don't.

INTERVIEWER: Sounds very sensible to me.

REVIEW AND DEVELOPMENT

REVIEW OF UNIT 14

Exercise 1

1. She broke it.
2. When I arrived he'd left.
3. He hadn't been before.
4. I was angry because she lost it.
5. They met a man who'd lived there.
6. She'd injured her ankle; that was the problem.
7. I hope she's gone.
8. We did it because he'd asked us to.

UNIT 17 PACKAGING

SACKS AND BARRELS

Exercise 3

NICK: Right – um, I've made a list of most things we'll need, but for the drinks, um, I'm not really sure how much we'll, we'll need.

AISHA: Well, um, I reckon we need about a dozen cartons of fruit juice, er, 5 or 6 bottles of wine and probably the same of, of mineral water.

NICK: OK, right. What, er, what about beer?

AISHA: Oh, yes, yes, yes. Get a few cans of beer … and some fizzy drinks as well, I think.

NICK: Right. Is that enough?

AISHA: Well, yes, I hope so. Er, now what about the food then?

NICK: Well, I've already got the sausages, chicken legs, mustard, etc. Um, how much bread do you think we'll need?

AISHA: Oh, I suppose about half a dozen loaves, yeah?

NICK: Yeah.

AISHA: And, and people will eat loads of salad stuff as well, so, so we need lots of green salad and a few tomatoes, something like that.

NICK: Yeah.

AISHA: Yeah.

NICK: Fine. Right, what else?

AISHA: Well, I'm a bit worried about what we're going to serve it on. I mean, I suppose we'll just have to borrow some things, won't we? Er, we could ask some people to bring plates and cutlery and maybe some glasses with them.

NICK: Yes, yeah. We'd better borrow a couple of large bowls for the salad too.

AISHA: Right, good. So that's it then, you think?

NICK: Yeah, I think so. Um, I bought the stuff for the games the other day, you know, the, er, the glue and the string …

AISHA: Oh, yes, and don't forget a large box of matches.

NICK: Yeah, yes, right, fine.

PACKAGING PRODUCTS

Exercise 5

This is a very visual advertisement. There is a very strong image which is also easily remembered.

The advert puts the product into a cultural and historical context. They don't give you an art history lesson on Picasso or Braque, though. It simply invites you to enter the Montparnasse café world of 1907, and lets your imagination run free.

The great artists have left the table. It gives you the opportunity to sit in those empty seats. If this cognac was good enough for Picasso, it is more than good enough for you. You feel that the people probably had animated discussions about art during their dinner.

Everything in the advert is saying something about the product. Here, all the things on the table, such as the half-drunk wines and coffee, the partly eaten peach, and so on, give a wonderful, warm atmosphere. The remains of the meal suggest quality and simplicity in the food, and not a big, expensive luxurious feast. Of course, the advertiser wants to show the product in the glass. But it is a natural, casual picture. You are told the company this cognac keeps, and its history and status.

REVIEW OF UNIT 16

Exercise 1

1.
A: Welcome to the programme. Did you drive here this evening?
B: I didn't.
A: You didn't come in a car?
B: I didn't - I came by train, David.
A: Was that a tube train?
B: It wasn't, David, it was a British Rail train.
A: Really? From which station did you get the, er, train?
B: From Henley.
A: From Henley. Is that Henley Central?
B: No, that's …

2.
C: Julia, is that Julia with a 'J'?
D: It is.
C: It is. And that's your first name?
D: It is indeed.
C: How many names do you have?
D: I have two names. Two Christian names.
C: Two Christian names.
D: I do.
C: Two Christian names?
D: That's right.
C: And your first one is Julia?
D: That's right.
C: And the second one is …
D: Gail.
C: Gail!
D: Correct.
C: Correct?
D: Absolutely.
C: You did say 'correct'?
D: I did indeed.
C: So it's Julia Gail.
D: It is, Julia Gail.
C: And where were you born, Julia?
D: I was born in Runcorn.
C: In Runcorn?
D: Hmm.
C: Sorry?
D: I was, yes.

3.
E: Juliet, do you live in London?
F: I do.
E: Whereabouts?
F: I live in Stoke Newington.
E: Stoke Newington?
F: That's correct.
E: In Stoke Newington?
F: Absolutely in Stoke Newington, yes …
E: And how did you get …

4.
G: Dominic, that's a very short haircut you've got there …
H: It is.
G: Do you always wear your hair that short?
H: Not always.
G: So have you had it recently cut?
H: About a month ago.
G: I see. And where did you go to have it cut?
H: The barber's shop.
G: Is it the same one you always go to?
H: It is.
G: And why do you like going there?
H: Because there is a man there who knows my head.
G: I see. Does he know it very well?
H: He does.
G: Right. So you always have the same hairdresser?
H: I do, yes. Oh!

UNIT 18 HONESTLY SPEAKING

Exercise 4

Please, God, let him telephone me now. Dear God, let him call me now. I won't ask anything else of you, truly I won't. It isn't very much to ask. It would be so little to you, God, such a little, little thing. Only let him telephone now. Please, God, please, please, please.

If I didn't think about it, maybe the telephone might ring. Sometimes it does that. If I could think of something else. If I could think of something else. Maybe if I counted five hundred by fives, it might ring by that time. I'll count slowly. I won't cheat. And if it rings when I get to three hundred, I won't stop; I won't answer it until I get to five hundred. Five, ten, fifteen, twenty, twenty-five, thirty, thirty-five, forty, forty-five, fifty … Oh, please let it ring. Please.

This is the last time I'll look at the clock. I will not look at it again. It's ten minutes past seven. He said he would telephone at five o'clock. 'I'll call you at five, darling.' I think that's where he said 'darling'. I'm almost sure he said it there. I know he called me 'darling' twice, and the other time was when he said goodbye. 'Goodbye, darling.' He was busy, and he can't say much in the office, but he called me 'darling' twice. He couldn't have minded my calling him up. I know you shouldn't keep telephoning them – I know they don't like that. When you do that, they know you are thinking about them and wanting them, and that makes them hate you. But I hadn't talked to him in three days – not in three days. And all I did was ask him how he was; it was just the way anybody might have called him up. He couldn't have minded that. He couldn't have thought I was bothering him. 'No, of course you're not,' he said. And he said he'd telephone me. He didn't have to say that. I didn't ask him to, truly I didn't. I'm sure I didn't. I don't think he would say he'd telephone me, and then just never do it. Please don't let him do that. God. Please don't.

'I'll call you at five, darling.' 'Goodbye, darling.' He was busy, he was in a hurry, and there were people around him, but he called me 'darling' twice. That's mine, that's mine. I have that, even if I never see him again.

Exercise 6

WOMAN: Hi, it's me.
MAN: Oh … uh … forgive me, I, I wasn't expecting your call.
WOMAN: Oh, I, I hope it's not inconvenient.
MAN: Not exactly, it's, er, no, it's fine go ahead.
WOMAN: I'm not bothering you, am I?
MAN: I just had to come out of a meeting, that's all.
WOMAN: Oh, I'm so sorry, it's just … well I, I just really wanted to see how you are. I mean I haven't … well, we haven't spoken in a few days.
MAN: No, that is true. I, I apologise.
WOMAN: Oh, I wasn't phoning for an apology. I just … I, I just wondered how you, how you are.
MAN: Oh, fine, fine, fine. Thank you.
WOMAN: Should I … should I … maybe call you later, or …?
MAN: Well, I don't really know where I'll be. Uh … except … well, um, I'll be here till four thirty … I think. Yes, why don't I … why don't I call you at five, darling?
WOMAN: Oh … oh, great, OK. Well, bye bye for now darling.
MAN: Goodbye … darling.

Exercise 3

Good morning. This is the 8 o'clock news and here are today's headlines.

Inflation falls for the third time this year.

The year-long industrial dispute at the Robinson factory has ended with massive redundancies.

The first peaceful multi-party elections in Atora have brought victory to the People's Party.

The drought in Zebrina is threatening to lead to famine in the coming months.

And defeat for Canada in last night's ice-hockey final.

REVIEW AND DEVELOPMENT

REVIEW OF UNIT 16

Exercise 2

He lives in Madrid, doesn't he?
You didn't see the others, did you?
They're coming this evening, aren't they?
It's a big place, isn't it?
You aren't married, are you?
You've got two brothers, haven't you?

UNIT 19 PLAIN ENGLISH

PLAIN ENGLISH OR GOBBLEDYGOOK?

Exercise 3

Version 1

The Plain English campaign really wants to make texts more readable. And things we look for include, first, texts which are clear and concise. And we don't like to see words used which are unnecessary really, um, words like 'we' and 'you' can be used instead of 'the insured', or 'the applicant', 'the society' and so on.

Texts are easier to read if they have a good average sentence length – about 15 to 20 words, and they're easier to read if there are no more than 7 to 12 words on each line. And of course, ideally, we like to see everyday English and no jargon. And clear helpful headings which stand out from the text – that breaks it down and just makes it easier to approach. Including that is, um, good typesize and clear typeface – anything that just makes it look simpler, instead of more complicated. And … included in the text we prefer to see active verbs instead of passive ones. For instance, a sentence like 'we will give you the best service possible' is quite direct and friendly, not too formal. But another way of putting it might be 'the customer will be given the best service possible', and this is more distancing and formal.

Version 2

A: So tell us Caroline, what exactly is the Plain English Campaign and what is it trying to achieve?

B: Well, what we're hoping to do is encourage companies and professions and government departments, etc., to produce literature which is clear and concise, and which – as far as possible – uses simple, everyday English and no jargon.

A: I see. And is it just the content of these documents you're concerned with or, or does the actual layout play a part in it?

B: Oh, yes definitely. It's very important that a text looks absolutely clear before you start reading it … that it, it looks as if it's going to be easy to read … with helpful headings that stand out from the text and good typesize and clear typeface … these things are all very important too.

A: I suppose for many people legal documents are the, um, the classic example of texts that people complain about which are utterly impenetrable and just seem to go on for ever without a single, single full stop anywhere.

B: Yes, absolutely. And we advise generally that sentences should be no more than average length – well that's to say about 15 to 20 words, and if there are no more than 8 to 12 words on each line, that also makes a text easier to follow.

A: And … could you give us an example of ways in which a document can be made easier to read and understand, actually in the way it's written?

B: Yes. One of the things we want to get away from is indirectness. Documents are always talking about 'the insurer' or 'the applicant' or 'the society', you know. And we think that if they could be more direct and use words like 'we' and 'you' instead, it would be much better. And along with that, we'd also like documents to use active verbs rather than passive verbs. Er, so let's take an example. An example might be 'the customer will be given the best possible service.' Now that makes sense, but it isn't very direct. If it said 'we will give you the best possible service', that's friendlier, more direct and less formal.

A: Well, that's, that's been very clear, very direct and very helpful. Caroline, thank you very much.

WRITING A CURRICULUM VITAE

Exercise 4

A good CV, a CV that's, that's going to work for you and get you interviews, should always be brief and to the point. You shouldn't include information that's not relevant to the job that you're applying for.

Um, sentences ought to be short and, and businesslike, and then they'll hold the reader's attention. It ought to start with your name, your address, phone number, and personal details including your age, your marital status, and then continue on with professional and educational qualifications. Previous jobs ought to be, ought to be listed in, in reverse order, that is with the, er, the most recent job at the top of the list, and then working down back to when your work life started. But again, bearing in mind that the CV has to be short – I mean, you needn't list everything. In my opinion the perfect CV shouldn't be longer than two pages. And, er, when you've finished it, er, you send it out with … you should send it out with a covering letter explaining why you think you're suitable for the job. And if you're not available for an interview at, at certain times, then you should also make that very clear in your letter. You don't want to be offered an interview and then have to say you can't make it because of some other commitment.

REVIEW AND DEVELOPMENT

REVIEW OF UNIT 18

Exercise 2

A: OK. Um, I've thought of one. I've got one.
B: Um.
C: Have you really got one?
A: Yes.
C: You yourself.
A: Ah, um, no, I haven't.
D: Is it, is it a big thing?
A: No.
B: Um, is it, is it very long?
A: No, not long or big.
C: Would you keep it indoors?

A: You could *keep* it indoors.
B: Could you read it?
A: Um, no.
B: Would it …would you be surprised to find it indoors?
A: No, not at all.
D: Is the colour of it important?
A: Yes.
B: Can you wear it?
A: Yes.
D: It's, er, it's something you'd wear outdoors?
A: Yes.
B: Aha!
A: Yes.
C: Would a man wear it or a woman wear it?
A: Both.
B: Would you wear it, um, on your feet?
A: No.
C: Your head?
A: Yes.
D: It's a hat.
A: No.
B: It's a scarf.
A: No.
D: A balaclava helmet?
A: No. … Definitely not.
D: Oh, it … does it serve a purpose?
A: It does.
D: Is it to protect your head?
A: Uh, sort of … well, yes.
B: Not a rain hat?
A: No.
D: A pair of sunglasses.
A: Yes, well done, Bob!

UNIT 20 ART AND SOCIETY

Exercise 2

After she left school, um, Julia went to live in the States and she managed to get a job there in a Beverley Hills nightclub where she was doing quick drawings of people for, well 20 dollars a time. Later on she moved to Arizona and she set up a small studio gallery and managed to do exhibitions of some of her portraits in galleries there – all around the southwest. But the thing that interested her most at that time was the idea of illustrating court cases. Now this was a practice that was quite common in America, and she managed to get an audition for NBC. And before she knew it she found herself in court. From then on she regularly reconstructed court scenes for television in California. In the United States it's not like in Britain, and the artist is allowed to work in court. But when she got back to Britain, she got a similar job for the BBC, but found out that it was very different, because you see in Britain there's a law that says that drawing in court is forbidden. So the thing that Julia has to do is she has fifteen minutes or so to study the subject, um, she can make notes about hairstyle or the colour of the tie, type of expression – all that sort of thing. And then she has to go into a different room where she has to draw the person and the court totally from memory. Usually she has about an hour and a half before it has to be ready for the next news broadcast. So you can imagine this is really difficult because she has to do it as accurately as she possibly can. I mean she has to be careful that she doesn't make the people look too mean or too sweet because she has to avoid making people look guilty or suspicious at all. Well, now what Julia's got planned is an exhibition of her work so that everyone'll be able to study the pictures that she's done for more than the fifteen seconds that they usually can on the television screen.

REVIEW OF UNIT 18

Exercise 2

famine	balance
third	hurt
industrial	justice
triumph	priority
police	achievement
dispute	refuse
rate	inflation
fair	area
threaten	success

UNIT 21 DARE YOURSELF TO SUCCEED

Exercise 2

MICHAEL: For me it was nothing but misery and it really destroyed my confidence. I remember … on the second day … it was freezing cold and raining, and we ended up at the top of a cliff and they wanted us to abseil down. I have a problem with heights and I just said I wouldn't do it. But then it became clear that abseiling was the only way down. I was exhausted and I just burst into tears. 'OK, let's have some team support,' said the trainers. But the 'team' just stood there looking embarrassed – it's not everyday they see one of their managers crying his eyes out at the top of a cliff. I'm an accountant. So what does it prove if I can climb down a cliff? Anyway, the following week I just didn't want to go to work … especially when I found boxes of Kleenex tissues on my desk every day. I even thought about leaving the company.

CAROLINE: I have mixed feelings about it. In some of the physical activities, I did feel that women were at a disadvantage … in a way that doesn't happen at work. I mean, at one point two men had to throw me over a wall because I wasn't physically strong enough to climb it.

On the other hand, most of the time it was fun, and by the end of the course I think there was a good team spirit – you know, we'd all been through the same problems together and survived. I think that will be good for our team morale when we're back at work.

JAMES: I think these courses are, are really useful. They help you to understand how to work as a group. You see, in our education system, success is based on individual achievement – but my course taught me that in a company, everyone has to work together to make a success of things. And it also gave me more confidence in myself. I know I won't have to abseil down a cliff in my job, but the fact that I did something I thought I couldn't do, has given me the confidence to believe now that nothing is impossible.

SONIA: Well, to be honest I thought it was a waste of time. I must admit I wasn't keen on going in the first place, and the conditions were pretty dreadful. I didn't get a shower all weekend and I felt really uncomfortable. Mind you, it was quite amusing to see my boss up to his neck in a river … I don't feel as frightened of him now as I did before. But I don't really see the point of it. After all, it's extremely rare for me to have to cross a river to get to work!

REVIEW OF UNIT 19

Exercise 1

Part A:
tomato
vase
magazine
address
hostile
inquiry
secretary
laboratory

Part C:
1. I'm visiting with her tomorrow.
2. Could I speak with Albert, please?
3. I just had some coffee.
4. I'll go get the car.
5. a half hour
6. I can't remember if it starts at twenty of four or five after five.

UNIT 22 FORCES OF NATURE

ONE MINUTE CHANGED OUR LIVES

Exercise 6

1.
SHEILA: Um, I think one of the biggest things that visitors to Britain would have trouble getting used to is queuing for everything. I mean we do, we queue everywhere – we queue for the cinema, we queue for the theatre if we haven't got a ticket, we queue for museums, and of course we queue for buses. And, I mean, visitors from abroad, particular … the continent, they, they just, well it's, it's, it doesn't happen over there. I remember going to Italy and people just sort of congregate in great masses and then when the bus comes along they just all run for it. And, I mean, I got left off several times; so I think they would probably wonder what we're all doing in these funny little straight lines, and, um, it would take some getting used to, I would think.

2.
BOB: Well I think, um, a lot of overseas visitors to this country wouldn't be used to driving on the left because there are very few countries that do. And when I go, when I go to the continent I know, er, it takes me a long time to get used to changing over. All right in the end.

3.
LORELEI: I'm an American but I live in London, and when I first moved here I had a lot of trouble getting used to the English sense of humour. My friends, who were English, would insult me a lot – they'd say mean things – and I asked them one day why they did this, and they said 'we insult you because we like you; you'd have to worry if we were polite to you'. In America we're not used to this …

Exercise 4

Version 1
Ginger root has a calming effect on the stomach, and helps counteract travel sickness and nausea.

Ginger tea is quite powerful – put three or four slices of thin ginger root in two cups of water and simmer for ten minutes, then leave to brew for fifteen.

Sellotape can make warts disappear. You have to put about four layers of tape over the wart so the bandage is airtight, but not too tight.

Cayenne pepper is good for warming feet – surprisingly it's not too irritating next to the skin. A lot of people find sprinkling it into their socks prevents frozen toes.

Ice can take the pain out of insect bites. Rub over the bite when you need it. It's also good for sinus infections. Put very hot and then very cold compresses on your face.

Bicarbonate of soda relieves itching. If you put a tablespoon of bicarb to every pint of cool water in a bowl or half a cup in the bath, you can calm the itchiness of rashes or stings.

Garlic fights colds and flu. Add two or three fresh cloves of garlic per person to whatever you are making. Or put it in a soup.

Tea bags soothe cold sores. You leave a tea bag in tepid water, take it out, hold it against the sore for 5 to 10 minutes. Repeat every 3 or 4 hours.

But with any of these remedies, if you have an unusual reaction, stop immediately!

Version 2
A: Hello, yes. Well I have a bit of a trouble with travel sickness.
B: Ah, travel sickness. Now what you need is ginger root. If you make yourself a ginger tea – it's quite powerful. Just put three or four slices of thin ginger root into two cups of water and simmer for about ten minutes, then leave to brew for fifteen minutes, and that should calm your stomach.
A: Oh, lovely.

B: Hello, and next on the line is Ian. Good morning, Ian.
C: Oh, hello. Good morning. Er, doctor, I've tried, I've tried everything to get rid of this, er, large wart that I have on the back of my neck, and it just won't go. Can you, can you help me?
B: Yes, well funnily enough, sellotape can help to make warts disappear. You have to put about four layers of tape over the wart so the bandage is airtight, but not too tight. And then you, you leave that on for between two and four weeks and it should disappear.
C: Sellotape?
B: Sellotape.
C: Sellotape?
B: Yes.
C: Gosh. Thank you very much, doctor.

B: Hello, and who's our next caller?
D: Oh, hello. My name's Mary. I'm ringing up to ask about my cold feet. I spend a lot of time watching my sons playing football and my feet get numb. Have you got any hints?
B: Now surprisingly enough cayenne pepper is very good for warming your feet. If you sprinkle some into your socks, it'll, er, stop your toes from freezing.
D: Really! Oh. I'll try it, thanks.

B: And good morning. Who's our next caller?
E: Oh, hello, yes. It's Shirley here. I've just got back from my holidays and I'm covered in insect bites and they're really sore. Is there anything you can suggest?
B: Yes, I can. I can suggest some ice. Now if you take some ice and rub it over the sore bits …
E: Yeah.
B: … that should ease the pain.
E: OK, I'll try it, thanks.
B: OK.

B: And our next caller is John. Good morning, John.

F: Oh, good morning, doctor. I'm, I'm really glad I've got through to you. I've got this, this rash, a red rash, all over my body and it is driving me mad. Er, er, I'm itching all the time, itching and scratching it and it's, I do need help desperately.

B: Well, what I would suggest you do is … if you take some bicarbonate of soda and if you put a tablespoon of bicarb to every pint of cool water into a bowl or, or perhaps half a cup in the bath, now that should help to calm the itchiness. OK?

F: Thank you.

B: And can we have our next caller, please.

G: Oh, yes, hello. My name's Joanna. I'm just asking – I expect you get a lot of questions like this at this time of year – if you've got any tips about fighting colds and flu?

B: Ah, yes. Now, what I always recommend for fighting colds and flu is garlic – and lots of it. If you add two or three fresh cloves of garlic, per person, yes, per person, to whatever you're making – put it in a soup or whatever – that should help to fight colds and flu. Also, it's very good at fighting off any kind of infection.

G: Thank you doctor.

B: OK.

B: And who's on the line now?

H: Oh, hello, yes. It's Audrey here. Could you help me, doctor? Cold sores, this is the problem. What can we do about them?

B: Now, I know this sounds like an old wives' tale, but in fact tea bags are very good for soothing cold sores. If you leave a tea bag in tepid water, take it out, hold it against the sore for five to ten minutes and repeat every three or four hours, this should soothe the pain of cold sores.

H: Super, thanks.

B: But remember, with any of these remedies, if you have an unusual reaction, you must stop immediately.

SEND FOR THE *FENG SHUI* MAN

Exercise 2

A: So what exactly is *feng shui*?

B: Well, in Chinese, *feng shui* literally means 'wind' and 'water', and the principle behind it is that human beings must live in harmony with these forces in nature, and your success or failure are dependent on them.

So, for example, the layout and the position of your home or your office in relation to the environment are very important. Every hill, er, wall, window, and the ways in which they face the wind and water have an effect.

A: Well, can people do anything about it?

B: Oh, yes. *Feng shui* aims to change and harmonise the environment – to improve people's health or wealth or fortunes, you know. Basically, if you change your surroundings, you can change your life.

A: Yes, but how do we go about this?

B: Well, in Hong Kong, where *feng shui* is widely practised, people consult the *feng shui* priest who advises them and tells them how they can change their environment.

A: Give me an example.

B: OK. Before any official building is constructed, the *feng shui* priest comes to see whether the structures are in line with wind and water. Remember, *feng shui*, wind, water …

A: Yeah, yeah, OK.

B: And if a building has bad *feng shui*, it's possible to do a number of things to improve it, like using mirrors or plants, for instance.

A: Really? Is that common only in Hong Kong?

B: Well, it isn't officially recognised in China, though it does exist, but it has begun to spread to the United States. OK, like there was this New York woman who lived in a luxury apartment for ten years, and she decided to consult a *feng shui* man. Now he told her that unless she moved, she wouldn't survive. So she moved out within a week. And you know what, she's still alive, as far as we know.

A: Really?

B: Yes. Oh, there was another interesting case in the States, um, of this graphic artist called Milton Glaser.

A: Yes, I've heard of him.

B: Now his off… you haven't!

A: I have.

B: His office was broken into and robbed six times. So he sent the layout and seating plan of his office to one of these Hong Kong experts on *feng shui*. Now, he followed the instructions he got back – he put in a tank with six black fish and hung a red clock up. And since then, he's had no problems.

A: Well he's a lucky guy, uh!

B: Or maybe good *feng shui*?

A: Maybe.

REVIEW OF UNIT 20

Exercise 2

Part A:
Example: replace   transaction
studio   portrait   taxpayer   sculpture   merchant   suspicious display   construction   engraving   drawing   landscape reproduction

Part B:
It was an exhibition of drawings and engravings.
The sculptures were part of a large collection.
He buys a lot of reproduction furniture.
It was a very intricate portrait.
She's a magnificent landscape artist.
The statue was on display in the entrance to the gallery.

ACKNOWLEDGEMENTS

Authors' acknowledgements

We would like to thank Stephen Slater for his original inspiration in the development of *True to Life*.

We are also very grateful to Gillian Lazar for her continued support and perceptive criticisms on the final manuscript.

Friends and colleagues have given us permission to use their ideas and activities – or in some cases given us inspiration. We would therefore like to thank Philip Dale, Claire Fletcher, Jackie Gresham, Frances Eales, Susan Barduhn, Terry Miles, Tim Shirra and Frances Gairns. As ever, a big thank you to all our colleagues at International House and The London School of English for their ideas, support and kindness.

We would also like to express our gratitude to writers whose work has influenced us in specific activities: Trisha Hedge, Jill Hadfield and Mark Bartram and Richard Walton.

At Cambridge University Press, we would like to thank James Dingle for his coordination of the pilot edition, and very sincere thanks to Kate Boyce for her excellent management of the project and unfailing support. Helena Gomm's contribution has been immense and we have much appreciated her humour; we are also most grateful to Nick Newton and Randell Harris for their impressive and stylish design and production work.

We would like to thank Martin Williamson for his considerable help and guidance on the listening material and to all the actors involved and to the staff of AVP.

Finally, our thanks go to the commissioning editor, Peter Donovan, who set the project in motion, and to the rest of the staff at Cambridge University Press.

The authors and publishers would like to thank the following institutions and teachers for their help in testing the material and for the invaluable feedback which they provided:

AVL, Paris, France; BTL, Paris, France; Diann Gruber, Paris, France; Associazone Culturale Delle Lingue Europee, Bologna, Italy; British Council, Milan, Italy; Civica Scuola di Lingue, Milan, Italy; Cambridge English Studies, La Coruña, Spain; Roger Scott, Bournemouth, UK; Hampstead Garden Suburb Institute, London, UK.

The authors and publishers are grateful to the following copyright holders for permission to reproduce copyright material. While every endeavour has been made, it has not been possible to identify the sources of all material used and in such cases the publishers would welcome information from copyright sources. Apologies are expressed for any omissions.

p. 131: *The Observer* for the extract from Room of my Own by Elspeth Thompson 8/5/94 © *The Observer*.

The authors and publishers are grateful to the following illustrators and photographic sources:

Illustrator: p. 124: Kathy Baxendale
Photographic source: p. 131: photo by permission of David Gamble / *The Observer*

Design and DTP by Newton Harris
Picture research by Marilyn Rawlings